# THE ENVIRONMENT

# THE ENVIRONMENT

**V K Ahluwalia**

The Energy and Resources Institute

ISBN 978-93-8653-012-7



**Suggested citation**

Ahluwalia, V. K. 2018. *The Environment.* New Delhi: TERI

**Published by**
The Energy and Resources Institute (TERI)
TERI Press
Darbari Seth Block
IHC Complex, Lodhi Road
New Delhi – 110 003
India

***Tel.*** 2468 2100 or 4150 4900
***Fax*** 2468 2144 or 2468 2145
India +91 • Delhi (0)11
***E-mail*** teripress@teri.res.in
***Website*** www.teriin.org
***Bookstore*** https://bookstore.teri.res.in

Printed in India

# Preface

The environment is defined, perceived, and valued diversely by different countries, cultures, and communities. A healthy environment ensures human security, which means everyone has the access to food and water, employment and livelihood stability, resilience to climate change and extreme weather events, and also social and political stability. As the demand for food, fodder, fuel, and raw material grows, it increases the pressure on the environment and the competition for natural resources. Both human and natural activities have caused the physical, chemical, and biological degradation of the environment. However, it is the unsustainable human activities that have put the environment at risk and at the same time threatened the ecosystem services on which all humanity depends. The loss of forest and other natural ecosystems directly affects biodiversity and ecosystem services, such as nutrient, carbon, and water cycles and climate regulation. It is important that large natural ecosystems for biodiversity and ecosystem services are protected. As far as possible, water resource should be used efficiently and recycled. It is also essential that pollution of land, water, air is cut down and climate mitigation and adaptation are maximized.

*The Environment* covers the basic components of environment, ecology, biomes, and biodiversity. Environmental degradation, pollution and conservation, environmental disasters and their management are some of the topics which have been discussed at length. The book also explains major crops and cropping pattern in India and environmental engineering including sustainable development. Each chapter is followed by exercises. These topics and exercises will help candidates appearing for competitive examinations such as civil services. The book is also extremely useful for readers interested in environment science, environment chemistry, and related subjects. The author thanks TERI for the publication of this book. Suggestions from readers are most welcome and will be gratefully acknowledged.

# Contents

# Basic Components of the Environment

## 1.1 INTRODUCTION

The term 'environment' is defined differently by different environmentalists. The environment means surroundings and is defined as the sum total of living and non-living components. It is made up of the abiotic (non-living) and biotic (living) components. The abiotic components of the environment are composed of light, precipitation, humidity and water, temperature, atmospheric gases, altitude, latitude, seasonal changes, and topography. The biotic components, on the other hand, comprise plants, animals (including humans, parasites, microorganisms), and decomposers. Besides the abiotic and biotic components, the environment also includes energy components, of which solar energy is of paramount importance, as it plays a vital role in sustaining life processes.

According to the Environmental Protection Act, 1986, the term 'environment' covers air, land, and the interrelationship that exists among and between water, air, land, human beings, plants, organisms, and other living creatures. It makes life possible by creating favourable conditions for the existence, growth, and survival of all living organisms including human. The environment never remains constant or static. It undergoes change. This change can be slow, rapid, or drastic. The change in the environment has a profound influence on its inhibitors which include all living organisms as well as human beings. Environmental changes can be beneficial as well as harmful. In fact, many species on earth, unable to adapt to the changing conditions of the environment have either died or are on the verge of dying out. For example, the extinction of dinosaurs occurred primarily due to the prevalence of adverse environmental conditions. This is generally attributed to the appearance of tiny primitive mammals that survived on dinosaur eggs. The environment which was conducive for primitive mammals became inhospitable for the dinosaurs and, thus, they became extinct.

## 1.2 TYPES OF ENVIRONMENT

The earth's environment can be broadly classified into two types—natural environment and human-made environment. Components of natural environment are air, water, soil, solar radiation, land, forest, wildlife, flora, and fauna. The constituent elements of human-made environment include housing, agricultural implements, industries, dams, and energy such as hydro, thermal, and nuclear.

## 1.3   SEGMENTS OF ENVIRONMENT

The environment consists of four principal segments: (i) atmosphere, (ii) hydrosphere, (iii) lithosphere, and (iv) biosphere.

### 1.3.1   Atmosphere

The cover of air enveloping the earth is known as the atmosphere. It is responsible for sustaining life on earth. It protects the earth from harmful radiations, especially ultraviolet (UV) radiations of the sun. It contains life-supporting gases such as oxygen for human beings and animals, and carbon dioxide for plants. These gases (oxygen and carbon dioxide) continuously cycle in nature via various cycles. The air in the atmosphere consists of a number of gases, such as nitrogen, oxygen, carbon dioxide, and inert gases. The atmosphere extends up to a height of about 500 km from the earth's surface. The total mass of the atmosphere is approximately $5 \times 10^{15}$ tonnes, which is about one millionth of the total weight of the earth. The temperature, pressure, and density vary considerably with altitude. On the basis of the altitude, the atmosphere can be divided into four major regions: (i) troposphere, (ii) stratosphere, (iii) mesosphere, and (iv) thermosphere (Table 1.1).

In addition to the above-mentioned regions, the atmospheric region that lies between 50 km and 100 km of altitude is called the ionosphere. This region is rich in ions such as $O_2^+$, $O^+$, $NO_2^+$, and electrons. UV radiations from the sun are primarily responsible for the formation of these ions. As this region does not receive any solar radiation during night-time, the ions combine with free electrons and form neutral species. The division of atmosphere into various regions in a simplified form is shown in Figure 1.1. As already stated, the atmosphere contains a number of gases. The actual composition of dry air at sea level is given in Table 1.2.

**Table 1.1**   Different regions of the atmosphere

| Region | Altitude (km) | Temperature (°C) | Main constituents |
|---|---|---|---|
| Troposphere | 0–11 | 15 to −56 | $O_2$, $N_2$, $CO_2$, $H_2O$ |
| Stratosphere | 11–50 | −56 to −2 | $O_3$ |
| Mesosphere | 50–90 | −2 to −92 | $O_2^+$, $NO^+$ |
| Thermosphere | 90–500 | −92 to 1200 | $O_2^+$, $O^+$, $NO^+$ |

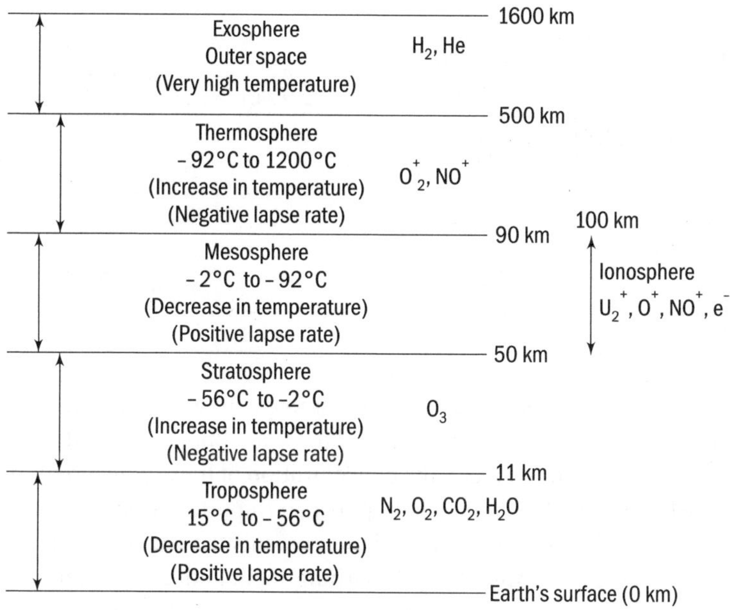


**Fig. 1.1**  Simplified representation of atmosphere into various regions

**Table 1.2**  Composition of dry air at sea level

| Components | Amount | |
|---|---|---|
| | Percentage (by volume) | Parts per million (ppm) |
| **(i) Major components** | | |
| Nitrogen ($N_2$) | 78.09 | 780,900 |
| Oxygen ($O_2$) | 20.98 | 209,400 |
| Water vapour ($H_2O$) | ~0.15 | 1,000–50,000 |
| **(ii) Minor components** | | |
| Argon (Ar) | 0.934 | 9,340 |
| Carbon dioxide ($CO_2$) | 0.032 | 320 |
| **(iii) Trace components** | | |
| Neon (Ne) | 0.00182 | 18.2 |
| Helium (He) | 0.000524 | 5.24 |
| Methane ($CH_4$) | 0.00018 | 1.8 |
| Krypton (Kr) | 0.00018 | 1.8 |
| Nitrous oxide ($N_2O$) | 0.000025 | 0.25 |
| Hydrogen ($H_2$) | 0.00005 | 0.5 |
| Xenon (Xe) | 0.0000087 | 0.87 |

*Contd...*

**Table 1.2** *Contd...*

| Components | Amount | |
|---|---|---|
| | *Percentage (by volume)* | *Parts per million (ppm)* |
| Sulphur dioxide ($SO_2$) | 0.0000002 | 0.002 |
| Nitrogen ($NO_2$) | 0.0000001 | 0.001 |
| Ammonia ($NH_3$) | 0.000001 | 0.01 |
| Carbon monoxide (CO) | 0.000012 | 0.012 |
| Ozone ($O_3$) | 0.000002 | 0.02 |
| Iodine ($I_2$) | Traces | Traces |

The most important constituents of the atmosphere are nitrogen, oxygen, and carbon dioxide along with water vapour. All these are important for the sustenance of life on earth. In the atmosphere, the concentration of these constituents remains, more or less, constant. The atmosphere plays an important role in the creation of different types of climates. The atmosphere prevents the harmful solar radiations from reaching the earth's surface by absorbing them and helps in supporting life on earth.

## 1.3.2  Hydrosphere

The collective mass of water found on, under, and over the surface of the earth is called the hydrosphere. It covers more than two-thirds of the earth's surface either as oceans or seas (saltwater) or as freshwater which includes waterbodies, such as rivers, lakes, and ponds. Oceans account for about 95% of the earth's water supply which is unfit for consumption due to high-salt contents. The polar ice caps and glaciers account for about 2% of the total water available on earth. Fresh potable water is available only to the extent of about 1% in rivers, lakes, and groundwater.

Water is the most essential component of life forms existing on earth and no life is possible without it. The high value of latent heat moderates the temperature of the biosphere. The solubility of oxygen in water is responsible for the survival of aquatic life.

## 1.3.3  Lithosphere

The layer of rock constituting the outer parts of the earth's atmosphere is called the lithosphere. It extends up to about 400 km of the earth's surface. About three-fourths of the surface of the lithosphere is covered with water. The earth's surface structure can be mainly divided into three layers: (i) crust, (ii) mantle, and (iii) outer and inner core (Figure 1.2). The core is the central fluid sphere; with a diameter of about 2500 km, it is composed of mainly nickel and iron. The mantle extends about 3000 km above the core and is also in the molten state. The outermost solid portion of the earth is the crust. It is about 30–40 km in thickness,

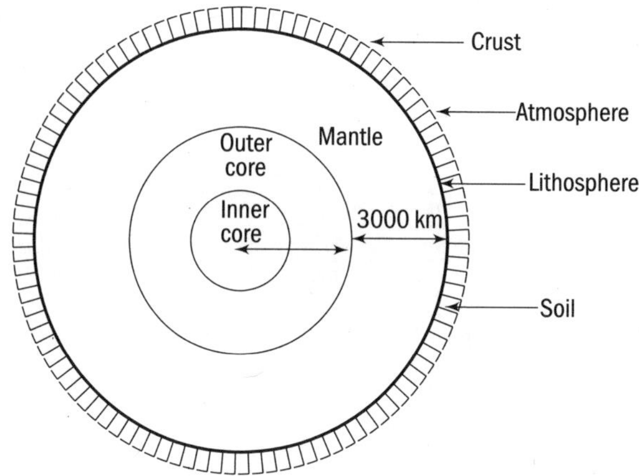


**Fig. 1.2**  Layers of the earth

mainly covered with soil, and is the most important part of the lithosphere from the environmental perspective.

The role played by the lithosphere is vital for the metabolic processes of organisms to take place as the layer provides most of the necessary minerals and nutrients essential for an organisms' growth. The formation of soil is another important function performed by the lithosphere.

The earth depends completely on the sun for its heat energy requirements. The earth loses a considerable portion of this heat energy through reflection and radiation. In this way, a nearly steady state of the average global temperature is maintained. The reflecting capacity of the earth is called albedo.

A number of industrial processes are responsible for the substantial release of greenhouse gases (GHGs), such as carbon dioxide, ozone, nitrous oxide, methane, water vapours, and particulate matter, into the atmosphere. Also deforestation, soil erosion, and eruption of volcanoes add to GHG release. Increase in GHG concentration leads to an increase in the earth's average temperature. In fact, pollutants discharged by anthropogenic activities create an imbalance in the global temperature. It has been observed that over the past few decades, the average global temperature has been rising steadily. This has disastrous effects on the environment.

## 1.3.4  Biosphere

The region of the earth where the lithosphere, hydrosphere, and atmosphere are present and where life—in the form of living organisms and their habitats—exists constitutes the biosphere. The biosphere extends from about 11,000 m below the sea level to about 2000 m above the sea level. The most densely populated region of the biosphere lies just above and below the sea level. A biosphere can be represented as shown in Figure 1.3.

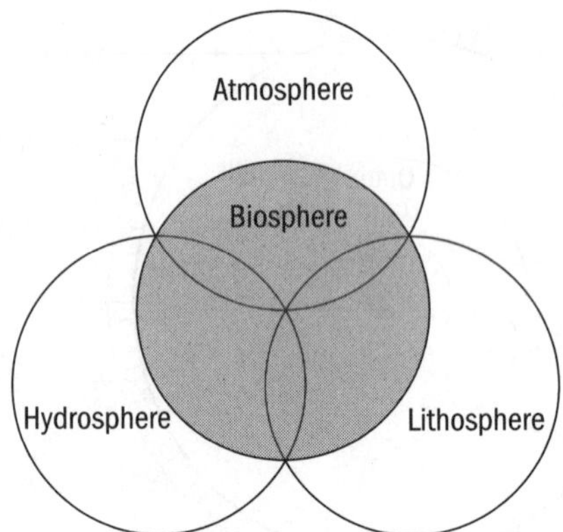



**Fig. 1.3**   Representation of biosphere (shaded portion)

The energy required for sustenance of life on the biosphere comes from the sun, without which it will collapse. The nutrients required for living organisms are sourced from air, water, and soil. In the biosphere, these nutrients get recycled over and over again so that they can be utilized for both survival and continuance of life. The biosphere provides food for all existing life forms. All the four segments of the environment: (i) atmosphere, (ii) hydrosphere, (iii) lithosphere, and (iv) biosphere are interlinked and dependent on each other. The interdependence of these segments is visible in the form of various biochemical cycles, such as water cycle, oxygen cycle, and nitrogen cycle.

## 1.4   ENVIRONMENTAL POLLUTION

The presence of any pollutant in the environment is referred to as environmental pollution. In other words, environmental pollution can be defined as the unfavourable alteration of the surroundings, mainly through the introduction of pollutants (contamination). The agent that contaminates the environment is called a pollutant. Even a normal constituent of the environment can become a pollutant if its concentration increases beyond manageable limits. For example, carbon dioxide, a normal constituent of the environment (atmosphere), becomes a pollutant if its environmental concentration reaches unmanageable limits.

A pollutant can be either a non-degradable pollutant or a biodegradable pollutant. Non-degradable pollutants remain in the environment in an unchanged form. Examples include pesticides, heavy metals, rubber, plastics, and nuclear waste. On the contrary, biodegradable pollutants can be broken down into simple products under bacterial decomposition; for example, paper, garden waste, domestic sewage, and fertilizers. These biodegradable pollutants become a potential threat to the environment, especially when their generation in the environment surpasses the decomposition capacity of the biosphere.

Pollutants can enter the environment either through a point source or a non-point source. Point source can be defined as a confined source of pollution which discharges pollutants (or effluents) through single, identifiable sources such as chimneys, pipes from industries, or municipal wastes. On the other hand, non-point sources are diffused sources that discharge pollutants over a large area. Examples include run-offs from agricultural fields, construction sites, and mines. Pollution from point sources, as compared to non-point sources, is easy to control by the application of on-site treatment.

Broadly, pollutants can be grouped into natural, primary, and secondary pollutants. Natural pollutants are released from natural sources or as a result of natural activity. Examples include pollens and volatile organic compounds (VOCs) released from plants, gases discharged by volcanic eruptions, and organic matter decay. Other examples include particulate matter released from wild fires and natural radioactivity. Primary pollutants get discharged in the environment from both natural and anthropogenic sources. Examples include sulphur dioxide, nitrogen oxides, carbon dioxide, carbon monoxide, hydrocarbons, and particulates released from burning of fossil fuels. However, it is important to note that secondary pollutants are produced as a result of chemical reactions between primary pollutants and normal atmospheric components in the presence of electromagnetic radiations from the sun. For example, sulphur trioxide which is obtained from sulphur dioxide, a primary pollutant, belongs to the class of secondary pollutants. Other examples of secondary pollutants include nitric oxide, ozone, peroxyacetyl nitrates (PANs), nitric acid, and sulphuric acid.

Environmental pollution can be caused by various factors. Some of the basic causative factors include the following:

(1) **Deforestation:** Deforestation is the indiscriminate cutting of trees for wood and expansion of cultivable land. Deforestation results in air, water, and soil erosion.

(2) **Animal killing:** Killing gentle animals for food and fierce animals for safety reasons may lead to the extinction of some of the animal species.

(3) **Industrial sector:** Industries engaged in the manufacture of medicinal products (drugs and antibiotics), dyes, and agrochemicals substantially pollute the natural environment.

(4) **Rapid growth:** Global-level advancements in technologies and their application in various sectors, especially industries, are accompanied with the release of momentous harmful pollutants.

(5) **Excessive use of agrochemicals:** The excessive use of agrochemicals in agriculture for increasing crop yield leads to environmental degradation.

(6) **Nuclear energy:** Nuclear power plants release a substantial amount of deadly toxic radioactive pollutants into the environment.

Environmental pollution includes air pollution, water pollution, and soil pollution. Apart from these major pollution types, we come across thermal pollution, noise pollution, and radioactive pollution (discussed at length in Chapter 5).

## 1.4.1 Air Pollution

Air pollution is described as an unwanted change in the quality of air caused by the emission of gases (such as carbon dioxide, nitrogen dioxide, and sulphur dioxide which are poisonous in nature). These poisonous gases are produced by various activities including burning of fossil fuels, volcanic eruptions, and discharge of particulate matter in the atmosphere by industrial activities. The presence of the contaminants in the air is called air pollution and the material responsible for polluting the air is called air pollutant. The major air pollutants are oxides of carbon (carbon dioxide and carbon monoxide), oxides of sulphur or $SO_x$ (such as sulphur dioxide and sulphur trioxide), oxides of nitrogen or $NO_x$ (such as nitric oxide, nitrogen dioxide, and nitrous oxide), hydrocarbons also called VOCs (such as methane, propane, butane, ethylene, benzene, and benzopyrene), other organic compounds (such as chloroform, formaldehyde, methylene chloride, vinyl chloride, ethylene chloride, and chlorofluorocarbons or CFCs), suspended particulates, and photochemical oxidants [such as ozone, peroxyacyl nitrates (PANs), acetaldehyde, and hydrogen peroxide].

Among the various air pollutants, sulphur dioxide is responsible for causing lung disease. Its short-term exposure may lead to irritation to nose, mucus lining, shortness of breath, oedema, and bronchospasm. Long-term exposure of sulphur dioxide can cause respiratory diseases such as chronic bronchitis, aggravated asthma, pulmonary fibrosis, and heart problems. The effect of sulphur dioxide increases manyfold when it settles on the particulate matter in the air and reaches deeper parts of the respiratory system. Thus, the effect of $SO_2$ increases significantly even at low concentration. The main sources of $SO_2$ in the atmosphere include (i) combustion of sulphur-containing fuels, for example, coal, (ii) extraction and refining of petroleum, and (iii) ore smelting for extraction of metals. In the atmosphere, $SO_2$ gets converted into $SO_3$ which is primarily responsible for causing acid rain.

Oxides of nitrogen are released in the atmosphere from the exhausts of automobiles such as cars, buses, trucks, and two-wheelers. If inhaled, $NO_x$ can cause inflammation of gums, internal bleeding, pneumonia, and even cancer. $NO_x$ have the ability to oxidize lipids, thus their exposure can disrupt cell membranes, which can lead to oxima. Exhausts released from diesel engines have been shown to cause chromosomal mutations which are responsible for causing cancer. Similar to $SO_2$, $NO_x$ are responsible for causing acid rain.

Carbon monoxide—a constituent of exhaust gases from vehicles—is extremely toxic. Once it enters the bloodstream, it inhibits the combining capacity of blood and gets attached to haemoglobin more strongly than oxygen, resulting in the formation of toxic carboxyhaemoglobin. Due to this, even low levels of carbon monoxide are unsafe. Higher concentration and prolong exposure to carbon monoxide can bring down physical and mental activities, eventually causing asphyxiation, heart ailments, brain damage, and even death.

Pollutants such as ozone and PAN which mainly arise from photochemical reactions between $NO_x$ and hydrocarbons in the atmosphere are responsible for causing a number of adverse biological effects. These pollutants can cause irritation in the eyes. Ozone is responsible for causing a number of ailments such as cough, headache, shortness of breath, bleeding, and constriction of respiratory passage. It is extremely harmful for people suffering from asthma, emphysema, and chronic bronchitis.

The extremely harmful fumes of toxic metals such as lead, mercury, zinc, and magnesium are released in the atmosphere from incinerators (where discarded tyres are incinerated). Lead exposure is known to damage the brain of young children. In adults, lead affects kidneys and liver, and can impair the central nervous system. Inhalation of mercury vapours causes lesions in the mouth. High-level exposure of lead may result in the development of neurological problems. Arsenic is known to be associated with skin cancer, peripheral vascular diseases, and other diseases.

Burning of tyres releases dioxins in the atmosphere, a well-known carcinogen. The suspended particulate matter (SPM), released in the air by diesel engine-equipped vehicles and electricity generators are responsible for chronic respiratory problems and can also increase the risk of cardiac arrest and premature death. The SPM can get coated with carcinogens and polycyclic aromatic hydrocarbons which can be fatal to humans.

It is a well-known fact that women who smoke or are exposed to smoke during pregnancy have a high chance of delivering an abnormal baby. As per a German study, air pollution from vehicular exhaust is equivalent to smoking as both reduce the immunity of the respiratory system. This is because vehicular exhaust contains carbon monoxide and benzene, which are the principal chemicals inhaled via cigarette smoking.

Chlorofluorocarbons—a group of organic compounds—contain chlorine, fluorine, and carbon, and are used in a number of applications. CFCs are stable compounds and remain in the atmosphere for 50–100 years. They are responsible for the depletion of the ozone layer in the stratosphere which has become one of the most serious problems of the earth, as life forms cannot survive in the absence of ozone. This aspect forms the subject matter of a subsequent section.

### 1.4.1.1 Air Pollution Episodes

Air pollutants pose a grave danger to all life forms on earth. Air pollution can be best described as a 'time bomb' which may explode any time, at any place causing severe, undetermined problems. This is clear from the various air pollution episodes (accidents due to natural or human-made causes) which have occurred since early times. The following are some of the world's major air pollution episodes:

(i) **Meuse River Valley fog:** The first episode of severe air pollution was recorded in 1930 in Meuse River Valley of Belgium. The incident occurred as a result of thermal inversion in which $SO_2$, mainly released from nearby factories, was trapped in the surrounding air at 38 parts per million (ppm) level. Due to this episode, about 60 people died and a large number of cattle were killed.

(ii) **Photochemical smog of Los Angeles:** In 1994, Los Angeles in California experienced serious air pollution, primarily caused by the formation of photochemical smog. It was characterized by reduced visibility, eye irritation, and plant damage.

(iii) **$SO_2$ poisoning in Donora:** In 1948, in Donora, Pennsylvania, the USA, about 40% of the population was severely affected as a consequence of $SO_2$ poisoning. The incident claimed 20 deaths.

(iv) **London smog:** On 5-9 December 1952, heavy fog engulfed London city for 5 days at a stretch affecting thousands of people. The incident was named 'Great Smog of London' and about 4000–5000 lives were lost. The peak $SO_2$ concentration was recorded at 1.3 ppm while that of smoke was 4 $mgm^{-3}$. Similar smog conditions also recurred in December 1962, and around 700 deaths occurred.

(v) **Poza Rica air pollution:** In November 1950, the Poza Rica air pollution episode resulted from an industrial accident of a refinery in which about 25 people died and many more became ill. The reason was the release of huge amounts of $H_2S$ from the refinery which spread over the ground around the refinery and seeped into nearby homes.

(vi) **Explosion in a chemical plant at Seveso, Italy:** In July, 1976, an explosion took place in a chemical plant (at Seveso, Italy) manufacturing the herbicide—2, 4, 5-trichlorophenoxy acetate. A white cloud of TCDC (2, 3, 7, 8-tetrachlorobenzo-10-dioxin) was released which contaminated buildings, ground, and soil. About 200 people suffered from skin diseases and many became prone to liver ailments. As an after effect of the episode, deformed and premature babies were born.

(vii) **Bhopas gas tragedy:** On 3 December 1984, in Bhopal, India, accident occurred in Union Carbide factory plant which manufactured carbamate pesticides. The starting material methyl isocyanate (MIC) was stored at low temperature in storage tanks. On 3 December 1984, a massive leak of MIC occurred in the storage tank and caused havoc. About 22,000 people residing in the area died and a very large number (about 120,000)

$$CH_3NH_2 + COCl_2 \longrightarrow CH_3{-}N{=}C{=}O + 2HCl$$

Methyl amine   Phosgene

$CH_3{-}N{=}C{=}O$
Methyl isocyanate

α-naphthol   1-naphthyl-N-methyl carbamide (carbaryl)

of people were disabled for the rest of their lives. This incident is now commonly known as Bhopal disaster, and Bhopal, where the episode occurred, is known as the city of death.

**(viii) Nuclear disaster at Chernobyl:** On 26 April 1986, the world's worst nuclear catastrophe occurred in Chernobyl, Ukraine. It is believed to be a result of human error in controlling fuel rods. The accident increased the reactor core temperature to more than 2000°C. Fuel and radioactive remains were shot into the air hitting the surrounding areas. The effect was felt over most of Europe. The accident resulted in the death of more than 200 people. Soil, water, and vegetation over 100 km$^2$ area around Chernobyl were severely damaged. The neighbouring countries such as Poland were also severely affected. Even after cleaning up operation and dumping tonnes of sand and clay to bury the molten core, more than 300,000 times the permissible dose of the radiation was continuously emitted.

**(ix) Three Mile Island nuclear accident:** A nuclear reactor in Three Mile Island in the USA made news due to an accident that took place on 26 April 1986 as a result of a complex operational failure, following human error.

**(x) Nuclear explosions in Japan:** A major nuclear disaster took place when a series of explosions occurred at three reactors in Japan on 11 March 2011, resulting in loss of human lives.

In view of the disastrous effects of atmospheric pollution, it is very important to make sure that suitable control measures are taken to prevent the release of atmospheric pollutants. However, in the case of nuclear catastrophes, adequate precautions and necessary steps should be taken so that the occurrence of nuclear disasters can be avoided to the extent possible.

## 1.4.1.2 *Environmental Crisis*

Large-scale dumping of pollutants in various environmental segments from industries and other activities of men have become a matter of serious concern, as they are responsible for causing environmental crises. Smog episodes of London and New York, mercury poisoning from contaminated seafood in a number of areas in Japan, disappearance of a number of species of birds due to the use of pesticides, such as dichlorodiphenyltrichloroethane (DDT), massive oil spills in oceans, and nuclear accidents are some of the fatal consequences of man-made disasters (discussed in the previous section). The problem compounded because of increase in human population, extensive use of natural resources, especially by some western countries who are depleting natural resources of the earth at a fast rate. All these have a profound influence on the survival of mankind. Owing to the environmental crisis, the world community is not only concerned about the survival of the present generation but also of the future generation. In order to prevent further degradation of the environment, the United Nations Conference on Environment and Development (UNCED), informally known as the Earth Summit, was held in Rio de Janeiro from 3–14 June 1992. The summit was attended by representatives of more than 150 nations and dignitaries from media and industrial sectors. It was unanimously agreed that degradation of the environment must be avoided to the extent possible. However, there were differences on the issue of 'who will pay' for cleaning up to the mess—the developed or developing countries.

In spite of differences in the opinion of various countries, certain resolutions were taken up in the form of Agenda 21. Some of these are listed here:

(1) All countries must adopt measures for international co-operation to achieve sustainable development

(2) Adoption of policies to combat poverty

(3) Take suitable measures in order to change consumption pattern of natural resources

(4) Take measures to promote and protect human health

(5) Take measures to protect the atmosphere

(6) Take integrated approach for planning and management

(7) Take appropriate measures for preventing deforestation

(8) Prevention of desertification and drought

(9) Promotion of sustainable agriculture and rural development

(10) Conservation of biodiversity

(11) Adoption of environmentally sound management of biotechnology

(12) Protection of oceans, seas, and other waterbodies

(13) Application of integrated approach for the development, management, and use of water resources

(14) Management of toxic chemicals

(15) Management of hazardous waste

### *1.4.1.3   Environmental Degradation*

Deterioration in the quality of the environment is referred to as environmental degradation. Natural processes as well as anthropogenic activities are responsible for degrading the environment. Besides the major air pollutants (such as oxides, carbon, nitrogen, sulphur, and particulate matter), the release of large amounts of GHGs (such as carbon dioxide, methane, and CFCs) are responsible for greenhouse effect, which in turn is responsible for global warming.

Uncontrolled growth of human population is another important factor of environmental degradation. In addition, Gulf War (16 January to 26 February 1991) is responsible for the large-scale degradation of the environment, and it took more than 10 years to restore the natural climatic conditions. In this war, more than one lakh one-tonne bombs were used for bombardment which released momentous amounts of black smoke and created deep craters in the earth's crust. About 700 oil wells were burnt and the burning continued for about a year, releasing about 80 million tonnes of $CO_2$ and 36 million tonnes of $SO_2$ on a daily basis. Besides this, about 8 million barrels of oil was dumped into the Persian Gulf, which proved disastrous for the marine ecosystem.

Nuclear waste is another man-made and dangerous pollutant and a severe environmental degrader. Generation of radioactive wastes, which mainly takes place at nuclear reactors, can cause numerous problems including health hazards. Industrial wastes which are discharged into different environmental segments without following proper waste treatment practices prior to disposal are hugely responsible for degrading the environment. It has been discussed in detail in Chapter 5 (Section 5.2).

## 1.4.2   Water Pollution

When the quality of water is unsafe or harmful for human beings, animals, or aquatic life, it is referred to as water pollution. Water pollution can take place through both natural and anthropogenic processes. Natural processes include pollution of waterbodies by decomposed vegetables, animals, and weathered products. Anthropogenic processes include industrial, agricultural, radioactive, and mining processes. Water pollution occurs by different types of pollutants which can be biological agents, chemical agents (including radioactive substances), and physical agents.

Biological agents include pathogenic agents such as virus, bacteria, and protozoans; all of these are harmful for human health. Some of the water-borne diseases, caused by biological agents, include cholera, bacterial and amoebic dysentery, gastroenteritis, typhoid, polio, viral hepatitis, worm infections, and flues. Apart from these, insects that have aquatic larvae transmit diseases such as malaria, dengue, yellow fever, and filariasis. In India, the onset of rainy season is accompanied by such epidemics. The main sources of biological agents of pollutants include human sewage, animal and plant wastes, decaying organic matter, industrial wastes, natural and urban land run-offs, and wastewater discharges from slaughterhouses. The contributory factors include overpopulation, unplanned industrial and human settlements, and lack of civic amenities. The bacteria require oxygen to survive on biological wastes and cause depletion of oxygen in the waterbody. This proves harmful for aquatic life.

Chemical agents of pollutants can be inorganic (such as nitrates, phosphates, salts, and toxic heavy metals) and organic (such as oil, gasoline, pesticides, dyes, paints, plastics, detergents, domestic sewage, and animal wastes). Organic wastes and inorganic nutrients such as phosphates and nitrates are responsible for eutrophication of waterbodies. Radioactive substances are released in waterbodies from sources such as processing of uranium ore, and wastes from research laboratories. The radionuclides enter the food chain and are chiefly responsible for birth and genetic defects. These are also causative agents for cancer.

The quality of water is affected by physical agents such as suspended solids, sedimentary solids, and temperature. These pollutants result in silting and clogging of waterways. The temperature lowers the solubility of oxygen in water; this has a direct influence on aquatic life.

On the basis of the source, water pollution can be of the following three types:

(i) Surface water pollution

(ii) Seawater pollution

(iii) Groundwater pollution

### 1.4.2.1   Surface Water Pollution

Surface water in the form of rivers, streams, and lakes is present to the extent of about 0.0091% of the total global water. Some sources of surface water pollution are listed in Table 1.3.

**Table 1.3**   Sources of surface water pollution

| Sources of contamination | Contaminants discharged on land |
| --- | --- |
| Agricultural run-offs | Agrochemicals (pesticides, herbicides, fungicides) |
| Accidental spillage of chemicals | Different chemicals |
| Leaks from surface, storage tanks, or pipelines | Gasoline, oil |
| Run-offs from industrial sites, such as factories, refineries, mines | Solvents and chemicals |
| Radioactive material processing plants | Radioactive material |

The harmful effects of surface water pollution are largely determined by the extent to which water has been polluted.

### 1.4.2.2 Seawater Pollution

Marine pollution or seawater pollution results from the discharge of waste substances into the sea which can degrade the water quality and, thereby, considerably harm aquatic organisms and human health. Seas and oceans are routinely used by humans as a dustbin for dumping all types of waste materials including industrial wastes, heavy metals, agrochemicals, mine tailings, urban and non-urban sewage, and farm and fossil fuel run-offs. These wastes contain non-biodegradable components, which is the root cause of marine pollution. Even radioactive wastes are dumped into the sea. Therefore, marine pollution is mainly caused by dumping oil, and radioactive and hazardous wastes in seawater.

Oil discharge is one of the major causes of marine pollution. It is estimated that per year about 250 million gallons of oil is discharged into oceans by various processes. The massive marine pollution often results from oil spillage, mainly caused by oil tanker accidents. Some of the adverse effects of oil discharge include the following:

- The oily surface markedly reduces the rate of oxygen uptake by water.
- Oil spill decreases the penetration of light which retards photosynthesis in aquatic plants.
- Lichens and algae along the shorelines get destroyed.
- Fishery is hampered.
- Soluble aromatics present in the oil affect the aquatic organisms. Some of the aromatic compounds are carcinogenic and affect plant metabolism.
- The aromatic compounds in oil can be very harmful to human health; their exposure can produce irritation, and liver and kidney damage.
- Birds are particularly vulnerable to damages from oil spill. Every year, thousands of birds die due to seawater pollution caused by oil spill incidents.

A number of procedures are available to clean up the mess created by oil spills in oceans. However, the best course is to avoid oil spills by taking adequate measures. Some of the methods of controlling oil spillage are the following:

**(i) Skimming:** The heavy oil fractions that float on the surface of the sea are best removed by skimming operation. This method is simple and offers very good results. It should be employed in the shortest possible time after the occurrence of the oil spill. Otherwise wind will spread the oil over a very large surface and as a result skimming will become very difficult to execute.

(ii) **Use of absorbents:** In this process, suitable absorbing materials such as polyurethane, saw dust, and chopped straw are spread on the surface of oil and then skimmed off.

(iii) **Burning of oil slick:** This method, though useful, causes extensive air pollution. In addition, thermal pollution is very much likely to occur because of oil slick burning.

(iv) **Chemical additives:** Chemicals can be used to solidify the oil spread on the water surface and then the solid material (containing oil) can be easily skimmed off.

(v) **Microorganisms:** The most-effective method of removing oil from seawater surface is the use of oil-eating bacteria. For example, oil-eating microbes were used with great success in cleaning up oil spills in Texas, the USA.

Radioactive pollutants enter waterbodies, especially seas and oceans, from various sources. Some of the important sources of radioactive pollutants are the following:

(1) Mining and processing of ores to produce unstable radioactive substances

(2) Nuclear power plants

(3) Nuclear reactors

(4) Nuclear weapons

(5) Use of radioactive isotopes in medical, industrial, and research applications

(6) Testing of nuclear weapons in the atmosphere and underwater releases radioactive fallout.

Nuclear weapon testing produces $Sr^{90}$, a long-lived component of radioactive fallout. It is chemically similar to calcium and accompanies calcium in soil, plants, and animals, and finally finds its way via food chain into humans and accumulates in bones and teeth. The presence of $Sr^{90}$ in bones is responsible for disorders in blood-cell formation, can cause anaemia, and more serious disorders.

Nuclear power plants generate liquid wastes (low-discharge-level radioactivity), gaseous wastes from fuel elements, fission products, and heat. The discharge of radioactive wastes in air and waterbodies causes problems in the long run. Table 1.4 lists some of the radioactive materials discharged from various activities.

The level of radionuclides found in water is measured in units of picocuries ($= 10^{-12}$ curie $= 3.7 \times 10^{-3}$ disintegrations per second). The permissible limit is 3 picocuries. The following are some of the serious consequences of the discharge of radioactive pollutants in water:

(i) They cause skin cancer, carcinoma, melanoma, breast cancer, leukaemia, breakage of DNA, and cataract.

**Table 1.4**  Radioactive material discharged from various activities

| Activities | Radioactive material obtained |
|---|---|
| Leaching of miners<br>Atomic reactors | $^{226}Ra$, $^{40}K$ $^{90}Sr$, $^{131}I$, $^{137}Cs$, $^{140}Ba$, $^{141}Cs$, $^{85}Kr$,<br>$^{60}CO$, $^{54}Mn$, $^{55}Fe$, $^{239}Pu$ |
| Neutron bombardment of atomic fuel | Radioactive Pu, Np, Am, Cm, Bk, Cs, Zn, Ru |

(ii) They cause radiation sickness which is characterized by nausea, vomiting, diarrhoea, anorexia, epilation, lethargy, and weakness.

(iii) They can cause genetic disorders, gene mutations, and blood abnormalities.

(iv) Radionuclides present in water get accumulated in soil sediments and this affects aquatic ecosystem.

### 1.4.2.3  Groundwater Pollution

Groundwater refers to the water below the water table (which is the level below the ground at which water is found). A portion of the rainwater that falls on the ground seeps through the soil and fissures in rocks, and forms a zone of groundwater. It constitutes about 0.31% of the total global water and is expected to be available for thousands of years; it is utilized for fulfilling water requirements.

Groundwater gets polluted due to human activities including industrial, domestic, and agricultural. The water contamination in groundwater is generally irreversible leading to degradation of water quality. Table 1.5 gives the sources of groundwater pollution.

## 1.4.3  Soil Pollution

Soil plays an important role in sustenance of various life forms on earth as it produces food for every inhabitant of this planet. The vital source—soil—is only six inches deep on earth's surface throughout. Besides natural causes, land

**Table 1.5**  Sources of groundwater pollution

| Sources of contamination | Contaminants discharged into groundwater |
|---|---|
| Domestic wastes | Pathogenic organisms, nutrients, and solids from domestic waste |
| Industrial wastes | Toxic heavy metals along with hazardous organic and inorganic effluents |
| Agricultural wastes | Fertilizers, pesticides, insecticides, herbicides. Leaches from agricultural land containing nitrates, phosphates, and potash pollute the groundwater. |

*Note:* Groundwater can also be polluted by septic tanks and refuse dumps.

utilization for agricultural and developmental activities carried out by humans is very much responsible for the degradation of land surface. Large-scale deforestation and waste disposal have been carried out by man on the pretext of development. Waste disposal is responsible for soil pollution.

Overindulgence of men with land results in loss of biodiversity and soil erosion, making the soil acidic or alkaline. In addition, deposition of waste pollutes the soil considerably.

*(i) Loss of biodiversity:* Deforestation of vast areas of forests for the fulfilment of agricultural and developmental needs destroys natural flora and fauna. According to International Union for Conservation of Nature (IUCN), by 2050, approximately 50,000 plant species are likely to become extinct or threatened. It is believed that at present, more than 4500 animal species and 20,000 plant species are threatened.

*(ii) Soil erosion:* The process of loosening and/or detachment of soil components, particularly, topsoil particles, is called soil erosion. It is caused by blowing wind and flowing water. These causative factors of soil erosion become more effective if the land is devoid of vegetation (for example, deforestation). The eroded soil reaches nearby waterbody such as lakes, rivers, ponds, and settles at the bottom, resulting in silting of the waterbody.

*(iii) Acidity and alkalinity:* Excessive use of fertilizers renders the soil acidic or alkaline, depending on the type of fertilizer used. The acidic or alkaline soil becomes unfit for subsequent crops.

*(iv) Pollution of land:* Humans have turned land into a dumping ground as a result of indiscriminate dumping of waste generated by anthropogenic activities. In India, most of the solid waste is land filled. During rains, leaching of wastes takes place, resulting in groundwater pollution. Burning of wastes in incinerators produces ash which has a high concentration of dangerous toxins, such as dioxins and heavy metals. When waste is buried in landfills, its ash leaches in the surrounding areas and causes pollution.

### 1.4.3.1 Water Quality Parameters

The quality of water can be assessed by a number of parameters. These include dissolved oxygen (DO), biological oxygen demand (BOD), chemical oxygen demand (COD), most probable number (MPN), and total dissolved solids (TDS).

**(i) Dissolved oxygen:** It is the amount of oxygen gas that is dissolved in a water source. Large amount of DO is an indicator of good quality water. Limited concentration of oxygen content in water signifies the presence of organic waste pollutant in water. Oxygen is soluble in freshwater to the extent of 14.6 ppm at 0°C, about 7.4 ppm at 20°C, and approximately 11.3 ppm at 0°C. A minimum of 4 ppm DO is necessary to support aquatic species.

**(ii) Biological oxygen demand:** BOD is the measure of oxygen used by microorganisms such as bacteria in order to decompose the organic matter including sewage, dead plant leaves, and food wastes. If the concentration of organic waste is high in a water source, then more bacteria will be present to consume the oxygen. Under such polluted conditions, the demand for oxygen is on a higher side, and the resulting BOD will be high. With high BOD, the DO level in water decreases.

**(iii) Chemical oxygen demand:** It is the amount of oxygen required to degrade or break down the organic chemical compounds of wastewater. A waterbody receiving effluents from chemical industries has a high COD value, between 0 and 5 $mgL^{-1}$. This signifies that the water quality is good and can be used for drinking (potable). However, COD value in the range of 200–100 $mgL^{-1}$ indicates that the water is unfit for drinking; however, it can be used for washing and agriculture purposes.

**(iv) Most probable number:** Water polluted with organic wastes such as sewage/sludge has high population of bacteria including *Escherichia coli* and coliforms. Using most probable number (MPN) test, both *Escherichia coli* and coliforms can be detected and enumerated. This method predicts the number of these organisms present in a waterbody. Coliform is present as human wastes in water and generally is not harmful; however, its presence indicates the existence of human wastes in water. Polluted water exhibits high MPN value.

**(v) Total dissolved solids:** It is a measure of the amount of salts and solids dissolved in water. Some of the dissolved substances that make the quality of water poor include calcium, phosphorus, iron, sulphates, carbonates, nitrates, and chlorides. Heavy metals also fall in this category. The quality of water is degraded in case excessive amounts of TDS are present. The following are the major types of wastes generated from different sources responsible for pollution of the land:

   **(a) Urban waste:** Municipal waste, sewage, industrial effluents, domestic effluents, and hospital wastes

   **(b) Industrial waste:** Slag, lime sludge, brine mud, scraps of metals, glass, ferrous and non-ferrous metals, wool, thread, paper, fly ash, plastics, wastes from tanneries and other small scale industries, and wastewater effluents

   **(c) Domestic waste:** Organic waste from kitchen, crockery, tin cans, plastic cans, bottles and bags, glass bottles, cloth rags, paper pieces, straw, board, boxes, and ash

   **(d) Rural waste:** Pesticides, herbicides, and agricultural run-offs

   **(e) Nuclear waste:** Radioactive hazardous wastes

### 1.4.4   Thermal Pollution

When the temperature of air or a waterbody gets altered, that is, when its temperature is either raised or lowered, this results in thermal pollution of the waterbody. The temperature of waterbodies is known to regulate aquatic life, for example, increase in just 1°C in the temperature of oceans can prove life threatening to some species of coral reefs. Increase in water temperature has similar effects on sensitive organisms. Thermal pollution is also caused by the release of waste heat into a waterbody. Some of the natural processes such as forest fires and eruption of volcanoes release large amounts of heat into the environment. In a number of industrial units such as smelters, petroleum refineries, paper mills, food processing units, and chemical manufacturing plants, water is used for cooling purposes. The hot water so obtained is released as an effluent into waterbodies. This changes the concentration of DO in the waterbody, affecting aquatic life. The only solution to thermal pollution problem is to retain the heated water and effluents in water-holding units to become cool and then discharge it into waterbodies. Alternatively, the waste heat generated from industrial units can be used to warm buildings in colder seasons.

### 1.4.5   Noise Pollution

Sound is an important element of the 'communication' process. It is not possible to lead day-to-day life without sound. In case, sound becomes noise, it is annoying. In fact noise is unwanted or high levels of sound can be annoying, stress causing, and impair the auditory perception (ability to hear). The main sources of noise include industrial operations, machines, vehicles, railways, aircrafts, construction work, and household appliances. Sound travels in the form of waves. The waves are known to exert pressure. The intensity of sound is measured by computing the pressure on a scale called decibel (db). A tenfold increase in the sound intensity is represented as 10 db on the scale. The instrument used to measure the pressure of sound wave is called decibel meter. Besides pressure, sound also has a pitch. A high pitched sound is louder than low pitched sound even if the pressure is the same. High-pitched sound is more annoying than low-pitched one of same intensity. The unit which measures both pressure and pitch of sound is called decibel–A (dbA).

Prolonged exposure to noise can cause health and behavioural disorders, and in extreme cases lead to permanent loss of hearing. According to the World Health Organization (WHO), noise can affect humans in a number of ways. These include physical, physiological, and psychological effects. Physical effects include high blood pressure and changes in cardiovascular and digestive systems. Prolonged exposure to noise can lead to deafness. Physiological effects include anxiety, insomnia, hypertension, nausea, and giddiness. Noise levels in 120–150 dB range can (i) affect respiratory system, (ii) cause dizziness, and (iii) result in loss of physical control. Psychological effects of noise include loss of working efficiency, which reduces output and higher rates in accidents and injuries. Table 1.6 gives some examples of sound levels on dB scale and their effects on human beings.

**Table 1.6**  Some examples of sound levels (on dB scale) and their effects

| Activities | Sound pressure (dbA) | Perceived loudness | Effect |
|---|---|---|---|
| Breathing | 10 | | |
| Whisper | 20 | | Very quiet |
| Quiet rural area (night-time) | 30 | | |
| Library, soft background music | 40 | | |
| Quiet suburb (daytime), conversation in living room | 50 | | Quiet |
| Conversation in a restaurant and office, background music | 60 | Moderately loud | Intrusive |
| Freeway traffic at 15 m, vacuum cleaner, noisy party | 70 | Moderately loud | Annoying |
| Garbage disposal machine, washing machine, freight train at 15 m | 80 | Very loud | Possible hearing damage |
| Busy urban street, diesel truck, food blender, cotton spinning machine | 90 | Very loud | Hearing damage (8 h) speech interfered |
| Jet takeoff (305 m away), power lawnmower, farm tractor, printing plant, garbage truck | 100 | Uncomfortably loud | Serious hearing damage (8 h) |
| Steel mill, riveting, automobile horn at 1 m, stereo held close to ear | 110 | Uncomfortably loud | |
| Thunderclap, live rock music, jet takeoff (161 m away), chainsaw | 120 | Uncomfortably loud | Human pain threshold |
| Jet takeoff (100 m away), earphone at loud level | 130 | Painful | |
| Aircraft career deck | 140 | Painful | |
| Jet takeoff (25 m away) | 150 | Painful | Eardrum rupture |
| Rocket engine | 180 | Painful | Eardrum rupture |

Noise pollution can be controlled by reducing noise at its point source, interruptions in the path of transmission, and by protection at the receiver's end. For this, awareness, motivation, and legislations including effective implementation are necessary.

## 1.4.6   Pollution by Radioactivity

Radioisotopes, also called radionuclides, are isotopes of chemical elements exhibiting radioactivity. The radioisotopes spontaneously emit high-energy electromagnetic radiation. This property of radioactive decay of elements is called radioactivity. The spontaneous disintegration of radionuclides is accompanied by emission of high energy radiations, that is, alpha particles, beta particles, and gamma rays. Radioactivity was discovered by French physicist Antoine Henri Becquerel, who shared the 1903 Noble Prize in Physics with Pierre Curie and Marie Curie. Radioactivity is measured in Becquerel or Bq (SI unit). 1 Bq is equal to the quantity of the radioactive material disintegrated per second. The rate of disintegration of radioisotopes is not influenced by any chemical change or change in temperature, pressure, or by the effects of electric or magnetic fields. Pollution caused by radioactive substances is called radioactive pollution. Undeniably, radioactive pollution is the worst type of environmental pollution and is responsible for untold misery to humans.

### 1.4.6.1   *Sources of Radioactive Pollution*

Sources of radioactive pollution are of two types—natural and human-made.

***Natural sources:*** Natural sources of radioactive pollution include rocks in the earth crust, which contain radioactive nuclides such as U-239, Th-234, and Ra-226. These nuclides continuously emit radiation. In fact, it has been found that buildings built using such rocks are unsafe for dwelling. Production of radioactive material before its use requires mining, milling, and processing. Environmental concerns are associated with each stage.

**(i) Mining:** Ores of uranium are extracted from mines and used in reactors. Uranium in the ore is associated with a number of toxic metals such as arsenic, cadmium, mercury, and other radioactive materials formed by the decay process. People involved in the mining activity are highly vulnerable to harmful effects of radioactivity. They are exposed to constant radiation which produces severe biological effects with time. This may lead to further health hazards. Adequate precautions such as using gas masks, spectacles, and gloves will safeguard the workers. No part of the body should be left exposed.

**(ii) Tailings:** Waste materials generated from mining are known as tailings. In the case of mining of radioactive material, tailings are to be safely disposed of or stored. The normal practice is to store this waste underground. Selection of the site is made carefully to avoid movement of this waste within the grounds or across other environmental segments (air and water). The usual practice is to bury tailings under a thick (1–3 m) layer of gravel, sand, or soil. These dumping sites cannot be used for any other activity for thousands of years. The problem with the disposal of radioactive waste has acquired global concern. Some nations, especially developed nations, export their radioactive wastes to developing countries. However, this is resulting only in shifting the problem from one location to another.

**(iii) Refining and fuel fabrication waste:** During refining and purification of uranium, radioactive wastes are generated; however, most of these wastes are cycled back. The chemical processing of uranium ore generates ammonium nitrate which is mixed with commercial fertilizers (for use in agriculture). In the fuel fabrication process, some waste is produced during pressing and grinding operations. This waste is also recycled into the fabrication process.

*Man-made sources:* Nobody can forget the terrible devastation caused by atomic bombings in the cities of Hiroshima and Nagasaki during World War II. This, in fact, formed the basis of man-made sources for the production of radioactivity.

Nuclear bomb is a device that can release a large amount of energy in a very short time. It is estimated that the energy produced by 1 g of $U^{235}$ is equivalent to that produced by about 3 tonnes of coal. The conversion of mass into energy releases fission fragments and large amounts of alpha radiation. Figure 1.4 shows the schematic representation of fission of $U^{235}$. In this process, a large amount of energy is released. This concept is also used in nuclear reactors where the energy

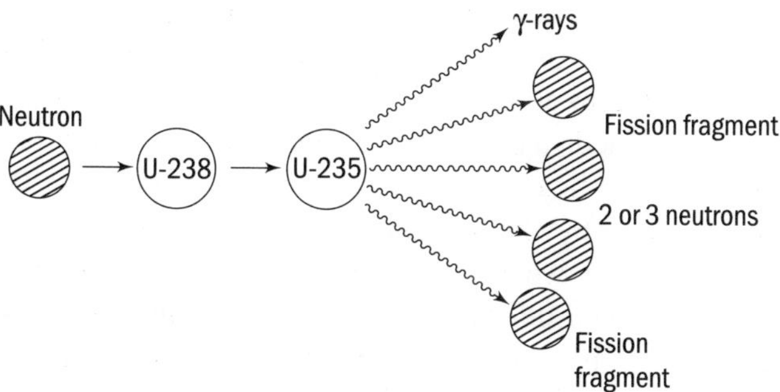


**Fig. 1.4**  Fission of U-235 and release of gamma energy and other particles

is used to produce electricity. The energy released in reactors is slow whereas in the case of atomic bombs, the energy released is instantaneous.

- Food crops grown on earth and water percolating through soil also contain some radioactive nuclides, such as K-40, C-14, and Rn-222. These enter the human body via food chain and drinking water. Although X-rays are used for diagnostic purposes, they should be used only when urgently needed and on the advice of a physician. X-ray exposure has cumulative effect on the body—a number of cases of disease caused by genetic damage from medical sources have been reported.

- Testing of a nuclear device in air, on ground, underground, and in sea greatly contributes to nuclear radiations. Considerable quantities of fission products (with the exception of underground tests), for example C-14, Sr-90, I-131, Cs-137, get released in the atmosphere. These radioactive products also enter the stratosphere where they stay for about 10 years. These nuclides may undergo further disintegration in the atmosphere and may spread all over the globe. Ultimately, they settle on earth's surface as radioactive fallouts and then find their way into the food chain. This type of nuclear pollution has considerably been reduced because of partial Nuclear Test Ban Treaty of 1963 between the USA, the USSR, and the UK to prohibit all types of nuclear tests in the atmosphere or on land. The treaty allows only underground nuclear tests.

- Radiations (including alpha, beta, and gamma rays) emitted from nuclear power plants at any stage of electricity production may enter the human body and transfer their energy to the tissues. The biomolecules present in the human system absorb this energy and undergo fragmentation. This causes a host of deleterious effects.

- Radioisotope is another source of radioactive pollution. Radioisotopes are increasingly used in industry, medicine, research, and nuclear reactors (for power generation). Radioisotopes may enter the human body either through direct inhalation from air or through food chain. Radioisotopes such as Rn-222 and Xe-133 (discharged into the atmosphere by any of the processes referred to above) are readily absorbed on suspended particles. When air is inhaled, these isotopes are deposited in the passageway of lungs where they release energy produced by their decay. Radioisotopes are also absorbed by the soil and taken up by plants. These enter the human body when we eat vegetables/plants or meat of animals that have consumed such plants. Radioisotopes can also be ingested through aquatic pathway by consuming contaminated sea animals. Different human organs are affected by different radionuclides. Table 1.7 gives an account of this.

**Table 1.7**  Effect of radionuclide on different organs

| *Radionuclide* | *Organ affected* |
|---|---|
| Radium-226 | Bones |
| Radon-222 | Lungs |
| Iodine-131 | Thyroid |
| Krypton-85 | Ovaries |
| Cobalt-60 | Liver |
| Potassium-42 | Muscles |
| Sulphur-35 | Skin |

The main concern of radioactive pollution is its severe biological effects. Radiations can alter the structure of the genetic material (DNA) and other biomolecules by ionization. This change in chemical structure is manifested at the functional level of these molecules. Alterations in the biomolecules change the cells that may die or function abnormally, leading to chronic health problems. Severe effects including cancer, and genetic defects get passed on from one generation to the next generation. In case, the effects are not severe, the person may show signs of allergy, asthma, minor muscular or bone defects, hypertension, or certain minor genetic aberrations.

## 1.5  ENVIRONMENTAL POLLUTION AND HEALTH

Environmental pollution is responsible for poor quality of the environment, which, according to the WHO estimates, contributes to about 25% of all preventable ill health in the world. According to the Centre for Science and Environment (CSE) reports, at least a million people die every year because of water pollution. In India alone, each year, about 50,000–100,000 people die due to diseases associated with air pollution. The cost of environmental damages in India, according to a World Bank study, is more than ₹34,000 crore. It is estimated that in India, respiratory infections, diarrheal diseases, tuberculosis, and malaria affects about 5 million, 3 million, 2 million, and 1.5 million people, respectively.

Besides environmental pollution, indoor air pollution in some countries (where people use fuels such as cow dung, wood, and coal for cooking) is a cause of severe health effects. It is estimated that in India more than 50,000 people die per annum due to premature deaths. This is attributed to indoor air pollution. The damage caused by indoor air pollution in the country has been considerably reduced by the widespread use of liquefied petroleum gas (LPG) as the cooking fuel.

According to the United States Environmental Protection Agency (USEPA), inhaling toxic chemicals increases cancer risk 10 times more than the safe limit.

A pregnant woman exposed to common pollutants is likely to deliver a child with heart deformities. Chemicals such as DDT and polychlorinated biphenyl (PCBs) are responsible not only for heart ailments and cancer, but also accountable for brain disorders, hormonal problems, and problems associated with reproduction that may become a concern for future generations. It has been confirmed that toxins present in the environment adversely affect every part of the human body.

## 1.5.1   Air Pollution and Human Health

Air pollutants which are mainly responsible for severe health problems include oxides of carbon ($CO_2$ and $CO$), oxides of sulphur ($SO_2$ and $SO_3$), oxides of nitrogen ($NO$, $NO_2$, and $N_2O$), VOCs, suspended particulate matter, and photochemical oxidants (for details, see Section 1.4.1). Dioxins are the most deadly pollutants known so far. Being fat soluble, these chemicals bioaccumulate in the food chain. According to USEPA (1984), dioxins may cause serious health problems such as lowering the immune system and cancer.

According to the WHO, the tolerable daily intake of dioxins is 1–4 picograms per body weight (one piogram is one trillionth of a gram). The dioxins are produced by burning of chlorinated compounds; for example, garbage, medical waste, and toxic chemicals. The released dioxins contaminate air and water. Dioxins are also produced when paper is bleached with chlorinated compounds and in the manufacture of polyvinylchloride (PVC) and chlorinated pesticides.

It is well documented that during Vietnam War (1970), the US military sprayed about 42 million litres of the herbicide, 'Agent Orange' [a mixture of 2, 4-dichlorophenoxyacetic acid (2, 4-D) and 2,4,5-trichlorophenoxyacetic acid (2,4,5-T)], a defoliant to destroy the forest cover, so that communist forces could not hide themselves in forest areas. Agent Orange was contaminated with dioxins, which created havoc in the life of victims of the war and other residents who were exposed to the herbicide. The dioxins got absorbed in the skin of victims. Children born to women who were exposed to Agent Orange were either mentally retarded or suffered from low IQ. A number of them suffered from skin tumours. In fact, dioxins are the most important carcinogenic agents tested so far.

Another incident involving dioxin was reported in Italy (1976). An accident in Roche Holding Ltd, a chemical factory in Italy, released a cloud of chemicals including dioxins. An area of about 150 $km^2$ with a population of about 40,000 was affected. A number of people exposed to dioxin suffered from skin injuries, which healed in about a month. A number of children born after the accident were premature and deformed.

## 1.5.2   Water Pollution and Human Health

As already stated (see Section 1.4.2), water pollution occurs through biological, chemical, and physical agents. All these are responsible for the pollution of surface water, seawater, and groundwater. The presence of various pollutants in water can have severe consequences on human health.

A number of microorganisms, for example, bacteria, viruses, protozoans, insects, and helminths are present in polluted water and can cause several types of infections. Table 1.8 lists the polluted water diseases caused by microorganisms.

The chemical agents which are known to cause water pollution include fluoride, arsenic, lead, nitrates, cadmium, and mercury. All these have profound effect on human health. Though fluoride in water is essential for protection against dental caries and weakening of bones, however, at higher levels, it causes a crippling and painful disease known as fluorosis, which can be further classified as non-skeletal fluorosis and dental fluorosis. The problem of fluorosis is very severe in India, particularly in Odisha, Rajasthan, Pavagada Taluk District, and villages of Kolar District, where the population depends upon groundwater. The prevalence of fluorosis can result in joint pains, irregular growth of limbs and spinal cord,

**Table 1.8**   Diseases caused by microorganisms

| Organisms | Diseases | Remarks |
|---|---|---|
| *Ascaris* sp. | Nematode worms | Danger to human from polluted water and dried sludge used as a fertilizer |
| *Bacillus anthracis* | Anthrax | Found in wastewater spores and resistant to treatment |
| *Brucella* sp. | Brucellosis, Malta fever in humans, contagious abortion in sheep, goat, and cattle. | Transmitted by infected milk, by contact, and by wastewater |
| *Entamoeba histolytica* | Amoebic dysentery | Spread by contaminated water |
| *Leptospira* sp. | Leptospirosis (Weil's disease) | Caused by sewer rats |
| *Mycobacterium tuberculosis* | Tuberculosis | Isolated from wastewater |
| *Salmonella paratyphi* | Paratyphoid fever | Common in wastewater |
| *Salmonella typhi* | Typhoid fever | Common in wastewater |
| *Salmonella* sp. | Food poisoning | Common in wastewater |
| *Shigella* sp. | Bacillary dysentery | Polluted water |
| *Vibrio cholerae* | Cholera | Polluted water |
| Virus | Poliomyelitis, hepatitis | Wastewater treatment plants |
| *Escherichia coli* | Diarrhoea | Polluted water |

formation of lumps on the body, resulting in the inability to even stand in certain cases.

Arsenic finds its way in waterbodies via the dissolution of minerals and ores, from industrial effluents, and atmosphere deposition. According to the WHO, the guideline value for arsenic in drinking water is 0.01 mg/L. The world's worst affected area due to arsenic contamination is the Indo–Bangladesh region. The WHO has cautioned Government of India to keep arsenic-related diseases under immediate surveillance, giving it the status similar to that of cancer. At higher levels, As (III) compounds coagulate proteins by attacking S-bond, retaining the secondary and tertiary structures of proteins. In biological systems, arsenic compounds complexes with coenzymes, resulting in coagulation of biological proteins and uncoupling at phosphorylated sites. The varying effects of arsenic on humans depend on the dose as summarized here.

| Dose | Effects |
| --- | --- |
| Mild dose | Nausea, fainting, salivation, vomiting, burning pain in stomach |
| Higher dose | Diarrhoea, peripheral neuritis, hyperkeratosis, conjunctivitis |
| Chronic dose | Severe gastroenteritis, loss of weight, skin lesions, black foot disease |
| Lethal dose | Death due to shock and vascular failure |

Toxicity of arsenic is known as arsenicosis, which develops in human body after 2 to 5 years of arsenic exposure, probably caused due to consumption of arsenic-contaminated drinking water. The initial symptoms are darkening of the skin (called skin melanosis) leading to appearance of dark spots at chest, back, and limbs (called diffuse melanosis). This is followed by leucomelanosis (appearance of black and white spots on the body) and keratosis (hardening of the skin). Arsenic can be removed from water by addition of aluminium and ferric salts. The precipitated arsenic salts are allowed to settle down and removed. Alternatively, arsenic can be removed by passing water through a membrane, which filters out the arsenic. The common membrane technologies include reverse osmosis and electrodialysis.

Lead finds its way into waterbodies during mining and metallurgical operations. Considerable amounts of lead are used as a pigment in paint in order to enhance their consistency and durability. According to a US study, about one-fourth of the houses in the country face considerable health hazards in the form of peeling paint chips. In fact, paints based on lead are the main cause of blood lead poisoning all over the world. According to the WHO, about 15–18 million children in developing countries suffer from irreversible brain damage due to blood lead poisoning. In view of this, some countries, particularly Canada, have considerably reduced lead concentration in paints, from 5000 ppm to 600 ppm. According to Prevention of Food Administration Act, 1954, the permissible limit of lead concentration is 2.5 mg/kg in both vegetables and food products. Lead has been shown to affect all parts of a human body. Exposure to lead results in reduced IQ, impaired neurobehavioural development, and restricted physical growth. The lead absorbed in the blood gets accumulated in liver, brain, kidneys, and bones. In case, a pregnant woman is exposed to lead, it may result in premature birth or low-birth weight. Higher levels of lead in blood (>70 mg/dL) can result in nephropathy and even death. Lead gets deposited in bones and is considered as a cumulative poison. It interferes with calcium metabolism both directly and by interfering with vitamin D metabolism (indirectly).

Nitrate is discharged in waterbodies by agricultural run-offs, that is, from fields treated with nitrate-containing fertilizers. Excess intake of nitrate through drinking water causes reduction in the oxygen-carrying capacity of the blood and damages alveolar tissues of lungs. Though nitrate is non-toxic, it gets converted to nitrite during metabolism in the digestive canal by bacteria under high pH conditions. The nitrite on reaching the blood oxidizes iron present in the haemoglobin of red blood cells to form methaemoglobin, which lacks the oxygen-carrying capacity. Also, during nitrate metabolism, free radicals of nitric oxide and oxygen are formed which can lead to alveolar damage in lungs. The intake of nitrite is severe in the case of infants (under six months) as their digestive tracts have high pH due to low secretion of gastric juices. Nitrate gets converted into nitrate under such circumstances while the infant appears blue due to lack of haemoglobin. The condition is called methaemoglobinaemia and the infants are called 'blue babies'. Cadmium is another toxic element which finds its way into waterbodies mainly through two routes: (i) processing of ores containing cadmium and (ii) metallurgical processes. Cadmium poisoning was first observed in Japan (1912) in the form of *Itai-itai* (meaning 'ouch-ouch') disease; in this condition, bones become fragile. Higher levels of cadmium can cause kidney problems, anaemia, disorders of bone marrow, hypertension, renal dysfunction, and even cancer. Cadmium in the body gets bound effectively to body proteins—metallothionein—present in kidneys. When excess of $Cd^{2+}$ is ingested, it replaces $Zn^{2+}$ at major enzymatic sites, causing metabolic disorders. Cadmium is a cumulative poison and affects mainly kidneys, lungs, and respiratory organs. Poisoning due to cadmium fumes causes cough, sore throat, vertigo, dyspnoea, cyanosis, and bronchopneumonia. Mercury is another well-known toxic element and a major water pollutant. Its source of origin includes mining and metallurgical processes involved in the extraction of mercury from its ores.

Mercury poisoning was first observed in Japan in the form of Minamata disease. The symptoms of the disease include numbness of limbs and area around the mouth, sensory disturbance and difficulty in hand movement, lack of mental coordination, weakness and tremors, slow and slurred speech, vision and hearing problems leading to paralysis. It was found that in Minamata Bay, mercury was discharged in large amounts by Chisso Corporation. In the aquatic environment, mercury compounds (discharged with effluents) were getting converted into highly toxic methyl mercury under bacterial action which was consumed by fish and bio-accumulated in high concentration. The consumption of mercury-contaminated fish led to Minamata disease.

On the basis of a US study, it was confirmed that mercury is the most lethal metal, responsible for severe neurological problems, particularly in children. It is potentially dangerous to the foetus of pregnant women. It was found that about 60,000 babies (in the USA) with low IQ were born to mothers who consumed mercury contaminated food. Being bio-accumulative, mercury moves up in the food chain. Mercury-causes irritability, depression, suicidal tendencies, Alzheimer's disease, and visual impairment.

Besides the above-mentioned chemical agents, a number of toxic chemicals are discharged in waterbodies. Some of such chemicals are suspected carcinogens and include PCBs, vinyl chloride, benzene, DDT, aldrin, chlorinated organic compounds, and nitrosamine.

### 1.5.3    Soil Pollution and Human Health

As already discussed (Section 1.4.3), soil pollution is caused by a number of sources such as industrial wastes, urban and domestic wastes, agrochemicals, and radioactive materials. All these wastes dumped on the soil are extremely harmful for human health. A typical example of the harmful effects of industrial waste dumping on soil is the case of Hooker Chemical Company at Niagara Falls, New York. It dumped its chemical waste (about 12,000 tonnes) in steel drums in the canal (called Love Canal). After dumping the waste products, the site was covered with sand and sold to Board of Education of Niagara Falls, who used the land as their school playground. Nearly, after about 20 years, the area turned into muddy swamp due to rains. It was contaminated with poisonous chemicals. Children and adults of nearby area suffered from health problems such as headache, skin sores, rectal bleeding, malfunctioning of liver, and epilepsy. Incidents of miscarriages and birth defects in newborns were also reported. It was subsequently found that the chemicals in the swamp were due to leakage in the drums that were buried by the chemical company earlier.

Hazardous pollutants can reach humans via several routes such as ingestion, skin absorption, and inhalation; this can result in allergies, sensory loss, and even cancer. Problems can become more acute when pollutants enter placenta and mutate genes, resulting in birth defects. It has been confirmed that pollutants have toxic effects on foetus. Some of the inorganic elements such as arsenic, cadmium, mercury, lead, nickel, fluorine are extremely harmful for human health. All these elements tend to accumulate in living tissues via food chain and interfere with the natural systems. The harmful effects of poisoning by mercury, cadmium, arsenic, and lead have been discussed earlier (Section 1.5.2).

Radioactive pollutants can cause skin cancer, cataract, and mutation in cells by breaking one or both strands of DNA. The damage depends on the nature of the radiation such as alpha particles, beta particles, and gamma rays (for details, see Section 1.4.6). The ionizing radiation causes cancer, has mutagenic (changes in genetic material, which can pass on to subsequent generations), and teratogenic effects (defects in the developing foetus resulting in birth defects).

Fertilizers such as sodium and potassium nitrates are responsible for methaemoglobin in children. In addition, excess use of fertilizers is accountable for eutrophication. Pesticides including DDT cause tumours and severely affect the central nervous system. Aldrin and dieldrin are known to damage kidneys and are suspected carcinogens. Meruric fungicides are also responsible for human poisoning and death. The harmful effects of herbicide, for example, Agent Orange which is a mixture of 2,4- dichlorophenoxyacetic acid and 2, 4, 5-trichlorophenoxyacetic acid has been already discussed (see Section 1.5.1).

The effects of pesticide exposure on human health can be very severe. People exposed to higher levels of pesticides suffer from headache, dizziness, irritability, nausea, impairment of nervous system, and even death. Chronic effects include development of long-term complications such as cancer.

## 1.5.4  Waste Disposal and Human Health

As already discussed, dumping of industrial, solid, and liquid wastes on land can pose serious threat to human health. Biomedical waste, due to its improper disposal, can also turn into a health hazard. It has become a common practice to dump biomedical waste with municipal waste in dustbins, open space, and waterbodies. Health care units such as nursing homes and private clinics do not dispose biomedical waste properly. Biomedical waste includes blood, fluids, and body secretions, which harbour many viruses, bacteria, and parasites that can cause severe and fatal infections. Rag pickers collect used syringes and blades; they therefore become prone to human immunodeficiency virus (HIV) infection (on being pricked by infected needles). Other diseases resulting from improper waste management include tuberculosis, pneumonia, diarrhoea, tetanus, and whooping cough.

The most dangerous pollutants are radioactive pollutants which fall on the land from radioactive fallouts. These pollutants have the ability to cause the most severe health problems.

# SUMMARY

- The environment is defined as the sum total of living and non-living components.
- The environment can be categorized into natural and human-made environment. The former includes air, water, soil, forest, wildlife and the later includes housing, industries, dams, and various forms of energy.
- The environment consists of four main segments: (i) atmosphere, (ii) hydrosphere, (iii) lithosphere, and (iv) biosphere.
- The atmosphere is the cover of air that envelopes the earth and is responsible for sustaining life on earth.
- The atmosphere can be mainly divided into four major layers: (i) troposphere, (ii) stratosphere, (iii) mesosphere, (iv) thermosphere. The ionosphere is the new addition to this layer classification.
- The collective mass of water formed on, under, and over the surface of the earth is called hydrosphere and covers about 75% of the earth's total surface area.
- Fresh potable water is available only to the extent of about 1% in rivers, lakes, and groundwater.
- Water is the essential component of life. Moreover, no life is possible without water.
- The layer of rock, constituting the outer part of the earth, extending up to 400 km, is called the lithosphere.
- The earth receives all its heat energy from the sun.
- The region of the earth where the lithosphere, hydrosphere, and atmosphere are present and where life can exist is known as the biosphere.
- The presence of any pollutant in the environment is called environmental pollution. Agents that contaminate the environment are called pollutants.
- A pollutant can exist in both degradable and non-biodegradable forms. Further, a pollutant can be a natural pollutant, primary pollutant, or secondary pollutant.
- Any unwanted change in the quality of air caused by the emission of various pollutants is described as air pollution.

- Most air pollutants such as oxides of sulphur, nitrogen, and carbon have profound effects on the health of humans.
- Air pollution can best be described as a 'time bomb' which may explode at any time, at any place, causing severe and undetermined problems.
- The large-scale dumping of pollutants in various environmental segments, released from industries and other anthropogenic activities has caused environmental crisis.
- The degradation of the quality of the environmental segments is referred to as environmental degradation. It is mainly caused by uncontrolled growth of human population which is marked by overexploitation of natural resources.
- The degradation of the quality of the water that makes it harmful to human beings, animals, and aquatic life is referred to as water pollution. Water pollution is caused by natural and anthropogenic processes.
- Eutrophication is caused by the discharge of organic wastes and inorganic nutrients such as phosphates and nitrates in waterbodies.
- Water pollution can be surface water pollution, seawater pollution, and groundwater pollution.
- Soil pollution is caused by both natural processes and human activities.
- Overindulgence of men with land results in loss of biodiversity, soil erosion, making the soil acidic or alkaline. In addition, deposition of waste pollutes the soil considerably.
- The quality of water can be assumed by a numbered of parameters such as DO, BOD, COD, MPN, and TDS.
- Thermal pollution occurs when there is an increase or a decrease in the temperature of atmosphere or hydrosphere.
- Noise pollution is caused by high levels of sounds.
- Radioactive pollution is caused by the discharge of radionuclides into environmental segments. It is the worst type of environmental pollution and responsible for untold misery to humans.
- Environmental pollution is responsible for affecting human health.
- Higher levels of fluoride in drinking water can cause fluorosis, a crippling and painful disease.
- Consumption of arsenic-contaminated drinking water can cause arsenicosis and is detrimental for human health.
- Lead, a cumulative poison, gets deposited in bones and can interfere with calcium metabolism.

- Nitrate exposure through drinking water can cause metheamoglobinaemia (blue baby syndrome) in infants.
- The presence of cadmium in waterbodies causes *Itai-itai* disease
- Mercury in drinking water is responsible for Minamata disease.

# EXERCISE

## [A] Multiple-choice questions

1. The components of natural environment include
   - (a) Air, water, soil
   - (b) Land, forest, solar radiation
   - (c) Industries, dams, energy
   - (d) All of the above

2. The most important segment of the environment is
   - (a) Atmosphere
   - (b) Hydrosphere
   - (c) Lithosphere
   - (d) Biosphere
   - (e) All of the above

3. Ozone is present as the main constituent in
   - (a) Troposphere
   - (b) Stratosphere
   - (c) Mesosphere
   - (d) Thermosphere
   - (e) Ionosphere

4. In mesosphere, the main constituents include
   - (a) $O_2^+$
   - (b) $NO^+$
   - (c) $O^+$
   - (d) All of the above

5. The layer of the atmosphere in the region 90–500 km is known as
   - (a) Troposphere
   - (b) Thermosphere
   - (c) Mesosphere
   - (d) Stratosphere

6. Nitric oxide is generated in the environment by
   - (a) Forest fires
   - (b) Lightening discharge
   - (c) Internal combustion engines
   - (d) All of the above

7. Which of the following is a secondary pollutant?
   - (a) $SO_3$
   - (b) $NO$
   - (c) $O_3$
   - (d) All of the above

8. Which of the following is a pollutant?
   - (a) $SO_2$
   - (b) $NO_2$
   - (c) $Cd$
   - (d) $Hg$
   - (e) All of the above

9. Which of the following statements is correct?
    (a) The presence of $O_2$ along with $N_2$ is necessary for sustaining life on earth.
    (b) The presence of $CO_2$ is essential for photosynthesis by green plants.
    (c) The most important role of the atmosphere is restricting harmful solar radiation from reaching the earth's surface.
    (d) The high value of latent heat of water moderates the temperature of the biosphere.
    (e) All of the above

10. Hydrosphere includes
    (a) Oceans and seas              (b) Rivers, lakes, and streams
    (c) Glaciers                     (d) Polar ice caps
    (e) All of the above

11. Freshwater sources include
    (a) Rivers, lakes, and streams   (b) Groundwater
    (c) Polar ice caps and glaciers  (d) All of the above

12. Fresh potable water is available to the extent of _____ in rivers, lakes, and groundwater.
    (a) 1%                           (b) 2%–3%
    (c) 5%–10%                       (d) None of the above

13. Which of the following statements is correct?
    (a) The earth receivers all its heat energy from the sun.
    (b) The heat energy received by the earth is lost by reflection and radiation.
    (c) The reflecting capacity of the earth is called albedo.
    (d) All of the above

14. The gas which absorbs infrared radiation is
    (a) $SO_2$                       (b) $NO_2$
    (c) $CO_2$                       (d) CO

15. Environmental pollution is also caused by
    (a) Deforestation                (b) Hunting of animals
    (c) Industrial revolution        (d) Agrochemicals
    (e) All of the above

16. Photochemical pollutants include
    (a) Ozone                        (b) Peroxyacetyl nitrate
    (c) Formaldehyde                 (d) Acetaldehyde
    (e) All of the above

17. Out of the following air pollutants, the most deadly air pollutant is
    (a) $SO_2$                              (b) $NO_2$
    (c) $CO_2$                              (d) CO

18. The worst air pollution episode is
    (a) The leakage of methyl isocyate from the Union Carbide pesticide factory, located in Madhya Pradesh, India in which 22,000 people died.
    (b) Nuclear catastrophe at Chernobyl in Ukaraine in which 2000 people died.
    (c) Nuclear disaster including explosions at three nuclear reactors in Japan in March 2011 resulted in tremendous loss of human life.
    (d) All of the above

19. Environmental crisis is attributed to
    (a) Dumping of various pollutants in environmental segments
    (b) Killer smog in London and New York
    (c) Mercury and cadmium poisoning in waterbodies
    (d) Oil spills in oceans
    (e) All of the above

20. Considerable environmental degradation has been caused by
    (a) Discharge of air pollutants in the atmosphere
    (b) Large-scale release of greenhouse gases (responsible for global warming) in the atmosphere
    (c) Gulf War (16 January to 26 February 1981)
    (d) All of the above

21. Water pollution occurs due to
    (a) Discharge of biological agents in waterbodies
    (b) Discharge of chemical agents in waterbodies
    (c) Discharge of radioactive substances in waterbodies
    (d) All of the above

22. Water pollution includes
    (a) Surface water pollution        (b) Seawater pollution
    (c) Groundwater pollution          (d) All of the above

23. Water pollution includes
    (a) Loss of biodiversity
    (b) Soil erosion
    (c) Making the soil acidic or alkaline
    (d) All of the above

24. The most important parameter for assessing the quality of water is
   (a) DO                     (b) BOD
   (c) COD                (d) TSD
   (e) MPN
25. metheamoglobinaemia is a result of poisoning by
   (a) Hg                     (b) Cd
   (c) As                     (d) Nitrates

### ANSWERS

| | | | | |
|---|---|---|---|---|
| 1. (a), (b) | 2. (d) | 3. (b) | 4. (a), (b) | 5. (b) |
| 6. (d) | 7. (d) | 8. (e) | 9. (e) | 10. (e) |
| 11. (d) | 12. (a) | 13. (d) | 14. (d) | 15. (e) |
| 16. (e) | 17. (d) | 18. (d) | 19. (e) | 20. (e) |
| 21. (d) | 22. (d) | 23. (d) | 24. (a) (b) (c) | 25. (d) |

## [B] Fill in the blanks.

1. The most important segment of environment is ——.
2. The main constituent of the stratosphere is ——.
3. The most poisonous pollutant of the atmosphere is ——.
4. Fresh potable water is available to the extent of about —— %.
5. The temperature of biosphere is moderated due to —— of water.
6. The survival of aquatic life is due to solubility of —— in water.
7. The reflecting capacity of the earth is called ——.
8. Acid rain is caused due to the presence of —— and —— in the atmosphere.
9. The harmful effects of $SO_2$ increases many folds when it settles on —— with the air and reaches deeper parts of the respiratory system.
10. Depletion of ozone by CFCs continues up to about —— years after being discharged in the atmosphere.
11. Discharge of organic wastes and inorganic nutrients are responsible for —— of waterbodies.
12. For aquatic species, a minimum of —— DO is necessary
13. A COD value of —— indicates that water is unfit for drinking.
14. Most deadly pollutant known so far is the ——.
15. Fluorosis is caused by higher levels of —— in drinking water.
16. The toxicity of arsenic is known as ——.
17. Lead is considered as a —— poison

18. Metheamoglobinaemia is caused by the presence of —— in drinking water.

19. Cadmium poisoning was first observed in Japan in the form of —— disease.

20. The presence of mercury salts in water causes —— disease.

**ANSWERS**

| | |
|---|---|
| 1. Biosphere | 2. Ozone |
| 3. CO | 4. One |
| 5. High latent heat | 6. Oxygen |
| 7. Albedo | 8. $SO_2$, $NO_2$ |
| 9. Particulate matter | 10. 100 |
| 11. Eutrophication | 12. 4 ppm |
| 13. 20–100 mg $L^{-1}$ | 14. Dioxins |
| 15. Fluorine | 16. Arsenosis |
| 17. Cumulative | 18. Nitrate |
| 19. *Itai-itai* | 20. Minamata |

## [C] Short-answer questions

1. What do you understand by the term 'environment'?
2. What are the different types of environment?
3. What are the segments of the environment?
4. What are the regions of atmosphere?
5. What is ionosphere?
6. What is hydrosphere?
7. Explain the term albedo.
9. What is a pollutant?
10. What are the causes of environmental pollution?
11. Is $CO_2$ a pollutant? Explain.
12. $CO_2$ is non-poisonous but a person kept in an atmosphere of $CO_2$ dies, why?
13. What caused Bhopal gas tragedy?
14. What do you understand by the terms 'environmental crisis' and 'environment degradation'?
15. How is Gulf War related to environmental degradation?
16. What is eutrophication?
17. How is marine pollution caused?

18. How does groundwater pollution take place?
19. What is soil erosion?
20. What are water quality parameters?
21. What is radioactive pollution?
22. Discuss environmental pollution and human health.
23. How is indoor air pollution caused?

# Ecology

## 2.1  INTRODUCTION

The term 'ecology' came into being in 1868. It is derived from two Greek words—*oikos* meaning home or estate and *logos* meaning study. Therefore, ecology can be defined as the study of the home or household of nature. In other words, ecology is the scientific study of the relationship of living organisms with each other and with their environment.

Ecology can be divided into three subdivisions: (i) autecology, (ii) synecology, and (iii) habitat ecology. Autecology is the ecological study of individual species in relation to the environment. Synecology is the study of the ecology of groups or communities in relation to their environment. Habitat ecology deals with the study of the habitat or environment of organisms. All organisms, including human, depend on the environment to sustain themselves. Their basic important needs, that of food, energy, water, oxygen, shelter, and so on, are fulfilled by the environment. The environment, as we know, is defined as the sum total of living and non-living components. The relationships/interactions between organisms and the environment are complex.

As already discussed in Chapter 1, the environment can be classified into abiotic (or non-living) and biotic (or living) components (Table 2.1).

**Table 2.1**  Components of the environment

| Abiotic components | Biotic components |
|---|---|
| Energy | Green plants |
| Radiation | Non-green plants |
| Temperature and heat flow | Decomposers |
| Water | Parasites |
| Atmosphere gases and wind | Symbionts |
| Fire | Animals |
| Gravity | Man |
| Topography | |
| Soil | |

The environment is not static—the biotic and abiotic components keep on changing continuously. Organisms can tolerate change in the environment within a certain range called 'range of tolerance'. For example, if a marine fish is transferred to a freshwater environment, it will not be able to survive.

The environment, as discussed in Chapter 1, is of two types—natural and human-made (or artificial). The components of natural environment are given in Table 2.1. Man-made environment includes housing, industries, dams, power plants for energy generation.

## 2.2   ECOSYSTEMS

The word 'ecosystem' was coined by Arthur Tansley—a British botanist—in 1935. According to Tansley, ecosystem is defined as a system resulting from the integration of living and non-living factors of the environment. The prefix 'eco' means the environment.

It is well known that human beings live or coexist with a variety of plants and animals on earth. The coexistence of various species is a highly ordered, dynamic, and complex system. Such a natural organization along with living and non-living components is called an ecosystem. The term 'ecosystem' is used to refer to both small and large ecological systems; for example, a small pond, a field, a grassland, a forest, and an ocean.

The interaction between living organisms and their environment is a two-way process. Organisms are influenced by their surroundings and the surroundings in turn influence the inhabitating organisms. The basic concept of an ecosystem is that at any place where organisms live, there is a continuous reaction between living and non-living components, that is, between plants, animals, and their environment. In fact, a continuous process of producing and exchanging material takes place between plants, animals, and the environment. For example, plants produce food, which is consumed by animals and humans, and is finally released into the environment.

### 2.2.1   Components of Ecosystem

Components of the ecosystem are abiotic or non-living and biotic or living components. The important abiotic components include the following:

(i) **Energy:** It is essential for maintenance of life. It is obtained—directly or indirectly—from the sun. Animals can obtain energy directly from the sun or they can obtain it indirectly by eating plants which utilize the sun's energy by photosynthesis.

(ii) **Materials:** *Organic compounds*, such as proteins, carbohydrates, lipids, humic substances, which are formed from inorganic substances, and reconverted into them on decomposition. *Inorganic compounds*, such as oxygen, nitrogen, carbon dioxide, water, sulphur, nitrates, phosphates, and ions of various metals are essential for the survival of organisms.

**(iii) Climatic factors:** These include light, heat, temperature, wind humidity, rainfall, and so on.

**(iv) Edaphic factors:** These deal with the composition of soil, along with its physical and chemical characteristics, that significantly influences organisms.

The biotic components of the environment include living organisms, comprising plants, animals, and decomposers. Plants are classified as producers or autotrophs while animals are classified as consumers or heterotrophs.

### 2.2.1.1  Producers or Autotrophs

Organisms, such as green plants, certain bacteria, and algae that can synthesize their own food in the presence of sunlight (through photosynthesis) are called producers or autotrophs. In a terrestrial ecosystem, producers are mostly herbaceous or woody plants. However, in marine and freshwater ecosystems, producers include some species of microscopic algae. Chemosynthetic bacteria are also producers. These bacteria are found in deep ocean trenches (where sunrays cannot reach) and derive their energy by chemosynthesis, mainly from hydrogen sulphide, which seeps through the cracks in the seafloor.

Producers can be divided into two types—primary and secondary. Green plants and some special types of bacteria that can trap solar energy and produce food are called primary producers. Heterotrophs that become food for other animals are called secondary producers.

### 2.2.1.2  Consumers or Heterotrophs

Organisms that cannot synthesize their own food (by photosynthesis) and depend on plants or animals or both are called consumers or heterotrophs. *Heterotroph* means other nourishing. Consumers are of two types—macroconsumers and microconsumers (also known as decomposers).

**Macroconsumers:**  These are of three types: (i) primary consumers, (ii) secondary consumers, and (iii) tertiary consumers.

(i) *Primary consumers* feed mainly on plants, such as cows and rabbits. They are also known as herbivores.

(ii) *Secondary consumers* are carnivores that feed on primary consumers. They obtain their food by capturing and killing their prey.

(iii) *Tertiary consumers* include carnivores that feed on secondary consumers; for example, lions eat wolves. Organisms that consume both plants and animals are called omnivores, such as human beings.

### *2.2.1.3   Microconsumers or Decomposers*

Bacteria and fungi are microorganisms that derive their energy and nutrients by decomposing dead organic substances (detritus) of plants and animals. The inorganic nutrients produced by decomposition are released in the ecosystem; these are reused by producers and recycled. Earthworms and some soil organisms, such as nematodes and arthropods, are also detritus feeders and take part in the decomposition of organic matter. As microorganisms decompose dead plants and animal remains, they are called decomposers. Both consumers and producers complete their life cycle in which the generation of a new population takes place and the old ones die. Breaking up or decomposition of dead organic matter is a very important feature of the ecosystem as it continues cycling of materials. The role of decomposers or microorganisms is significant. Certain decomposers are also called scavengers. The by-products of microbial activity include water, carbon dioxide, phosphates, and a number of organic compounds, which are released in the environment and recycled.

## 2.2.2   Size of an Ecosystem

An ecosystem may be as small and simple as a cow dung cake or as complex and large as an ocean. An interesting point is that an ecosystem may occur within an ecosystem. As an example, the cow dung ecosystem may be contained in a forest ecosystem which itself is contained in the biosphere. In some ecosystems, as in a pond ecosystem, boundaries are well defined. However, in other ecosystems, for example, forest, grassland, and desert ecosystems, there are no clear boundaries. Such ecosystems are separated from adjacent ecosystems by a transition zone or diffused boundary zone called ecotone. Organisms of adjacent ecosystems intermingle in the ecotone zone. This may lead to greater diversity of species than the neighbouring ecosystems.

## 2.2.3   Types of Ecosystems

The ecosystems can be natural or artificial (man-made). Natural ecosystems can be further classified into terrestrial or aquatic. Examples of terrestrial ecosystem include deserts, grasslands, crop fields, forests, and glaciers. Aquatic ecosystems are oceans, estuaries, mangroves, coastal marshes, rivers, lakes, ponds, and swamps.

Natural ecosystems are mostly free from human disturbances, such as tropical forests, grasslands, oceans, lakes, and deserts. However, artificial or man-made ecosystems are formed due to human modification of natural ecosystems. For example, humans transform natural forests into crop fields for agriculture. In fact, increasing human interference has destroyed many natural ecosystems and replaced them with artificial ecosystems, such as crop fields and industrial estates.

Every ecosystem influences and is influenced by its neighbouring ecosystem(s). Communications between ecosystems is mainly through exchange of energy and nutrients (Figure 2.1). Ecosystems also possess self-regulating ability as a result of which they are able to recover from minor perturbations. This is known as homeostasis.

Ecosystems undergo change over a period of time. This process is called ecological succession. It is related to seasonal environmental changes that bring changes in the species structure of an ecological community over time. For example, cold-blooded animals are the worst affected by changes in temperature. Their body temperature fluctuates with variation in the environmental temperature. These cold-blood animals undergo hibernation during the cold season and stay active during the hotter periods of the year.

## 2.3  BIOGEOCHEMICAL CYCLES

Energy flows through an ecosystem. This energy flow enables organisms of an ecosystem to carry out various kinds of activities. Ultimately, the energy is lost as heat (see Figure 2.1). However, the nutrient materials do not get exhausted and can be recycled indefinitely. Some of the nutrient materials are required in relatively larger amounts and, hence, called macronutrients. These include carbon, hydrogen, oxygen, nitrogen, and phosphorous. It is worth mentioning here that nutrients move from the non-living to living components of an ecosystem and subsequently return to the non-living components, more or less coming to a full circle. This is known as biogeochemical cycling. These biogeochemical cycles are also called nutrient or mineral cycles.

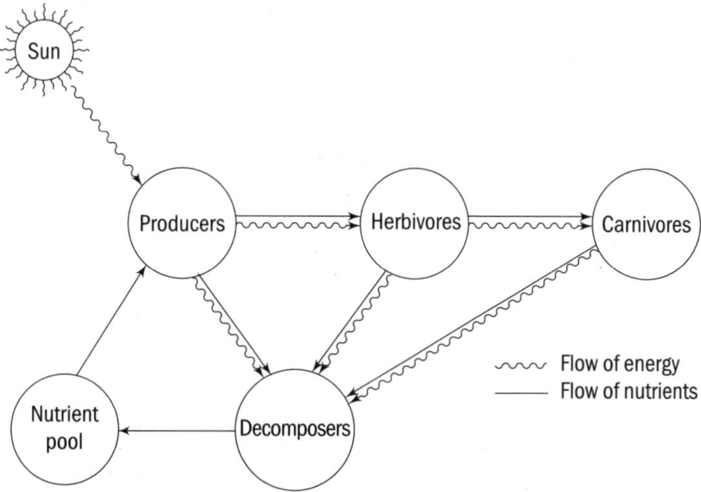


**Fig. 2.1**  Representation of energy and mineral movement in ecosystems

Each nutrient is usually concentrated in a source called a reservoir or pool. For example, nitrogen is concentrated in the atmosphere. In other words, atmosphere is the reservoir of nitrogen.

The biogeochemical cycles are of the following two types:

(i) **Sedimentary cycles:** The main reservoirs in these cycles are soil, sedimentary rocks, and other rocks found in the earth's crust. Examples include phosphorous cycle and sulphur cycle.

(ii) **Gaseous cycles:** The chief reservoir in these cycles is the atmosphere or hydrosphere. Examples include water cycle, carbon cycle, nitrogen cycle, and oxygen cycle.

The energy required for various biogeochemical cycles is obtained from the sun. A brief account of the various biogeochemical cycles is given in the ensuing sections.

## 2.3.1   Carbon Cycle

Carbon is one of the most important constituents of all organic compounds. It is the building block of life and is found in carbohydrates, fats, proteins, and nucleic acids. The chief reservoirs of carbon are as follows:

(i) The atmosphere in which carbon is present as carbon dioxide.

(ii) Oceans/seas in which carbon is present as carbon dioxide dissolved in water, and also as calcium carbonate in seashells and rocks at the ocean bed/seabed.

(iii) Land in which carbon is present in some ores, such as dolomite and other carbonates.

The carbon cycle involves circulation of carbon dioxide from the above three sources, as shown in Figure 2.2. The following processes are involved in the carbon cycle:

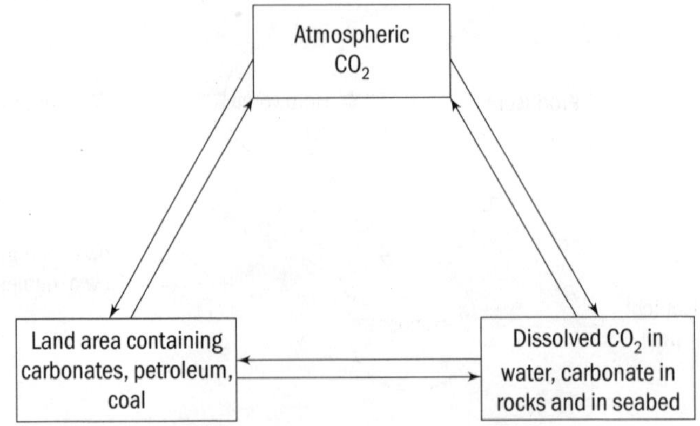


**Fig. 2.2**   Reservoirs of carbon

(i) Plants take in carbon dioxide from the atmosphere during photosynthesis—carbohydrates are formed by plants and oxygen is released in the atmosphere.

(ii) Animals receive the carbon in the form of carbohydrates from plants.

(iii) The remains of dead animals and plants on putrefaction and decomposition by bacteria (decomposers) release carbon dioxide back to the atmosphere.

(iv) The atmospheric carbon dioxide gets dissolved in oceans by the simple diffusion process. Marine algae and photosynthetic bacteria utilize water-dissolved carbon dioxide. Some of the dissolved carbon dioxide is also trapped in the form of limestone (calcium carbonate) and other carbonate-containing rocks.

(v) By respiration and combustion of fuels, such as coal, wood, diesel, natural gas, and gasoline, carbon dioxide returns to the atmosphere.

(vi) Weathering of carbonate-containing rocks (particularly by water-containing dissolved carbon dioxide as carbonic acid and by acid rain) and volcanic eruptions release carbon dioxide into the atmosphere.

The basic features of the carbon cycle are depicted in Figure 2.3. It should be understood that the release of excessive amount of carbon dioxide into the atmosphere is chiefly responsible for greenhouse effect and global warming.

## 2.3.2 Oxygen Cycle

Oxygen, the second most abundant element on earth, has atmospheric concentration of about 21%. It is essential for all the life processes. The main pools

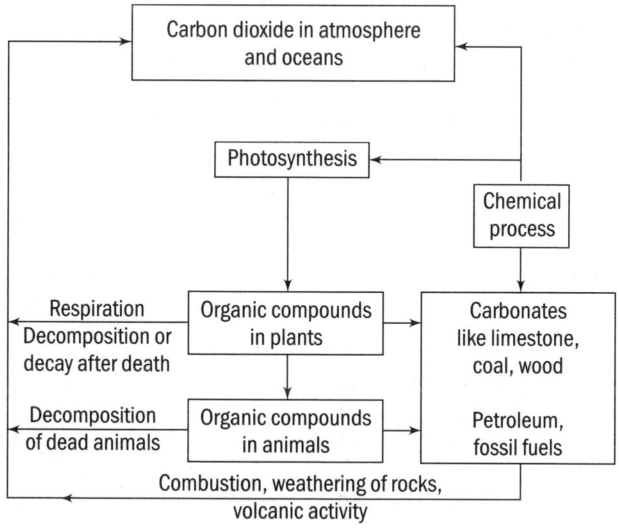


**Fig. 2.3**   Schematic of the carbon cycle

of oxygen are the atmosphere and oceans. The oxygen dissolved in waterbodies is responsible for sustaining aquatic life. It is also a common constituent of oxide ores in the earth. The various steps involved in the oxygen cycle are as follows:

(i) During respiration, organisms including animals and human beings breathe in oxygen from the air and release carbon dioxide into the atmosphere.

(ii) Carbon dioxide is used by plants to carry out photosynthesis. In this process, carbon dioxide reacts with water in the presence of solar energy and a catalyst (chlorophyll which is present in plants) to produce carbohydrate and oxygen, which are released into the atmosphere (Figure 2.4).

$$6CO_2 + 6H_2O + \text{solar energy} \rightarrow C_6H_{12}O_6 + 6O_2$$

(iii) Oxygen is needed by bacteria and fungi for decomposing dead matter. The products of decomposition (carbon dioxide and water) are released into the atmosphere. Oxygen is also needed for burning of fossil fuels, such as wood, coal, petroleum, and natural gas, and the products of combustion (carbon dioxide and water) are released into the atmosphere. The released carbon dioxide and water are utilized by plants during photosynthesis.

In the upper part of the atmosphere, solar energy splits water to give hydrogen and oxygen, which are released into the atmosphere.

$$h\gamma + 2H_2O \rightarrow 2H_2 + O_2$$

The above processes complete the oxygen cycle in nature. The oxygen content in the atmosphere remains more or less constant.

At times, imbalance may occur in the oxygen cycle, largely due to deforestation. Deforestation reduces the number of trees in the environment and, thus, the extent

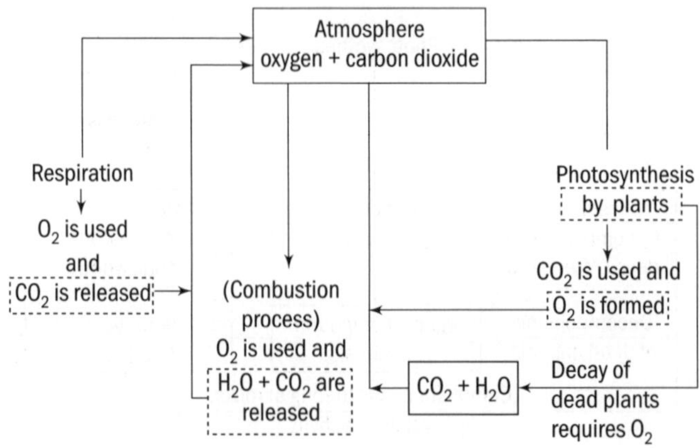


**Fig. 2.4**   Schematic of the oxygen cycle

of photosynthesis (which is a major source of oxygen in the atmosphere). This reduces the concentration of oxygen in the atmosphere.

## 2.3.3  Nitrogen Cycle

Nitrogen is essential for synthesizing amino acids and proteins in both plants and animals. Proteins are the building blocks of all living tissues. It is present to the extent of 80% in the atmosphere, which is the main source of nitrogen. However, elemental nitrogen cannot be used by most living organisms. Plants can take up nitrogen either as nitrates or as ammonia in the form of salts, such as ammonium nitrate. This is achieved by the fixation of atmospheric nitrogen through either a natural process or a synthetic process.

In the natural process of atmospheric nitrogen fixation, gaseous nitrogen, during periodic thunderstorm and lightening, is converted into nitric oxide, which gets oxidized into nitrogen dioxide. Both nitric oxide and nitrogen dioxide are washed down with rain, and reach the soil and form nitric acid. The nitric acid combines with salts present in the soil, such as sodium and calcium salts, to form the corresponding nitrates. During thunderstorm, atmospheric nitrogen may also combine with hydrogen present in the atmosphere to produce ammonia, which is also washed down to the earth with rain and may combine with nitrates and sulphates of the soil to form ammonium salts. As an alternative route, certain microorganisms convert atmospheric nitrogen into ammonium ions. These microorganisms include nitrifying bacteria, such as aerobic *Azotobacter* and anaerobic *Clostridium*, symbiotic nitrifying bacteria living in association with leguminous plants and symbiotic bacteria living in non-leguminous rod nodule plants, such as *Rhizobium,* as well as blue-green algae, such as *Anabaena, Spirulina.* Some plants can directly take up ammonium ions—a source of nitrogen. Alternatively, ammonium ions can be oxidized to nitrites and nitrates by specific bacteria. For example, *Nitrosomonas* bacteria promotes oxidation of ammonia into nitrite, which is further oxidized into nitrate by *Nitrobacter* bacteria. The nitrates, thus, obtained in the soil are taken up by plants and converted into amino acids—the building blocks of proteins. During the decay of dead plants, nitrogen is released and returned to the soil in the form of ammonia. Some of the nitrates (being soluble in water) find their way into waterbodies, such as rivers and oceans. Denitrifying bacteria, such as *Pseudomonas,* are present in soil and in oceans. These bacteria convert nitrates into elemental nitrogen, which escapes into the atmosphere and completes the cycle. Figure 2.5 depicts the various steps involved in the nitrogen cycle.

At times, imbalance may occur in the nitrogen cycle primarily due to the following two reasons:

(i) Soil erosion results in the loss of nitrifying bacteria (present in the top layer of the soil), which are the essential components of the nitrogen cycle.

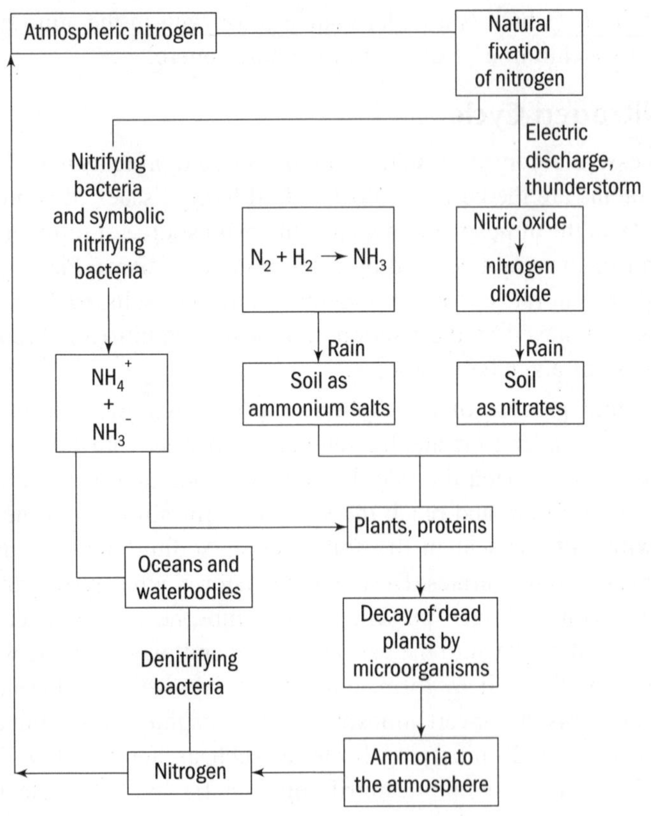


**Fig. 2.5**   Various steps involved in nitrogen cycle

(ii) The nitrogen components in the form of fertilizers may be washed away from the soil and may not be available for plants.

## 2.3.4  Phosphorus Cycle

Phosphorus is essential for living organisms. Phosphorus, in the form of phosphates, is necessary for growth and maintenance of bones and teeth in animals. It is also necessary for plant growth. It is a constituent of nucleic acids, phospholipids, adenosine triphosphate (ATP), and adenosine diphosphate (ADP). Rocks and other deposits are the main reservoirs of phosphorus. From these deposits, mainly via weathering of rocks, phosphorus is made available to living organisms. Plants absorb phosphorus through their roots. From plants, phosphorus finds its way to living organisms.

Dead organisms and decaying plants release phosphorous back to the soil, which is again recycled. A small amount of phosphorus also finds its way to waterbodies. In oceans, phosphorus is consumed by fish and sea birds. Figure 2.6a shows the flow chart of the phosphorus cycle.

In fresh waterbodies, the floating algae (phytoplankon) absorb soluble inorganic phosphate, which is converted into organophosphates. The algae are eaten by zooplankton, which are subsequently eaten by other aquatic animals, such as fish. Aquatic animals after their death decompose and phosphate is released. Thus, phosphates return to waterbodies and the phosphorus cycle continues (Figure 2.6b).

Excessive use of phosphate-containing fertilizers in agricultural fields has led to serious environmental concern. As run-offs from fields enter the waterbodies (for example, rivers, ponds, lakes), it results in population explosion of photosynthetic bacteria and blue-green algae. As time progresses, the whole waterbody gets covered by a thick layer of algae, resulting in depletion of oxygen in waterbodies. This results in the death of algae, bacteria, and fish. This process is called eutrophication.

### 2.3.5 Sulphur Cycle

Animals and plants use sulphur and its compounds to synthesize sulphur-containing amino acids and proteins. Sulphur is mainly found in the lithosphere, where it exists as sulphide ores of different elements and as free sulphur. Sulphur is also present in coal and oil in sedimentary rocks. Weathering of sedimentary

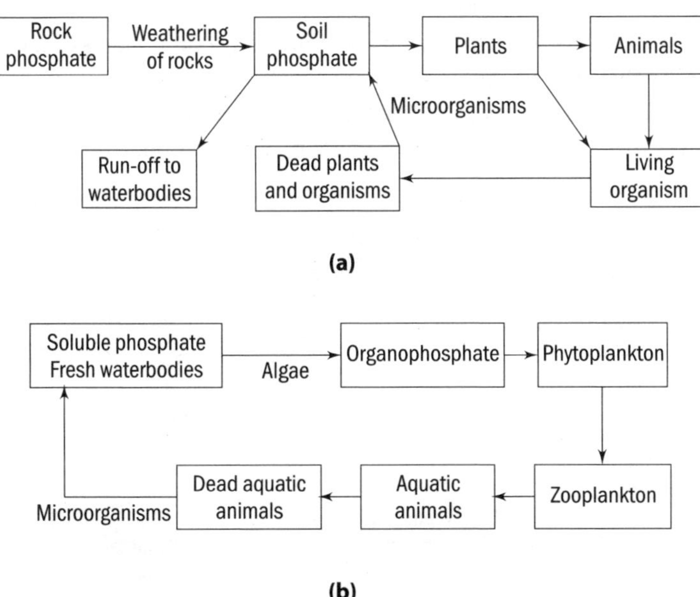


**Fig. 2.6**  Phosphorus cycle in waterbodies

rocks releases sulphur, which finds its way into the soil. In the soil, sulphur-containing compounds release $H_2S$ and $SO_2$ on bacterial decomposition.

In the atmosphere, $SO_2$ and $H_2S$ are released by volcanic eruptions, combustion of fossil fuels, and putrefaction of organic matter. In addition, $SO_2$ is oxidized to $SO_3$ and is released as acid rain (diluted $H_2SO_4$). $H_2S$ in the atmosphere is oxidized to $SO_2$ by ozone in the presence of particulates.

$$H_2S + O_3 \xrightarrow{\text{Particulates}} H_2O + SO_2$$

The various stages of the sulphur cycle is shown in Figure 2.7.

## 2.3.6    Water Cycle

Also known as the hydrological cycle, the water cycle is the most important cycle among the various cycles of the environment. This is because water carries materials that also move through other nutrient cycles. Water is one of the most important substances required for the sustenance of various life processes. Living organisms contain about 75% of water in them, although, some plants contain less water. On the other hand, algae and jellyfish are made up of 95% of water. Water covers about 75% of the earth's surface in the form of oceans, seas, rivers, lakes, and so on. Oceans alone contain about 97% of the total water content of the earth. A sizeable amount of the remaining water is locked in frozen form in the polar regions and glaciers. Only about 1% is available as freshwater (potable water). The global distribution of water is given in Table 2.2.

Water circulates between the living and non-living components of the biosphere (biosphere is that part of the earth where living organisms exist) in the form of an unending cycle. The water cycle is depicted in Figure 2.8. In the water cycle, water moves from oceans to the atmosphere by evaporation, from the atmosphere

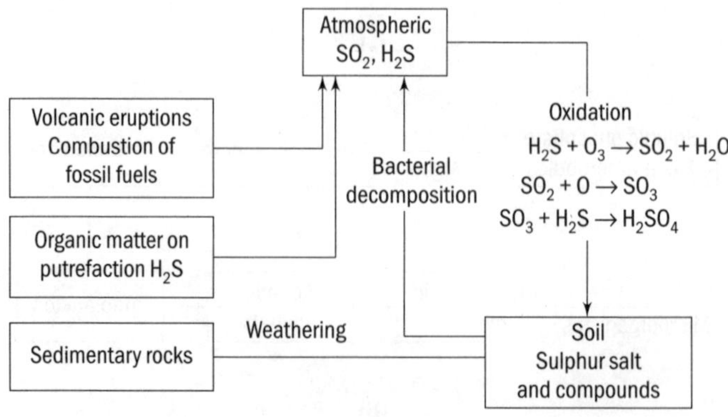


**Fig. 2.7**  Sulphur cycle

**Table 2.2**  Global distribution of water

| Source | Amount of water (%) |
|---|---|
| Oceans | 97.6 |
| Ice in polar regions and glaciers | 1.8699 |
| Groundwater | 0.5 |
| Rivers, lakes, inland seas | 0.02 |
| Soil moisture | 0.01 |
| Atmosphere | 0.0001 |

to oceans and land by precipitation, from land to oceans by run-offs from streams and rivers, and from land to the atmosphere by evaporation. The cycle is driven by solar energy. The water cycle does not involve any living organisms, and the water circulates between waterbodies, that is oceans, seas, and lakes, and the atmosphere.

An alternative pathway of the water cycle is soil water or underground water circulated by plants, animals, and the atmosphere. Plants absorb soil water through their root system. A portion of the water is used by plants for photosynthesis, and the excess water is released into the atmosphere through transpiration (the loss of water from the leaves of plants via evaporation). Transpiration is the major source of water in the atmosphere. The decay of dead plants by microorganisms (decomposers) releases water back to the soil.

Animals consume water by drinking from various water sources and also through the plants they eat. Water vapour is released into the atmosphere through exhalation, prespiration, and excretion. The water vapour thus released is lighter and rises in the air. At a higher altitude, it cools down and condenses into tiny droplets to form a cloud. These droplets ultimately fall on earth in the form of

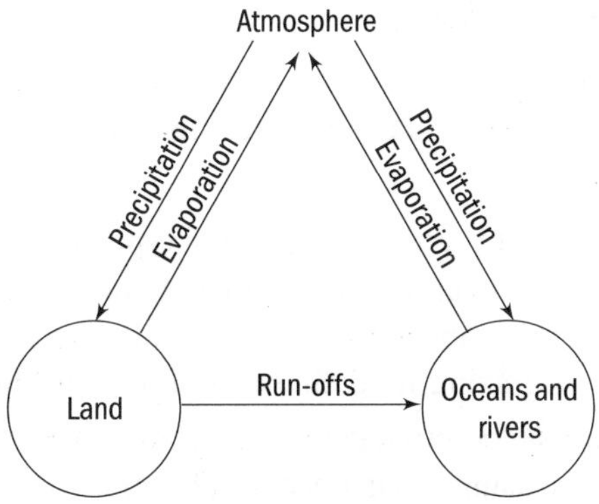


**Fig. 2.8**  Water cycle

rain, part of which is absorbed by the soil and the remaining finds its way into waterbodies.

Water is also used in large amount by industrial units engaged in manufacturing processes and power generation units. After use, the wastewater is discharged into the waterbodies; however, is should be kept in mind that discharging contaminated water is harmful to the environment and causes water pollution.

## 2.4  FOOD CHAINS, FOOD WEBS, AND ECOLOGICAL PYRAMIDS

As already stated, the energy flow in an ecosystem is unidirectional (a one-way process). The sequence of organisms through which the energy flows is known as food chain. There are a number of food chains, which are not isolated events but interconnected with each other. This interlocking pattern is known as food web. Each step in the food web is called a trophic level. These trophic levels combine together to constitute the ecological pyramid.

### 2.4.1  Food Chain

The transfer of energy from the plant source through a series of organisms, by eating or being eaten, constitutes a food chain. During energy transfer, a large amount of energy is lost in the form of heat. In a food chain, the food energy is transferred from a given source through a series of species, each of which eats the one existing before it in the chain. This cycle is repeated. The sequence of eating and being eaten is invariably initiated with plants as they convert the sun's energy into chemical energy and store it.

Energy is lost as heat at each transfer and the number of links or steps in a food chain is usually 4 or 5. In aquatic ecosystems, microscopic plants called phytoplankton and algae play the same role as grasses in a pasture or trees as producers.

#### *2.4.1.1  Types of Food Chain*

Depending on the type of organisms (producers) that constitute the first trophic level, there are three types of food chains: grazing food chain, detritus food chain, and parasitic food chain.

**(i) Grazing food chain:** It is the most common type of food chain. A cow, deer, or sheep grazing in a field represents a grazing food chain. Similarly, eating phytoplankton or algae by zooplankton and fish is another example of the grazing food chain. Example of grazing food chains is shown in Figure 2.9.

In Figure 2.10, grass is the producer (first trophic level) which makes its own food by photosynthesis using solar energy. The grass is consumed by a deer which is a herbivore (second trophic level). Finally, the deer is consumed by a

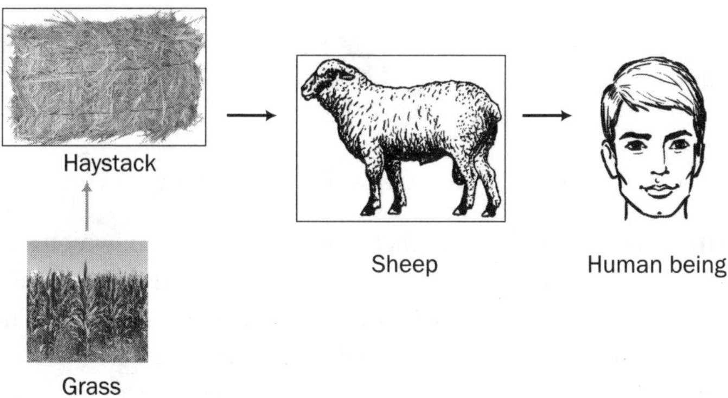



**Fig. 2.9**  A typical grazing food chain

lion which is a carnivore (third trophic level). A grassland food chain may involve five steps as represented in Figure 2.11.

In general, ocean food chains (marine food chains) are the longest. One of the reasons for the longer length of grazing food chain in aquatic ecosystems is the small size of phytoplankton and zooplankton that mainly comprise the first 10 trophic levels. Also, the carnivores at level 3 can be relatively small and numerous. A typical marine food chain is shown in Figure 2.12.

**(ii) Detritus food chain:** The detritus food chain starts from the dead or decomposed organic matter called detritus. The organic matter is decomposed by microorganisms, such as bacteria and fungi. Certain animals (consumers) that feed on this detritus form part of the detritus food chain. In fact, the detritus food chain is an inbuilt system in nature to clean up the environment from the dead and decaying matter. Vultures that feed on dead animals and in turn clean up the environment are also active participants in the detritus food chain.

The detritus food chain is responsible for releasing various nutrients locked in dead organic matter to the soil, which are used again by plants. The detritus food chains are essential components of the natural ecosystems and are, in fact, responsible for maintaining the ecological balance in the nature.

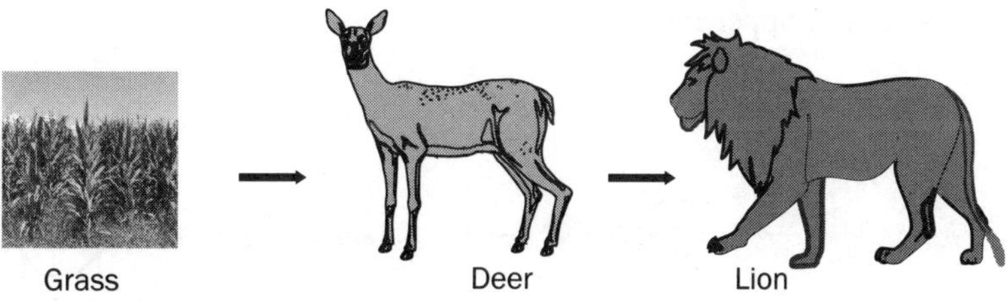



**Fig. 2.10**  A three-step grassland food chain

**Fig. 2.11**  Five-step grazing food chain

**(iii) Parasitic food chain:** It is another type of food chain in which parasites live on or inside the body of a host, such as a plant or tree, and derive food from it. In this process, the parasite gets nourished whereas the host is harmed. The parasitic food chain occurs in human beings when they get infected with worms. Here, the worms drain nourishment from the huaman body which leads to deficiencies of many vital minerals and nutrients. The result is that the infected human becomes prone to many diseases.

Food chains are not as simple as have been described above. There is a possibility that several different species may use the same item for food and one species may feed on different species for its food requirements.

## 2.4.2  Food Web

A food chain represents only one part of food or energy flow through an ecosystem. No food chain, in nature, is isolated or is as simple as described in the previous section. An ecosystem may consist of several interrelated food chains, which are interlocked with each other. This interlocking pattern is known as food web. Each step in the food web represents a trophic level. In the food web, the same food resource can be a part of more than one chain, especially, when that particular food resource is at one of the lower trophic levels. For example, a plant species may serve as a food source for many herbivores at a time. For example, grasses can support a rabbit, grasshopper, goat, or cow. In a similar way, a herbivore may be a food source for many different carnivores. Thus, interconnected networks of feeding relationships exist that make up a complete food web. A food web illustrates all possible transfers of energy and nutrients among organisms in an ecosystem, whereas a food chain traces only one pathway of food (Figure 2.13).

A simplified scheme of a food web is shown in Figure 2.14. In a food web, the largest amount of food energy is found in the lowest level. The amount of energy decreases in upper levels.

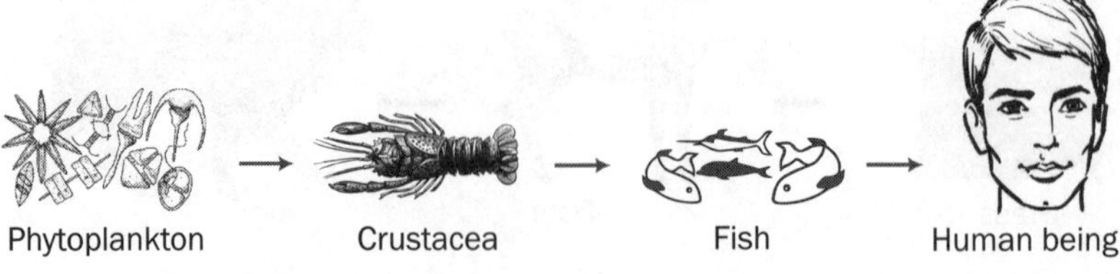


**Fig. 2.12**  A typical marine food chain

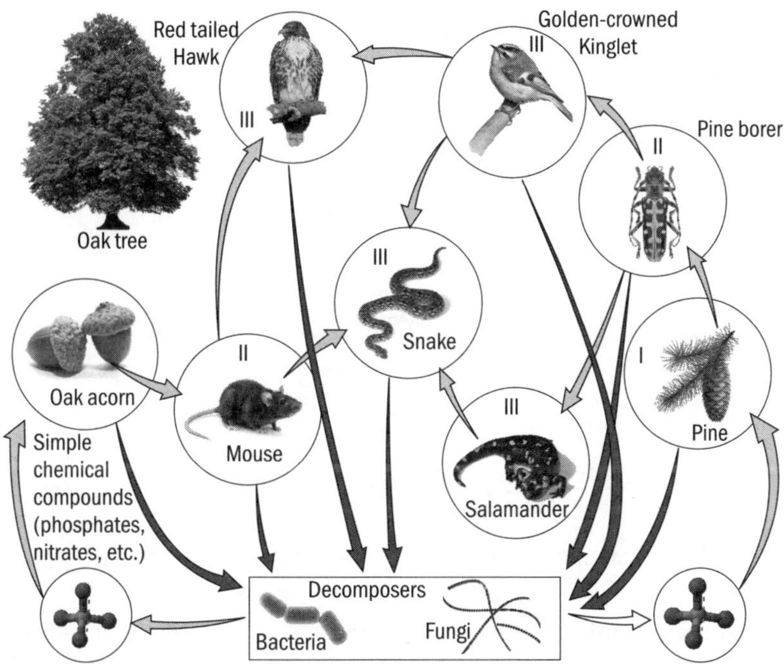


**Fig. 2.13**    A complex network or web of primary producers, consumers, and decomposers in a typical terrestrial food web

*Note:* Trophic levels are depicted by roman numerals

## 2.4.3  Ecological Pyramid

The trophic levels have been already discussed in the chapter. These trophic levels, combined together, constitute the ecological pyramid. The food producers form the base of the pyramid while the carnivores form the top of the pyramid.

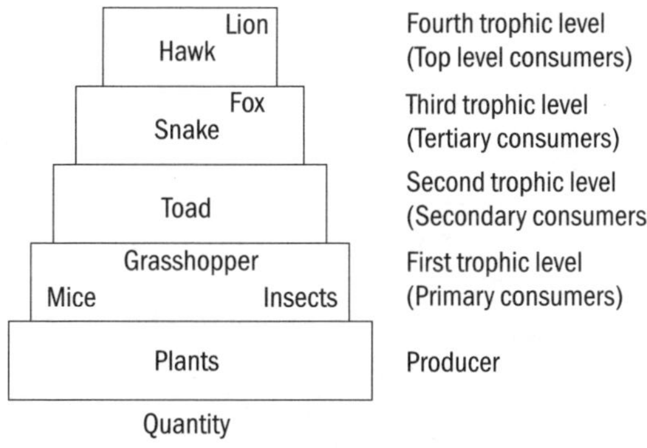


**Fig. 2.14**    A simplified scheme of a food web

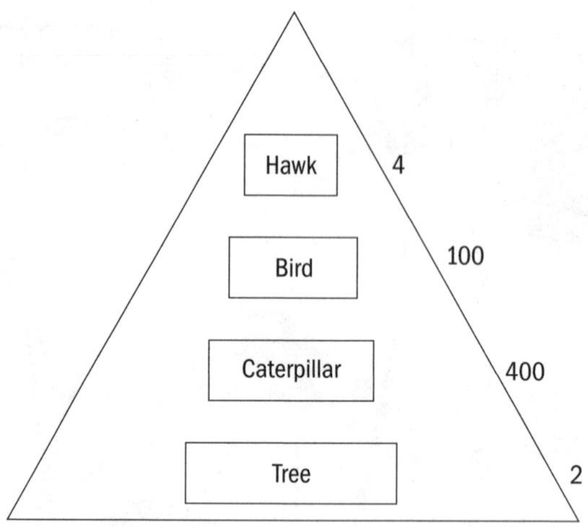


**Fig. 2.15**   Pyramid of numbers

The ecological pyramids can be divided into three categories: (i) pyramids of numbers, (ii) pyramids of biomass, and (iii) pyramids of energy.

**(i) Pyramid of numbers:** It deals with the relationship between the number of primary producers and the number of consumers of different trophic levels. Figure 2.15 represents the pyramid of numbers. In this, the base of the pyramid represents the food production base for higher trophic levels. As it is very difficult to count all the organisms, a pyramid of numbers cannot define the trophic structure of an ecosystem correctly.

**(ii) Pyramid of biomass:** A comparatively simple approach to assess the energy passed on at each trophic level is to weigh the individuals at each trophic level. This gives a pyramid of biomass, which is the total weight of all the organisms at any level. The pyramid of biomass has a large base of primary producers. This is represented in Figure 2.16.

In an aquatic ecosystem, the producers are tiny phytoplankton that grow and reproduce at a rapid rate. In such a situation, the pyramid of biomass can have a small base, with the consumer biomass, at any instant, exceeding the producer biomass.

**(iii) Pyramid of energy:** The pyramid of energy is the most informative method of assessing energy flow in an ecosystem. An energy pyramid reflects the laws of thermodynamics, and so the pyramid is always right side up with a large energy base at the bottom. A pyramid of energy based on determination of the actual amount of energy that organisms take in should be able to answer the questions, such as how much energy organisms burn during their metabolism, how much energy remains in their waste products, and how much energy they store in body tissues? The energy inputs and outputs are calculated so that the energy flow can be expressed per unit of land or water per unit time.

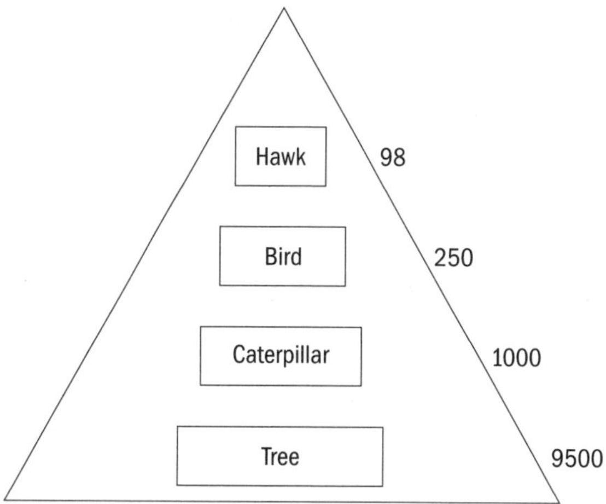



**Fig. 2.16**  Pyramid of biomass [biomass (g/m$^2$)]

Let us understand this with the help of an example. Assume that an ecosystem receives 1000 calories of light energy in a given day. Most of this energy is not absorbed and is reflected back in space. Out of the energy absorbed, only a small amount is used by plants in carrying out natural processes, such as photosynthesis and respiration. Out of 1000 calories, only 100 calories get stored in energy-rich materials. Next, suppose an animal, say a deer, eats a plant that contains 100 calories of food energy. The deer uses some of this energy (100 calories) for its own metabolism and stores only 10 calories of energy. A lion, in turn, eats the deer and gets even smaller amount of energy. Thus, the usable energy is on a constant decline in the energy pyramid. It decreases from sunlight to producer, to herbivore, and to carnivore. Therefore, as already stated, the energy pyramid always stays in an upright position (Figure 2.17).

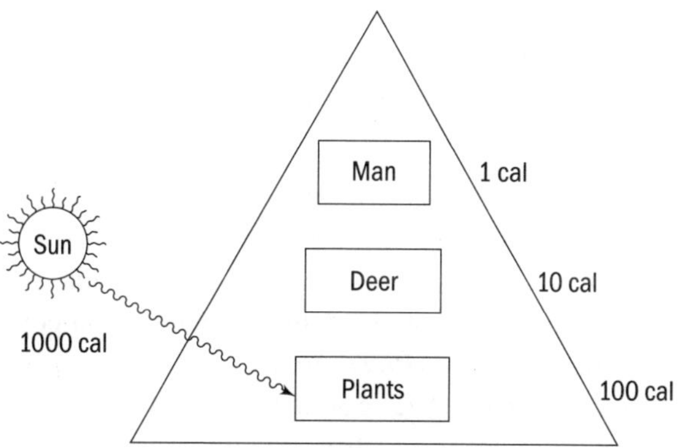



**Fig. 2.17**  Pyramid of energy

The two laws of thermodynamics that form the basis of the energy pyramid are as follows:

**First law of thermodynamics:** Energy is neither created nor destroyed; it only gets converted from one form to another.

**Second law of thermodynamics:** When energy changes from one form to another, some of it is lost.

## 2.5　FUNCTIONS OF ECOSYSTEMS

Ecosystems are many; however, this section discusses the following four important ecosystem types that have a profound influence on both existence and sustenance of life on earth:

　(i) Forest ecosystem

　(ii) Grassland ecosystem

　(iii) Desert ecosystem

　(iv) Aquatic ecosystem

### 2.5.1　Forest Ecosystem

Forests are the treasure house of resources. They provide a wide variety of commodities, such as timber, fuel, wood, fodder, fibre, fruits, herbal drugs, and raw materials for industries. In addition, a great variety of animals and birds inhabit forests and serve as useful living resources. Forests play a vital role in soil formation, water conservation, and regeneration of oxygen that are important factors for the climate. Overexploitation of forests for timber, firewood, and other forest products, without putting in efforts to regenerate them, is resulting in fast depletion of the forest cover which in turn is causing environmental imbalance. A serious consequence of deforestation is the loss of rainwater due to surface run-offs. This results in the increased rate of floods. Excessive washing away of the topsoil results in low fertility and reduces crop yields.

#### 2.5.1.1　Types of Forests

Forests have been classified into three major categories: coniferous forests, tropical forests, and temperate forests.

**(i) Coniferous forests:** Coniferous forests are characterized by high rainfall and strong seasonal climates with long winters and fairly short summers. These are transcontinental, that is, adjacent to tundra regions (Canada, Sweden, Finland, and Siberia). The coniferous forest vegetation is mainly composed of species of evergreen plants, such as spruce (*Picea glauca*), fir (*Abies balsamea*), and pine (*Pinus resinosa/Pinus strobus*). The prominent animal species that inhabit these forests include lynx, wolf, beer, red fox, porcupine, squirrel, and amphibians, such as *Hyla* and *Rana*.

**(ii) Temperate deciduous forests:** Temperate deciduous forests are characterized by moderate climate and broad-leaved deciduous trees that shed their leaves in fall, are bare in winter, and grow new foliage in spring. These forests are typically found in North America, Europe, Eastern Asia, Chile, part of Australia, and Japan. Rainfall varies from 70 cm to 150 cm while temperature lies in the range of 10–20°C. The trees are tall (40–50 m), and their leaves are thin and broad. The common genera of trees inhabitating these forests include maple (*Acer*), beach (*Faqus*), oak (*Quercus*), hickory (*Caryd*), basswood (*Tilia*), chestnut (*Castriea*), and cotton wood (*Populus*). Temperate vegetation, including pine, fir, and juniper, grows in the Himalayas.

Animal species typical to temperate forests are deer, beers, squirrels, grey foxes, bobcats, wild turkey, and woodpeckers. The common invertebrates found include earthworms, snails, millipedes, Coleoptera, and Orthoptera while vertebrates include amphibians, such as toad, salamander, and frog. Reptiles, such as turtle, lizard, and snake; mammals, such as raccoon, opossum, pig, and mountain lion; and birds, such as horned owl and hawks, are found in temperate forests.

**(iii) Temperate evergreen forests:** Mediterranean-type climate is required for temperate evergreen forests. Such forests are characterized by warm, dry summers and cool, moist winters. The common inhabitants include broad-leaved low evergreen trees. The characteristic animals of temperate evergreen forests are mule, deer, brush rabbit, wood rat, chipmunk, and lizard.

**(iv) Temperate rainforests:** Temperate rainforests are colder than any other rainforests. Rainfall in these forests is high, and fog is very heavy, which may represent a more important source of water than rainfall. The animals of temperate rainforest are similar to those of deciduous forests, but show a somewhat high diversity.

**(v) Tropical rainforests:** Tropical rainforests are found near the equator. Both the temperature and the humidity remain high and more or less uniform. The annual rainfall exceeds 200–225 cm and is generally distributed throughout the year.

The flora is diversified—as many as 300 different species of trees may be found in 1 km$^2$ area. The common vertebrates inhabitating tropical rainforests are arboreal amphibians, aquatic reptiles, chameleons, agamids, geckos, and many species of snakes and birds. Mammals include insectivores, leopards, jungle cats, anteaters, giant flying squirrels, monkeys, and sloths.

**(vi) Tropical seasonal forests:** Tropical seasonal forests are found in regions where the total rainfall is high but segregated into wet and dry periods. Such forests are found in South East Asia, Central and South America, Northern Australia, Western Africa, tropical islands of South Pacific, and India. Teak is a major large tree found in the best-known tropical seasonal forests of India (central India) and South East Asia.

**(vii) Subtropical rainforests:** Subtropical rainforests are found in fairly high rainfall regions; however, the temperature difference between winter and summer seasons is not much. The vegetation of such forests includes mahogany, gumbo-limbo, bays, palms, oaks, magnolias, tamarind, pineapple, and figs. Animals inhabitating these forests are very similar to those of tropical rainforests.

Table 2.3 lists the types of forests in India, along with plants and animals found in these forests.

### 2.5.1.2  Importance of Forests

Forests have supported human civilization since time memorial. Some of the most noteworthy contributions of forests are listed here:

(i) Forests are renewable resources of energy and provide a variety of commodities to the humankind.

(ii) If planned properly, then they can be a continuous source of firewood.

(iii) They provide raw material for various wood-based industries engaged in the production of pulp and paper products, rayon, and other human-made fibres, matches, furniture, and sports items.

**Table 2.3**  Types of forests in India

| Forest type | Plant examples | Common animals | Rare animals |
|---|---|---|---|
| Himalayan coniferous | Pine, Deodar | Wild goats and sheep, Himalayan black bear | Snow leopard, Himalayan brown bear, musk deer, Himalayan wolf |
| Himalayan broad-leaved | Maple, Oak | | |
| Evergreen North-east, Western Ghats, Andaman | Jamun, Ficus, *Dipterocarpus* | Tiger, leopard, sambar, Malabar whistling thrush, Malabar pied hornbill, tree frogs | Pigmy hog, rhinoceros, lion-tailed macaque |
| Deciduous dry | Teak, Ain, *Terminalia* | Tiger, chital, barking deer, babbles | |
| Deciduous moist | Sal | | |
| Thorn and scrub, semi-arid forests | Babul, Ber, Neem | Blackbuck, chinkad, partridge, monitor lizard | Bustard, florican |
| Mangrove delta forests | Avicennia | Crocodiles, fish, crustaceans | Water monitor lizard |

Leopard, tiger, and tree frog are found in Evergreen North-east,
Western Ghats, and Andaman type of forests

(iv) Indian forests also provide other minor products, such as essential oils, medicinal plants, resins and turpentine, lac and shellac, *katha* and catechu, *biri* wrappers, and tasar silk.

(v) Tropical countries, such as India, are a source of abundant timber and heartwood. In fact, timber accounts for 25% of all photosynthetic materials produced all over the world and about 50% of the total biomass produced by forests.

(vi) Forests play a vital role in regulating the earth's climate.

(vii) Forests provide habitat and food as well as protection to wildlife species against extremes of climate. They also help in balancing carbon dioxide and oxygen in the atmosphere.

(viii) Forests improve the water-holding capacity of soil, regulate the water cycle, and maintain soil fertility by returning nutrients to the soil through litter.

(ix) Forests prevent soil erosion and landslides, and reduce the intensity of floods and droughts.

(x) Being home to the wildlife, forests provide important aesthetic assets for tourism and add cultural value to the society.

### 2.5.1.3  Deforestation

The indiscriminate felling of trees due to urbanization, industrialization, mining, and use of wood for domestic and other purposes has resulted in heavy depletion of forests. This is a global phenomenon. India alone is losing more than 1.5 million hectares of good forest cover every year. If the present rate of depletion is allowed to continue, the country will have no forests in about 20 years.

Deforestation results not only in lowering of groundwater level but also in the reduction of rainfall. Forests recycle moisture back into the atmosphere by transpiration. Due to deforestation, this natural water cycle is broken and water is lost rapidly as run-offs.

### 2.5.1.4  The Chipko Movement

The Chipko Movement was launched in 1970 by villagers of the then Uttar Pradesh (now Uttarakhand) to save trees from felling. This movement was led by people, such as Sunderlal Bahuguna and Chandi Prasad Bhatt. The Alaknanda Valley, in which the movement started, was the scene of unprecedented floods in 1970. People realized that deforestation due to felling of trees resulted not only in the loss of fuelwood and fodder resources but also in frequent floods and loss of the precious topsoil. People (local women and men) prevented the cutting of trees by hugging them. This unique initiative was the world's most well-known grassroots eco-development movement. This non-violent, action-oriented movement helped the people to unite and draw the attention of the government towards mismanagement of forests. The Chipko Movement practised Gandhian thoughts of non-violent resistance (Satyagraha). The movement not only helped preserve forests but also inculcated awareness among the people.

## 2.5.2  Grassland Ecosystem

Grasslands are found where annual rainfall is about 25–75 cm, which is not enough to support a forest but sufficient to prevent land from turning into a desert. Grasslands are typical vegetation formations and are usually found in temperate climates. In India, grasslands are found mainly in the higher altitudes of the Himalayas. In other parts of India, grasslands are composed of steppes and savannahs. Steppe formation is found in sandy and saline soil, as in western Rajasthan where the climate is semi-arid, the average rainfall is less than 20 cm a year, and with a dry season of 10–11 months. Forage is available only during the brief wet season. Dry savannah grazing ecosystems are found in eastern parts of Rajasthan, where the rainfall is about 50 cm per year and dry season is of 6–8 months.

### 2.5.2.1  Types of Grasslands

Grasslands are found in both temperate and tropical regions where the rainfall is relatively low or uneven. Based on the climatic conditions, grasslands found in India can be categorized into six types (Figure 2.18). Of these, the four major types of grasslands are discussed here.

**(i) *Sehima-Dichanthium* grasslands:** *Sehima-Dichanthium* grasslands cover the whole of Peninsular India (dry sub-humid zone, except Nilgiri). The grass in this region has thorny bushes; for example, *Acacia catechu*, *Mimosa rubicaulis*, *Ziziphus*, *Anogeissus latifolia*, and other deciduous species. The flora includes 24 perennial grasses and 124 other herbaceous species, of which 56 are legumes.

**(ii) *Dichanthium–Cenchrus-Lasiurus* grasslands:** In India, *Dichanthium–Cenchrus-Lasiurus* grasslands are found in semi-arid zones and extend to the northern parts of Gujarat (excluding Aravalli Hills), western Uttar Pradesh, Delhi, and Punjab. About 11 perennial grasses and 45 other herbaceous species are found in this region. Besides these, shrubby growths of *Acacia senegal* and *Calotropis gigantea* are also found.

**(iii)** ***Phragmites–Saccharum-Imperate* grasslands:** *Phragmites–Saccharum-Imperate* grasslands are found in moist sub-humid zones, covering the Gangetic alluvial plain in Northern India. These grasslands comprise about 19 main grass species and 58 herbaceous species, including 16 legumes. Some common trees and shrubs include *Acacia arabica, Anogeissus latifolia, Butea monosperma.*

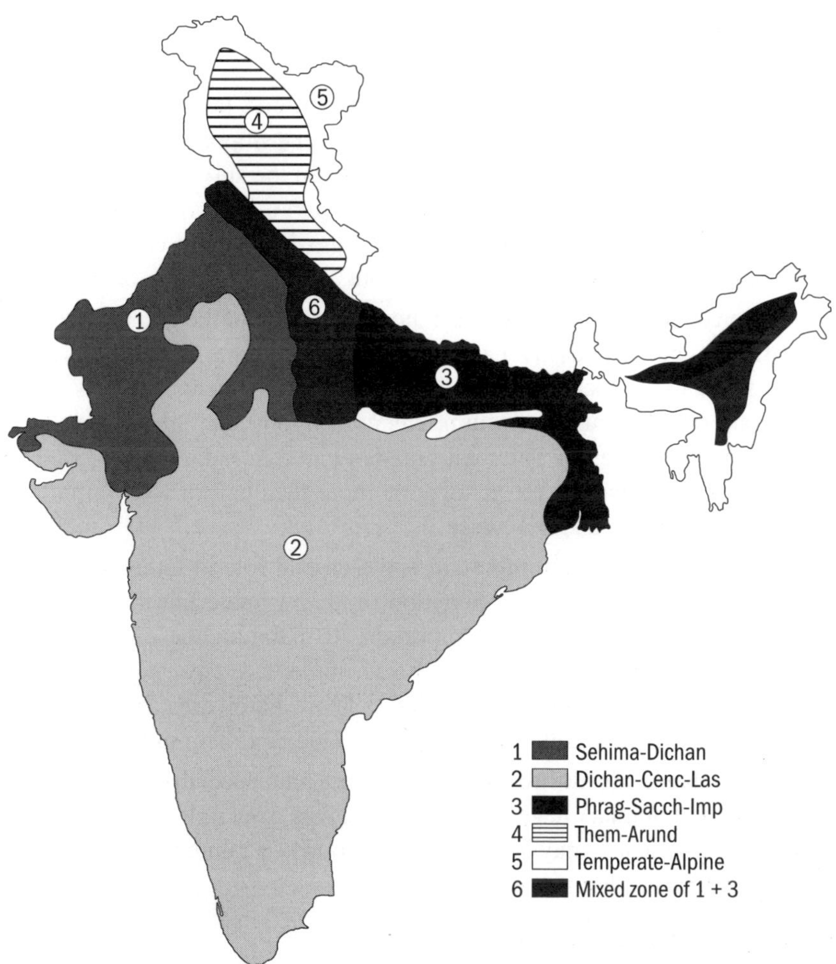


**Fig. 2.18** Types of grasslands and their locations

**(iv)** *Themeda–Arundinella* **grasslands:** *Themeda–Arundinella* grasslands cover the humid montane regions and moist sub-humid areas of Manipur, Assam, West Bengal, Uttar Pradesh, Punjab, Himachal Pradesh, and Jammu and Kashmir.

### 2.5.2.2   Importance of Grassland Ecosystem

Generally, grasslands are utilized by rural communities, farmers, and shepherds for the purpose of grazing their cattles. It is very important that grasslands should not be overgrazed because this may threaten the survival of the grassland ecosystem itself. It is best not to use a particular part of the grassland for grazing purposes for a specific time so that rotational grazing pattern can be practised. Also, fires must be prevented or, if broken out, must be rapidly controlled.

In addition to people and cattle, the major component of the grazing ecosystem is vegetation. Its herbaceous layer and the non-ligneous parts of woody shrubs and trees constitute the fodder. Fodder with chemical constituents, such as proteins and minerals (phosphorus, potassium, calcium, lignin, and silica) are the best choice for grazing material. The total grassland area in India is just 25% of the total land area of the world. Yet, it supports more than half of world's buffaloes, 15% cattle, 15% goats, and 4% sheep.

Livestock wealth plays an important and a crucial role in India. It is a major source of fuel, draught, power, nutrition, and raw materials for the village industries. Grassland biomes are important to maintain the crop that many domestic and wild herbivores, such as horse, mule, ass, cow, pig, sheep, goat, buffalo, camel, deer, and zebra use as food. These herbivores are important to humans as they provide food, milk, wool, and hide, and help in transportation.

If our grasslands are destroyed, we will lose our specialized ecosystem to which plants and animals have adapted themselves over millions of years. The destruction of grasslands may lead to the extinction of a number of species which will be a great loss to humankind.

## 2.5.3   Desert Ecosystem

Normally, a desert forms where low annual rainfall (less than 25 cm) or sporadic rainfall with low humidity is received. The sun's rays in the range of visible light penetrate the atmosphere easily, making the ground temperature very high, especially during daytime; in contrast, nights are often cold. Drought-resistant vegetation, such as cacti, euphorbias, and sagebrush are found in deserts. A number of animals live in deserts; but they are mostly nocturnal. Many species of reptiles and mammals, and some bird species are also found in deserts. As water is the dominant limiting factor, the productivity of any desert is directly proportional to the rainfall it receives.

### 2.5.3.1  Desertification

Desertification is responsible for the degradation of about 73% of the world's total rangeland. A drop in the biological potential of a land ultimately leads to desert-like conditions. Desertification has become a worldwide environmental problem. In fact, it threatens the future of about 628 million people around the world. Desertification is caused not because of natural disasters, such as climate change and drought; it is a result of human activities.

Increase in population and lack of employment opportunities have left people with no choice but to continue grazing cattle even in inhospitable conditions. Another cause of desertification is the increase in agricultural land, thereby decreasing grazing land. Also, felling of trees for fuel and increase in cattle production have multiplied the process of desertification.

## 2.5.4  Aquatic Ecosystem

Ecosystems consisting of water as the main habitat are known as aquatic ecosystems. There are three kinds of aquatic ecosystems—freshwater, saline water, and brackish water. Freshwater ecosystems are of two types—static water ecosystems (lentic systems) and flowing water ecosystems (lotic systems).

Water covers 75% of the earth's surface either as freshwater where the salt content is less than 0.5% in concentration, as saline water where the salt content is more than 3.5%, or as brackish water where the salt content is intermediate between freshwater and saline water. On the basis of the salt content, aquatic ecosystems can be of two types— saline and fresh waterbodies. Seas and oceans come under saline waterbodies. Estuaries and brackish waterbodies have the salt content between 5 ppm (parts per million) and 35 ppm. The salt content is the prime factor for adaptation and evolution of aquatic organisms. The different aquatic ecosystems are given in Figure 2.19.

A desert ecosystem

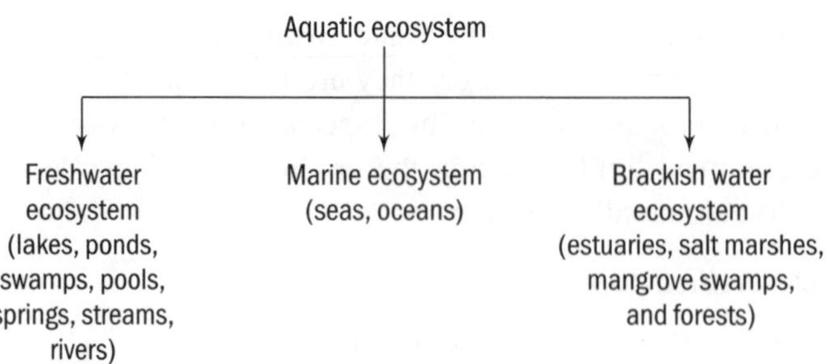


**Fig. 2.19**   Different aquatic ecosystems

There is an uneven distribution of organisms in different ecosystems. Each aquatic ecosystem has certain unique characteristics. Every aquatic ecosystem varies in size, light penetration, temperature, and the amount of dissolved oxygen (DO). All these factors are responsible for the environment and biota of an aquatic ecosystem.

### 2.5.4.1 Freshwater Ecosystems

Freshwater ecosystems are of the following two types:

(i) Lentic (from 'lenis' meaning calm), or standing, or basin series ecosystems. Examples of lentic aquatic ecosystems include lakes, pools, ponds, swamps, marshes.

(ii) Lotic (from 'lotus' meaning washed), or running, or channel series ecosystems. Examples of lotic aquatic ecosystems include rivers, streams, springs.

**(i) Lentic ecosystems:** Lentic ecosystems include all those systems that have a static body of water, such as lakes, impoundments, and wetlands.

*Lakes* are inland depressions that are filled with water (standing). They vary considerably in area and depth. The largest lake of the world is Lake Superior in North America, with surface area of 83,000 $km^2$ and maximum depth of about 5000 feet. The deepest lake in the world is Lake Baikal in Siberia which is nearly half the size of Lake Superior but twice its depth. Most lakes are a result

A lentic ecosystem

of geological changes that took place within the past 20,000 years. However, Lake Baikal and Lake Tanganyika in Africa are believed to have originated about 20 million years ago. Algae, a large constitutent in lakes, derive their energy from the sun (photosynthesis). This energy is transferred to microscopic animals that feed on algae. Fish that are herbivores also feed on algae and aquatic weed. The fish, in turn, are preyed upon by larger carnivorous fish. In the lake ecosystem, energy circulates from sunlight (that penetrates the water) to plants and then to herbivorous animals and finally to carnivores. The waste products of animals settle at the bottom of the lake (lakebed) and act as a nutrient supplier for aquatic plants. These plants also use carbon dioxide for their growth and in the process release oxygen, which is used by aquatic animals for respiration.

In addition to natural lakes, there are waterbodies (both small and large) or reservoirs formed by a dam. These **impoundments** are created with the aim of fulfilling specific requirements, such as hydroelectric power generation, fisheries, water supply, irrigation, industries, recreation, and control of floods.

**Wetlands** are permanently or periodically water-covered bodies and can be defined as submerged or saturated lands, either artificially or naturally. These can be up to 6 m deep and may be fresh, brackish, or saline. ***Inland wetlands***, as the name suggests, occur inland and contain freshwater, such as bogs and swamps. ***Coastal wetlands*** occur near the coast and contain saline or brackish water such as mangrove swamps and mangrove forests.

**(ii) Lotic ecosystems:** Lotic ecosystems include all those systems in which the water flows. Some typical examples include rivers, streams, brooks.

## 2.5.4.2  River Ecosystems

In rivers (and streams), water flows continuously and, therefore, the volume of the river water keeps changing, causing variation in its velocity. The physical, chemical, and biological conditions of rivers gradually change with distance along the main channel in a definite direction. Unlike lakes (which are closed or self-contained systems), rivers are open or heterotrophic systems. The nutrients in a lake may be used several times. In contrast, in rivers, at any point, due to water flow, nutrients become available to plants and animals on a temporary basis.

A lotic ecosystem

As rivers and streams are flowing water ecosystems, all living forms are specially adapted to different flow rates. The flora and fauna of rivers and streams depend on their clarity, flow, and oxygen content as well as the nature of their beds.

### 2.5.4.3  Marine Ecosystems

Marine ecosystems cover about 75% of the earth's surface and have an average depth of about 3750 m. These are the largest reservoirs of water, living beings, and essential nutrients needed by both marine and land organisms.

Marine ecosystems are of great ecological significance. The producers in these ecosystems vary from microscopic algae to large seaweeds. There are millions of zooplankton and different varieties of invertebrates that are food for fish, turtles, and marine mammals. In coastal areas, the sea is shallow; the depth of the sea increases with the increase in its distance from the coast. Some of the important features of marine ecosystems are as follows:

(i) **Salinity:** Seawater is saline. The salinity is fairly constant, averaging about 3.5% (35 PPT). The main constituent of seawater salt is sodium chloride (27%). Calcium, potassium, and magnesium salts are also present in small concentrations in the form of chloride, bicarbonate, carbonate, and bromide.

(ii) **Light:** It penetrates to a certain extent and is responsible for the production of organics (photosynthesis).

(iii) **Temperature:** The temperature of oceans remains fairly constant, ranging from about 2°C in the polar seas to about 32°C in the tropics.

(iv) **Nutrients:** The concentration of dissolved nutrients is low in the marine environment. This low quantity is a major limiting factor in determining the size of marine population.

(v) **Dissolved gases:** The marine environment is a gigantic reservoir of dissolved oxygen and carbon dioxide. These two gases help to regulate the composition of air (with respect to oxygen) we breathe in and the temperature of the atmosphere (carbon dioxide is a greenhouse gas).

(vi) **Alkalinity:** The seawater is alkaline and has a pH of about 8.2.

(vii) **Pressure:** The pressure changes from 1 atm (at the surface) to about 1000 atm at the greatest depth. This change in pressure has a pronounced effect on the distribution of aquatic life.

(viii) **Currents:** Sea is in a continuous state of circulation. These currents may be driven either by wind (surface currents) or by variation in temperature and salinity (deeper currents).

(ix) **Waves and tides:** There are several types of waves and tides in the marine ecosystem. These are produced by the pull of the moon and sun.

### 2.5.4.4  Productivity of Aquatic Habitats

Sunlight and oxygen play the most prominent roles in aquatic habitats. In fact, these two factors distinguish aquatic habitat from terrestrial habitat in which moisture and temperature are the driving factors. Some of the important factors responsible for the productivity of aquatic habitats are sunlight, transparency, temperature, and oxygen.

**Sunlight** has a profound influence on waterbodies. It rapidly diminishes as it passes down the column of water. Photosynthetic activity takes place up to the water layer where sunlight reaches. This zone is called photic zone. The depth of this zone depends on the transparency and temperature of the water.

**Transparency** affects the extent of light penetration and is indirectly related to turbidity. Turbidity is caused by suspended particulate matters, such as clay, silt, and phytoplankton. In fact, transparency limits the extent of light penetration and influences underwater photosynthetic activities.

Aquatic organisms have narrow **temperature** tolerance. Even a small variation in the water temperature can be a threat to the survival of aquatic organisms. However, slight temperature changes are not much of a concern for terrestrial organisms.

In aquatic systems, the **dissolved oxygen** concentration varies constantly and depends on parameters that influence the input and output of oxygen in the water. In freshwater, the average concentration of dissolved oxygen is 10 ppm. Oxygen enters the water through two pathways: (i) air–water interface and (ii) photosynthetic activities of aquatic plants.

The factors discussed apply, in general, to all aquatic ecosystems including lakes, ponds, rivers, streams, estuaries, oceans, and seas.

### 2.5.4.5  Uses of Aquatic Ecosystems

Three most important uses of aquatic ecosystems include the following:
  (i) Aquatic ecosystems are the source of freshwater which is essential for sustenance of life on earth.
  (ii) All agricultural crops rely heavily on water (besides other nutrients).
  (iii) The livelihood of a large number of people depends on ocean ecosystems, which are used for fishing purposes.

### 2.5.4.6  Threats to Aquatic Ecosystems

The main threat to an aquatic ecosystem is the pollution caused because of the discharge of municipal wastes, and wastes and by-products from industrial units. Hence, these anthropogenic activities are primarily responsible for the degradation of aquatic ecosystems.

Discharge of municipal waste is the main
threat to an equatic ecosystem

### 2.5.4.7  Estuaries

All rivers and lakes ultimately drain into the sea. Many rivers develop a highly specialized zone before joining the sea. This zone is called an estuary. In other words, estuaries are transitional zones between rivers and seas. Estuaries possess unique ecological features and biotic communities. In fact, they are the most productive aquatic ecosystems of the world. An estuary is a semi-enclosed part of the coastal ocean containing brackish water. On the one hand, estuaries connect with the seas, while on the other hand, they connect with the river mouth and receive freshwater. In India, estuaries are seen along the coast of Kerala.

Each ecosystem consists of producers and consumers. In fact, the ecosystem functions due to the presence of these producers and consumers. The producers (plants) make their own food from solar energy, carbon dioxide, and water (photosynthesis). With the help of minerals, such as carbon, hydrogen, nitrogen, phosphorus, calcium, magnesium, zinc, and iron (which are obtained from the edaphic soil), plants build up complex organic matters, including carbohydrates, fats, and proteins to produce their food. Thus, plants convert solar energy into food energy.

Consumers, such as animals, cannot make their own food and eat plants and other animals. Consumers can be herbivores (feed on plants), carnivores (feed on animals), or omnivores (feed on both plants and animals). Thus, the energy is transformed through food to animals.

When plants and animals die, their remains are acted upon by decomposers (microconsumers), such as bacteria and fungi. Decomposers decompose the dead matter into simple materials, such as carbon dioxide, water, and minerals, which are released into the air, waterbodies, and soil. Plants reuse these materials from air, water, or soil (Figure 2.20).

The right proportion of producers, consumers, and decomposers in an ecosystem is very important for its continuous functioning. This also helps in maintaining the ecological balance in the nature. Any malfunctioning of

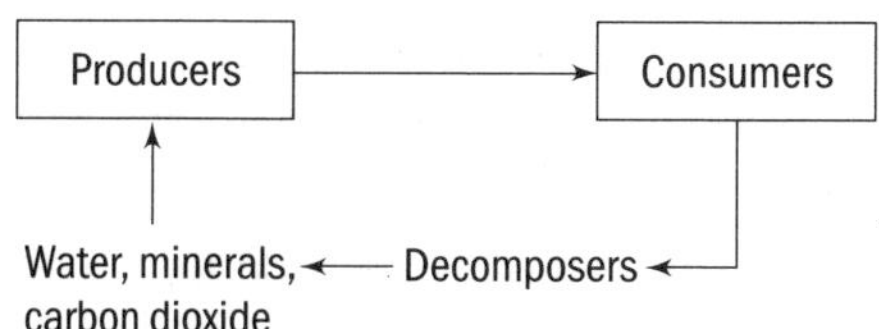

**Fig. 2.20**   Recycling in an ecosystem

the ecosystem—whether owing to imbalance in the population of producers, consumers, and decomposers or owing to various other human activities—leads to ecological crises, such as global warming, deforestation, loss of biodiversity, acid rain, depletion of ozone layer, soil erosion, and floods. The main cause for the occurrence of ecological crises is the explosion in human population.

## 2.6   DEGRADATION OF ECOSYSTEMS

Ecosystems should not be allowed to degrade as they sustain life. Ecosystems degrade because humans overexploit them. Deforestation, overgrazing, agriculture, mining, and urbanization are some of the contributing factors of ecosystem degradation.

### 2.6.1   Deforestation

Deforestation is a broad term which means removal or destruction of forest cover or vegetation in a forest area. It involves felling of trees, removal of forest litter, or grazing. Four main causes of deforestation are (i) shifting cultivation, (ii) development projects, (iii) fuel requirement, and (iv) raw materials for industries.

(i) **Shifting cultivation:** Shifting cultivation involves clearing a land (in the forest area), burning of vegetation, mixing ash with soil (this adds nutrients to the soil) for the purpose of using the land for cultivation for 2–3 years. This is the most common and globally employed agricultural system. Once the soil runs low in nutrients and minerals, the area is abandoned and the same practice is followed on a fresh piece of land. In this way, a substantial amount of forest cover gets removed. In the absence of any protective layer of tree cover in the abandoned area, there occurs soil erosion (due to rainfall), and the nutrients present are washed away in the river. When the area is used many times, there is permanent degradation in the soil quality.

(ii) **Development projects:** Development projects, such as hydroelectric projects, large dams, reservoirs, and laying down of railway lines require large-scale deforestation. The deforestation not only affects the biota and neighbouring ecosystems, but also erodes the soil.

**(iii) Fuel requirements:** There is an increasing demand for fuelwood due to the ever-increasing human population. This leads to the degradation of forest ecosystems.

**(iv) Raw materials for the industry:** In addition to its use as fuel, wood has numerous applications, such as making packing cases, furniture, paper, and plywood. Also, industries that manufacture drugs, scents and perfumes, gums, waxes, turpentine, latex, and rubber procure their raw materials from plants; this may ultimately lead to the destruction of plants.

## 2.6.2  Overgrazing

Overgrazing exerts pressure on vegetation and ultimately leads to deforestation, which is the cause of soil erosion and desertification.

## 2.6.3  Agriculture

An ecosystem also degrades due to the adoption of ineffective agriculture practices. Some of these bad practices are as follows:

- Deforestation (removal of trees) destroys the habitat of many kinds of organisms. This also leads to soil erosion, loss of nutrients, and desertification.

- Irrigation without proper drainage leads to excessive accumulation of water and salts because of which the soil quality degrades.

- Excessive and indiscriminate use of agrochemicals, such as fertilizers and pesticides, has harmful effects on the soil and underground water resources. All these chemicals ultimately degrade the quality of the ecosystem.

## 2.6.4  Mining

The process of extraction of mineral resources (mining) and its use in divergent ways leads to a wide range of environmental changes, which ultimately results in the degradation of ecosystems (Figure 2.21).

## 2.6.5  Urbanization

Due to population explosion, urbanization has sharply increased. As a result, forest areas have to be cleared and result in environmental degradation. Floods and fires cause considerable destruction of forests. Even termites, pests, and diseases affect forests adversely.

**Fig. 2.21**    Mining leads to degradation, loss of biodiversity, and pollution

# SUMMARY

- Ecology is the scientific study of the relationship of living organisms with each other and with their environments.
- All organisms are dependent on the environment from which they derive their sustenance.
- The environment is classified into biotic and abiotic components.
- The environment is not static. It undergoes constant change.
- The biotic and abiotic components keep on changing continuously.
- The environment can be natural or artificial.
- The important abiotic components of an ecosystem include energy, materials, climatic, and edaphic factors.
- Producers synthesize their own food.
- Consumers cannot make their own food, and can be macro- or micro-consumers.
- The natural organization along with living and non-living components is called an ecosystem.
- An ecosystems can be simple or complex.
- Every ecosystem influences and is influenced by its neighbouring ecosystem(s).
- Ecosystems possess self-regulating ability called homeostasis.
- Energy flows through ecosystems and enables organisms to perform various kinds of work. Ultimately, the energy is lost as heat energy.
- The nutrients never get exhausted and can be recycled indefinitely.
- Biogeochemical cycles can be sedimentary cycles or gaseous cycles
- The main reservoirs of carbon include atmosphere, oceans, and land.
- Excessive amount of carbon dioxide is responsible for global warming.

- The main source of oxygen in the atmosphere is photosynthesis.
- Imbalance in the oxygen cycle may occur due to deforestation.
- The sequence of organisms through which the energy flows is known as food chain.
- Food chains are of three types: (i) grazing food chain, (ii) detritus food chain, and (iii) parasitic food chain.
- An ecosystem may consist of several intermediate food chains which are interlocked with each other. This interlocking pattern is known as food web.
- A number of ecosystems exit. These include forest ecosystem, grassland ecosystem, desert ecosystem, and aquatic ecosystem.
- The forests of the world have been classified into three major categories: (i) coniferous forests, (ii) tropical forests, and (iii) temperate forests.
- The indiscriminate felling of trees due to various anthropogenic activities, such as urbanization, industrialization, and mining, is called deforestation.
- The freshwater ecosystems are of two types: lentic and lotic.
- Lentic ecosystems include all those systems that have a static body of water, such as lakes, impoundments, and wetlands.
- Lakes are natural but impoundments are artificially created waterbodies.
- Wetlands are permanently or periodically water-covered bodies. Wetlands are of two types—inland wastelands and coastal wastelands.
- Lotic ecosystems include all those systems in which the water flows. Examples include rivers, streams, and brooks.
- In aquatic systems, oxygen dissolves in water to the extent of 10%.
- Ecosystems get degraded because of deforestation, overgrazing, mining, and urbanization.

# EXERCISE

## [A] Multiple-choice questions

1. The subdivisions of ecology are
   - (a) Autecology
   - (b) Synecology
   - (c) Habitat ecology
   - (d) All of the above
2. The abiotic components of the environment are
   - (a) Energy, water
   - (b) Soil, atmospheric gases
   - (c) Plants, animals
   - (d) Human
3. In an ecosystem, the source of energy is
   - (a) Sun
   - (b) Wind

(c) Water

(d) None of the above

4. Producers include

   (a) Plants

   (b) Certain bacteria

   (c) Algae

   (d) All of the above

5. Which statement is true about an ecosystem?

   (a) Ecosystems may be small and simple.

   (b) Ecosystems may be complex and large.

   (c) An ecosystem may occur within an ecosystem.

   (d) All of the above

6. In a living organism, the most likely combination of elements is

   (a) C, H, O, N, P

   (b) C, H, O, N, S

   (c) H, O, N, S, P

   (d) C, O, N, P, S

7. The most important function of an ecosystem is

   (a) Regulation of water

   (b) Regulation of climate

   (c) Regulation of gas

   (d) Production of food

8. In a human body, the most abundant element is

   (a) Hydrogen

   (b) Oxygen

   (c) Nitrogen

   (d) Carbon

9. For carrying photosynthesis, plants need

   (a) $CO_2$

   (b) $H_2O$

   (c) Sunlight

   (d) All of the above

10. The fixation of nitrogen from the atmosphere is done by the bacterium

    (a) Rhizobium

    (b) *E.coli*

    (c) Nitrosomonas

    (d) Nitrobacter

11. An ecosystem comprises

    (a) Producers

    (b) Consumers

    (c) Decomposers

    (d) Abiotic factors

    (e) All of the above

12. The most stable ecosystem is a/an

    (a) Desert

    (b) Forest

    (c) Ocean

    (d) Mountain

13. Which of the following are examples of an ecosystem?

    (a) Forest

    (b) Ocean

    (c) Desert

    (d) Mountain

    (e) All of the above

14. In the lithosphere, the chief elements present are
    (a) Al, O
    (b) Si, N
    (c) Al, Si
    (d) Fe, Al

15. The main reservoirs of carbon are
    (a) Atmosphere
    (b) Oceans
    (c) Land
    (d) All of the above

16. Pine, hemlock, cedar, and fir are found in
    (a) Tundra
    (b) Moist deciduous forest
    (c) Boreal forest
    (d) Tropical evergreen forest

17. Teak, oak, and maple trees are found in
    (a) Tropical rainforests
    (b) Moist deciduous forests
    (c) Savannah
    (d) Temperate deciduous forests

18. In India, tropical forests are found in
    (a) Kerala and Assam
    (b) Jammu and Kashmir
    (c) Rajasthan
    (d) All of the above

19. The food chain in which microorganisms break down matter is called
    (a) Consumer food chain
    (b) Parasitic food chain
    (c) Detritus food chain
    (d) All of the above

20. The major grasslands in India are
    (a) *Sehima-Dichanthium*
    (b) *Dichanthium–Cenchrus-Lasiurus*
    (c) *Phragmites–Saccharum-Imperate*
    (d) *Themeda–Arundinella*
    (e) All of the above

### ANSWERS

| | | | | |
|---|---|---|---|---|
| 1. (d) | 2. (a) (b) | 3. (a) | 4. (d) | 5. (d) |
| 6. (a) | 7. (d) | 8. (b) | 9. (d) | 10. (a) |
| 11. (e) | 12. (c) | 13. (e) | 14. (c) | 15. (d) |
| 16. (c) | 17. (d) | 18. (a) | 19. (c) | 20. (e) |

## [B] Fill in the blanks.

1. All organisms derive their ______ from the environment.

2. Organisms can tolerate changes in the environment within a certain range called ______.

3. The word 'ecosystem' was coined by ______.

4. The most important abiotic component of an ecosystem is ______.

5. Organisms which can synthesis their own food are called the ______.

6. Consumers that feed mainly on plants are called ____.

7. Microorganisms which decompose dead plants and animal remains are called ______.

8. Ecosystems that are separated from adjacent ecosystems by a transition zone or a diffused boundary zone are called ______.

9. All ecosystems communicate with each other through import and export of ______ and ______.

10. The self-regulating ability of an ecosystem is called ______.

11. The energy required for various biogeochemical cycles is obtained from ______.

12. For sedimentary cycles, the main reservoir is ______.

13. The main consumers of carbon dioxide in the atmosphere are ______.

14. Excessive amount of carbon dioxide in the atmosphere is responsible for ______.

15. The main source of oxygen in the atmosphere is ______.

16. Agricultural run-offs contain fertilizers which can lead to the ______ of waterbodies, particularly lake and pond.

17. In an ecosystem, the flow energy is ______.

18. A number of food chains are interlocked. This interlocking pattern is known as ______.

19. The food chain starting from dead or decomposed organic matter is called ______.

20. The indiscriminate felling of trees is known as ______.

21. Lakes which are created artificially are called ______.

22. During photosynthesis ______ gas is produced.

23. Each stage in a food chain is called ______.

24. Carbon dioxide constitutes ______ % of the air.

### ANSWERS

| | |
|---|---|
| 1. Sustenance | 2. Range of tolerance |
| 3. Arthur Tansley | 4. Energy |
| 5. Producers | 6. Primary producers |
| 7. Decomposers | 8. Ecotone |
| 9. Energy nutrients | 10. Homeostasis |
| 11. Sun | 12. Light |

| | |
|---|---|
| 13. Plants | 14. Global warming |
| 15. Photosynthesis | 16. Eutrophication |
| 17. Unidirectional | 18. Food web |
| 19. Detritus food chain | 20. Deforestation |
| 21. Impoundments | 22. Oxygen |
| 23. Tropical level | 24. 0.03 |

## [C] Short-answer questions

1. Explain the term 'ecology'.
2. What are the components of the environment?
3. What are the different types of the environment? Give examples.
4. Explain the term 'ecosystems'.
5. What are the abiotic components of the ecosystem?
6. Explain the term 'producers'. Give example.
7. What are consumers?
8. What are decomposers?
9. How many types of ecosystems are there? Give examples.
10. What is homeostasis?
11. Explain ecological succession.
12. What do you understand by geochemical cycling?
13. Give an example of a sedimentary cycle.
14. What are the main sources of oxygen in the atmosphere?
15. Explain hydrological cycle.
16. Explain food chain, food web, and ecological pyramid.
17. What are the functions of a forest ecosystem?
18. What is the difference between deforestation and desertification?
19. What are the different types of freshwater ecosystems?
20. What are impoundments, wetlands, and estuaries?
21. How photosynthesis takes place in aquatic ecosystems?
22. What is a biome?

# Biomes

## 3.1 INTRODUCTION

A biome is defined as a large geographical biotic community, chiefly controlled by climate. It has an assemblage of plants and animals whose survival depends on their adaptability to the prevailing conditions of the biome. The earth can be divided into various biologically distinct zones; these zones are nothing but biomes. As already stated, each biome has its own distinct and unique assemblage of plants and animals. However, regional variations occur within each biome.

Biomes are classified on the basis of the dominant vegetation type found in them, for example, deciduous forests or grasslands. The biomes such as ecosystems have fuzzy edges. Aquatic areas such as tidal zones and oceans are also characterized by temperature and light. These are not called biomes, but they function in a similar way.

## 3.2 MAJOR BIOMES ON EARTH

The major biomes on earth include tundras, taigas, temperate deciduous forests, grasslands, deserts, and tropical rainforests. The salient features of these biomes are discussed next.

### 3.2.1 Tundra

The tundra covers about 10% of the earth's total land mass and stretches across the northernmost portions of North America, Europe, and Asia. It lies between a region of perpetual ice and snow to the north and coniferous forests to the south. The tundra is not known by the trees but by the grasses, shrubs, and mat-like vegetation such as mosses and lichens which have successfully adapted to the harsh climate of tundra.

Rain in the tundra occurs mostly during summers, to the extent of about 25 cm per year. During winters, the temperature remains below zero. Due to harsh winters, deep-rooted plants do not grow in tundra. However, during summers, insects (such as mosquitoes and black flies) and birds appear. The birds feed mostly on the swarms of insects. In spite of harsh conditions, a variety of animals such as ptarmigans, musk oxen, and Arctic hares are found in tundra.

## 3.2.2   Taiga

The taiga extends across Canada, parts of Europe, and Asia. The trees in the taiga are mostly coniferous trees (pines, firs, and spruces). The climate of the taiga is mild and its life forms are more diverse as compared to the tundra's. The taiga has a large population of wild animals. However, the forests in this region are not able to meet the rising demands for wood and wood products.

## 3.2.3   Temperate Deciduous Forest Biome

It is located in the eastern USA, Europe, and the northeast of China. About half USA's population lives in this biome which supports a variety of plants and animals. This biome receives abundant rainfall (75–150 cm per year) and has a long growing season (about 6 months).

The vegetation of the temperate deciduous forest biome is dominated by maple, oak, black cherry, and beech trees. The fertile soil in this region supports a varied population of insects, microorganisms, birds, reptiles, amphibians, and mammals. The mammals commonly found in this region include raccoons, white-tailed deer, red fox, and black bears.

## 3.2.4   Grassland Biome

Grasslands are normally found in North America, South America, Africa, Europe, Asia, and Australia. A small stretch of grasslands is also present in the Great Basin. The grasslands are mostly formed to exist in temperate and tropical regions which receive intermediate levels of precipitation, that is, less than in forest regions but more than in deserts (Table 3.1).

The soil in grasslands is the richest in the world. This is attributed to thousands of years of plant growth and decay. The grasslands, in general, are devoid of trees due to the lack of annual precipitation. The richness of the soil in grasslands has been exploited by humans mainly for agriculture.

**Table 3.1**   Precipitation in some biomes

| Biome | Annual precipitation (cm) |
|---|---|
| Tundra | <25 |
| Taiga | 300–100 |
| Temperate deciduous | 75–150 |
| Grassland | 25–75 |
| Desert | <25 |
| Tropical rainforest | 150–400 |

## 3.2.5  Desert Biome

Deserts are known to be present in various parts of the globe. Some deserts cover vast regions. For example, the Sahara stretches across North Africa and is about the size of the USA. The desert biome covers more than one-third of the earth's total land area. It is worth mentioning that dry deserts are not devoid of rains. Generally, rain in these areas comes in violent downpours which often result in flash floods and soil erosion.

The plants in deserts are adapted to low-soil moisture. The cactus is the prime vegetation species of deserts. Desert biomes are home to a number of insects and other animals including desert snakes, lizards, and mice. Each year, deserts the size of millions of acres are formed on semi-arid grasslands.

## 3.2.6  Tropical Rainforest Biome

Tropical rainforests exist near the equator in South and Central America, Africa, and Asia. These are the richest and most diverse biomes on earth due to the abundance of rainfall and warm climate. Tropical rainforests support a large number of plants, animals, and microorganisms.

Many rainforests cannot be used for farming due to the presence of large amounts of iron in the soil. According to a UN study, it is found that tropical deforestation is occurring at the rate of 17 million hectares per year. At this rate, the remaining tropical forests will vanish in about 100 years. This may affect the global rainfall pattern, which in turn will affect global climate as a substantial amount of $CO_2$ will get removed from the atmosphere each year.

## 3.3  AQUATIC ECOSYSTEMS

As already discussed, aquatic ecosystems are not biomes, though they function as biomes. Ecosystems where water is the main habitat are known as aquatic ecosystems. Depending on the salt content, the aquatic ecosystems are of three types: (i) freshwater ecosystem (salt <0.5%; examples include lakes, ponds, swamps, pools, springs, streams, and rivers), (ii) marine ecosystem (salt >3.5%; examples include seas and ocean), and (iii) brackish water ecosystem (salt content 0.5%–4.5%; examples include estuaries, salt marshes mangroves, and swamps).

An aquatic ecosystem comprises different organisms which are unevenly distributed. These organisms vary in size, light penetration, temperature, and the amount of dissolved oxygen (DO); these are all responsible for a particular type of environment and biota and, thus, a specific type of ecosystem.

Freshwater ecosystems are of two types: (i) lentic (originating from the Latin word *lentic,* meaning calm) or standing ecosystem (examples include lakes, pools, ponds, swamps, marshes) and (ii) lotic (originating from the Latin word *lotus,* meaning washed) or running ecosystem. (Examples include rivers, streams, and springs.)

The lentic freshwater ecosystem refers to all the static bodies of water such as lakes, impoundments, and wetlands. Lakes are described as inland depressions that contain standing water. They vary in depth and area. The world's largest lake is Lake Superior in North America, with a surface area and depth of about 83,000 $km^2$ and 5000 ft, respectively. The deepest lake in the world is Lake Baikal in Siberia, which is about 100 ft deep and has a surface area of 31,722 $km^2$. Most lakes have formed due to geological changes that took place in the past 20,000 years (approximately). However, some lakes are believed to have originated about 20 million years ago, for example, Lake Baikal and Lake Tanganyika in Africa.

In lakes, the plant materials constitute algae which derive energy from the sun. The energy is transferred to microscopic animals that feed on algae. Algae, along with aquatic weeds, are food for fish (that are herbivores). These fish in turn are consumed (or preyed upon) by larger carnivorous fish.

In a lake ecosystem, the energy transfers from sunlight (which penetrates the water) to plants, then to herbivorous animals, and finally to carnivores. All waste products of animals settle down at the bottom of the lake (lakebed), which acts as a nutrient supplier for the aquatic plants and supports their growth. Aquatic plants also use carbon dioxide for their growth (photosynthesis) and in turn release oxygen, which is used by aquatic animals for survival.

Artificially created lakes (small or large) are called impoundments or reservoirs. They are made to meet specific requirements such as generation of hydroelectric power, fisheries, irrigation, industries, recreation, water supply, and flood control.

Wetlands are land areas covered with water, periodically or permanently. They can be submerged or saturated lands and can be artificial or natural. The water contained in wetlands can be brackish or saline. Wetlands can be up to 6 m deep and can be of two types: (i) inland wetlands (which occur inland and contain freshwater such as bogs and swamps) and (ii) coastal wetlands (which occur near the coast and contain saline or brackish water such as mangrove swamps).

The lotic ecosystems refer to those aquatic systems in which water flows. Examples include rivers, streams, and brooks. In a river ecosystem, there is a continuous flow of water and the strength of the flow changes continuously, resulting in variations in its velocity. The physical, chemical, and biological conditions of a river change gradually as it covers its course along the main channel in a definite direction. Rivers are described as open or heterotrophic systems. Unlike lakes, plants and animals in rivers can only avail nutrients on a temporary basis. As water in a river ecosystem flows continuously, the living forms adapt to different rates of flow. The flora and fauna of a river ecosystem depend on its transparency, flow, DO content, and the nature of its beds.

The marine ecosystem comprising seas and oceans covers about 75% of the earth's surface and has an average depth of about 3750 m. In fact, a marine ecosystem is the largest reservoir of water, living things, and some of the essential nutrients needed by both marine and land organisms. Marine ecosystems are of great ecological significance. The producers in these ecosystems vary from microscopic algae to large seaweeds. In a marine ecosystem, there exist millions of zooplankton and different varieties of invertebrates, which serve as food for fish, turtles, and marine mammals. Some of the important features of marine ecosystems are:

(i) **Salinity:** Seawater is saline with 3.5% concentration of salt. Marine water is composed of many salts, with sodium chloride as its chief constituent (27%). Other salts present in seawater include salts (chloride, bicarbonate, carbonate, and bromide) of calcium, potassium, and magnesium.

(ii) **Light:** The extent of light penetration in marine water largely influences the process of photosynthesis.

(iii) **Nutrients:** Although water-dissolved nutrients are present only to a small extent, they are a limiting factor in the determination of the size of marine population.

(iv) **Temperature:** The temperature of oceans remains fairly constant—ranging from about 2°C in the polar seas to about 32°C in the tropics.

(v) **Dissolved gases:** The marine environment contains considerable amounts of DO and $CO_2$. Both these gases are helpful in regulating the composition of air and the temperature of the atmosphere. $CO_2$ is a greenhouse gas (GHG).

(vi) **Alkalinity:** Seawater is alkaline and has a pH of about 8.2.

(vii) **Pressure:** The pressure changes from 1 atm (at the surface) to about 1000 atm (at the greatest depth). This change in pressure has a profound effect on the distribution of aquatic life.

(viii) **Currents:** A marine ecosystem exhibits a continuous state of circulation due to currents. The currents are caused either by wind (surface currents) or by variation in temperature and salinity (deeper currents).

(ix) **Waves and tides:** There are several types of waves and tides which are produced by the pull of the moon and the sun.

Important factors responsible for the productivity of aquatic habitats are sunlight, transparency, temperature, and DO. Aquatic ecosystems are sources of freshwater, which is essential for sustaining life. Also, all agricultural activities are dependent on water (besides other nutrients). The livelihood of a large number of people (fishing communities) depends on oceans.

The aquatic ecosystem is severely degraded due to anthropogenic activities, which include the discharge of municipal wastes and by-products from industrial units.

The transitional zones between rivers and seas are known as estuaries. A number of rivers are known to develop highly specialized zones (estuaries) before joining the sea. Estuaries possess unique ecological features and biotic communities. In fact, they are the most productive aquatic ecosystems of the world.

## 3.4   THREAT TO AQUATIC ECOSYSTEMS

The prime threat to aquatic ecosystems is due to water pollution which results mainly from sewage, dumping of garbage, and mismanagement of solid and liquid wastes. The sewage disposal in aquatic ecosystems results in eutrophication. Eutrophication is caused by the discharge of large amounts of nutrients, especially phosphates and nitrates, in waterbodies, particularly ponds and lakes. Due to this, the oxygen content in waterbodies is considerably reduced which is responsible for destroying aquatic life. Fish and crustaceans cannot breathe and get killed. The flora and fauna of aquatic ecosystems are also destroyed due to the foul odour produced by eutrophication. Also, excessive use of chemical fertilizers also increases nutrients' concentration and causes eutrophication. In India, Dal Lake, Wular Lake, and Manasbal Lake of Kashmir, wetlands of Assam, and Loktak Lake of Manipur are facing the problem of eutrophication.

# SUMMARY

- A biome is a large geographical biotic community which is controlled by climate.
- Each biome has a distinct climate and a unique assemblage of plants and animals.
- Biomes are named after the dominant type of vegetation that grows in them.
- The major biomes on earth include tundras, taigas, temperate deciduous forest biomes, grassland biomes, desert biomes, and tropical rainforest biomes.
- The tundra covers about 10% of the earth's land mass and is character-ized by grasses, shrubs, and mat-like vegetations such as mosses and lichens, which are adapted to harsh climate. The rainfall in tundra is about 25 cm per year and occurs during summers. As the summer is the growing season for the tundra, insects; birds; and a variety of animals such as ptarmigan, rusk oxen, and arctic hares can be found during this time.

- The taiga extends across Canada, parts of Europe, and Asia. It is characterized by coniferous trees such as pines and firs. It receives mild climate and supports a large population of wild animals.

- The temperate deciduous forest biome supports a variety of plants and animals and is inhabited by about 50% of the population. It has abundant rainfall (75–150 cm per year) and its growing season is of about 6 months.

- Grassland biomes are found in North America, South America, Africa, Europe, Asia, and Australia. Grasslands also exist in temperate and tropical regions which receive intermediate levels of precipitation (25–75 cm per year).

- Desert biomes are present in various parts of the globe and cover more than one-third of the world's total land area. Although these are dry regions, they receive some rainfall. The plants in the desert are, in general, adapted to low soil moisture contents. The cactus is the prime vegetation species of deserts. A number of insects and other animals such as snakes and lizards inhabit the desert biome.

- Tropical rainforest biomes exist near the equator in South and Central America, Africa, and Asia. These are the richest and most diverse biomes on earth and support a large number of plants, animals, and microorganisms.

- Aquatic ecosystems also function as biomes. These are of three types: (i) freshwater ecosystem (salt <0.5%; examples include lakes, ponds, swamps, pools, springs, and rivers), (ii) marine ecosystem (salt >3.5%; examples include seas and oceans), and (iii) brackish water ecosystem (such as salt contents, mangroves, and swamps).

- Aquatic ecosystems have different organisms which are unevenly distributed.

- Freshwater ecosystems are of two types: (i) lentic or standing ecosystem (having a static body of water, for example, lakes, impoundments) and (ii) lotic ecosystem (a running ecosystem, for example, rivers and streams).

- Marine ecosystems comprising seas and oceans cover about 75% of the earth's surface and are of great ecological significance.

- The main threat to aquatic ecosystems is due to water pollution which results mainly from sewage, dumping of garbage, and mismanagement of solid and liquid wastes.

- Sewage disposal in aquatic ecosystems results in eutrophication.

# EXERCISE

## [A] Multiple-choice questions

1. Which of the following statements is/are correct about biomes?

   (a) A biome is a large biotic community.

   (b) Each biome has a distinct climate and a unique assemblage of plants and animals.

   (c) The earth's surface is divided into biologically disinct zones called biomes.

   (d) All are correct

2. Out of all biomes, the most important biome is

   (a) Tundra                          (b) Taiga

   (c) Grassland biome                 (d) Desert biome

   (e) Tropical rainforest biome

3. Which of the following biomes receives the maximum annual precipitation?

   (a) Tundra                          (b) Taiga

   (c) Grassland                       (d) Tropical rainforest

   (e) Desert

4. In desert biomes, the plant that is found in abundance is

   (a) Cactus                          (b) Grass

   (c) Maple                           (d) None of the above

5. The richest soil is present in

   (a) Tundra                          (b) Taiga

   (c) Grassland                       (d) Desert

   (e) Tropical rainforest

6. Deforestation

   (a) affects the global rainfall pattern

   (b) reduces $CO_2$ concentration in the atmosphere

   (c) is destructive for various species

   (d) All are correct

7. A marine ecosystem has a salt content of

   (a) <0.5%                           (b) More than 3.5%

   (c) 0.5%–4.5%                       (d) None of the above

8. A lentic ecosystem includes

   (a) Lakes                           (b) Impoundments

   (c) Wetlands                        (d) Streams

   (e) All except streams

**ANSWERS**

| 1. (d) | 2. (e) | 3. (d) | 4. (a) | 5. (c) |
|---|---|---|---|---|
| 6. (a) | 7. (b) | 8. (e) | | |

## [B]  Fill in the blanks.

1. Each biome has a distinct ——.
2. The tundra covers about —— of the earth's land mass.
3. In the tundra —— do not grow.
4. The rainfall in the tundra is about —— per year.
5. In the taiga, the trees are mostly ——.
6. In the USA, about 50% of the population lives in the —— biome.
7. The common mammals in temperate deciduous forest biomes are white ——.
8. In the grassland biome, the per-year rainfall rate is —— cm.
9. The soil in —— is the richest in the world.
10. The desert biome covers more than —— % of the world's land area.
11. Aquatic ecosystems function as ——.
12. The largest lake in the world is ——.
13. Aquatic ecosystems are under threat mainly due to —— .

**ANSWERS**

| 1. Climate | 2. 10% |
|---|---|
| 3. Trees | 4. 25 cm |
| 5. Coniferous | 6. Temperate deciduous forest biomes |
| 7. deer | 8. 25–75 |
| 9. Grassland | 10. 33 |
| 11. Biomes | 12. Lake Superior |
| 13. Water pollution | |

## [C]  Short-answer questions

1. Define a biome. How biomes are named?
2. What types of vegetation grow in tundras and taigas?
3. Write a note on the temperate deciduous forest biome.
4. Compare the precipitation of tundra, taiga, grassland, desert, and tropical rainforest biomes.
5. What types of plants are found in desert biomes?
6. Write a note on aquatic ecosystems.

# Biodiversity

## 4.1 INTRODUCTION

The term 'biodiversity' attempts to describe 'biological diversity'. In fact, biodiversity refers to that part of nature which includes all forms of life such as plants, animals, and microorganisms. These life forms vary in shape, size, and colour. For example, plants range from very tiny plants to large trees and animals from tiny insects to elephants. Similarly, microorganisms include different types of bacteria. Different living forms exist in oceans, deserts, cold snowy regions, and high mountains. All life forms together constitute the earth's biological wealth and are useful for the benefit and further development of humanity. In fact, biodiversity is a precious resource; it must be preserved, that is, various species should be protected against extinction not only for the present but also for the future generations.

Biodiversity can also be measured by the number of species found in an area. The more the number of species per square metre, the higher is the biodiversity. Biodiversity is classified into three types: (i) genetic diversity, (ii) species diversity, and (iii) ecosystem diversity.

(i) **Genetic diversity:** It arises because of the combination of a large number of different genes and is responsible for every specific characteristic (genetic make-up) of a species. This is well understood because each individual is unique from the other. Genetic diversity is essential for the health of a species. Biotechnology is helpful in developing better-yielding crops (which has resulted in the Green Revolution) and also more effective medicines.

(ii) **Species diversity:** It refers to the number of plant and animal inhabiting a region. This type of diversity occurs in various ecosystems. Some habitats are richer in particular species as compared to other habitats. For example, a natural ecosystem yields a large number of non-wood forest products (NWFPs), whereas a timber plantation does not provide a large variety of NWFPs. It is believed that about 1.8 million species of plants exist on earth. However, only a fraction of this has been identified so far.

Many new species of flowering plants and insects are being identified. Areas rich in different species are known as the hotspots of diversity.

**(iii) Ecosystem diversity:** It arises because of the difference in species and their habitats across different ecosystems. The diversity of ecosystems depends on the diversity of environmental conditions and also, to a large extent, on human interferences. As an illustration, clearing a mixed forest and planting a single variety of pines (for a paper mill) results in lower plant and animal diversity in the new pine forest than in the mixed natural forest.

## 4.2 VALUE OF BIODIVERSITY

Biodiversity is of enormous value to human beings. This is attributed to the various species and the number of ecosystems. For example, when green plants utilize carbon dioxide for carrying out photosynthesis, they help reduce the carbon dioxide concentration of the atmosphere and in turn produce oxygen, an essential element for the survival of living beings. Carbon dioxide and other gases released from various industrial processes contribute to the 'greenhouse effect', leading to global warming, which further results in the melting of ice caps. Owing to the melting of ice caps, the sea level rises and consequently causes floods. Major atmospheric changes are also attributed to global warming.

The ecological processes are preserved by biological diversity, of which recycling of nutrients and biochemical cycles are two very important aspects. The survival of human beings depends on the preservation of biological resources. Biodiversity offers us a number of benefits. Some of the values of biodiversity include consumptive use; productive use; and social, ethical, aesthetic, and option values. These are briefly discussed here:

- It is a well-known fact that forests offer a number of products such as timber, food, fuelwood, and fodder, mainly utilized by the local communities. People living in and around forests rely heavily on them for fulfilling their daily needs including food, building material, medicines, and so on. This is attributed to the biodiversity contained in ecosystems. An aquatic ecosystem offers an abundant amount of food in the form of fish and shellfish. In fact, the biodiversity of a region influences each and every aspect of the people inhabiting it.

- Genetic engineering has made possible the development of better varieties of plants and animals. It mainly involves selecting genes from one plant and introducing them into another.

Many drugs are extracted from medicinal plants. Some of the drugs obtained from medicinal plants are given in Table 4.1.

**Table 4.1**  Drugs obtained from medicinal plants

| Drug | Medicinal plant | Use |
| --- | --- | --- |
| Atropine | Balladonia | Anticholinergic |
| Bromelain | Pineapple | Controls inflammation in tissue due to infection |
| Camphor | Camphor tree | Analgesic |
| Cademi | Opium poppy | Analgesic |
| Morphine | Opium poppy | Analgesic |
| L-DOPA | Velvet bean | Controls Parkinson's disease |
| Quinine | Yellow cinchona | Antimalarial |
| Reserpine | Indian snakeroot | Reduces blood pressure |

- In early times, the traditional societies, being small, could preserve biodiversity as they needed less resources. However, modern humans desire more than what they really need. This has resulted in the large-scale depletion of natural resources. Moreover, a number of species (both plants and animals) have gone extinct because of the extensive human interference with nature.

  In traditional agriculture, a wide range of products were grown and marketed throughout the year. In case, one crop failed, the other helped overcome the loss. This acted as an insurance against the failure of one crop (the present-day monoculture). The failure of one crop—as seen in recent times—often results in food shortages with the increased possibility of drought.

- The approach that 'only human beings have the right to exist' is a misconception. All forms of life, such as plants, animals, and small creatures, also have the right to exist. In fact, all these life forms are essential for the survival of human beings. Several cultural, moral, and ethical values are associated with the different forms of life.

- The importance of biodiversity is not limited to its inherent value, beauty, and contribution to our knowledge pool. It has an undeniable importance in aesthetics and creativity. Though wild animals are killed by humans for many heinous reasons, they also serve as a tourist attraction. It is fascinating to watch wildlife and the way numerous forms of life survive. In India, the holy basil plant (*tulsi)* has been grown in households since centuries and is, thus, a part of our cultural history.

- It is keeping the future possibilities for their use. It is not possible to determine which of our species or traditional crops and domestic animals will be of maximum use in the future. The preservation of biodiversity must also include all our species (past and present) of crops and animals.

## 4.3   USES OF BIODIVERSITY

The survival of human beings depends on biodiversity, which provides a variety of services through its various species and ecosystems. For example, oxygen is produced through photosynthesis by green plants and carbon dioxide is greatly reduced by plants and oceans. Deforestation leads to the shortage of oxygen and abundance of carbon dioxide. The latter factor, along with the release of carbon dioxide through industrial processes, is responsible for the 'greenhouse effect', which in turn is responsible for global warming and, consequently, global climatic changes.

Biodiversity or biological variety, directly or indirectly, helps us meet our requirements of food, clothing, housing, energy, and medicines. Animal species—from both land and aquatic ecosystems—help us meet our need of animal-derived foods. The timber produced by forests is useful for construction purposes. Animal wastes are useful for obtaining biogas, which is used for heating and also for making crop fertilizers. A number of drugs are obtained from medicinal plants such as atropine (belladonna plant), caffeine (tea/coffee), cocaine (cocoa), codeine, and morphine (opium poppy), L-DOPA (velvet bean), penicillium (*Penicillium* fungi), quinine (cinchona bark), and reserpine (Indian snakeroot). Plants, fungi, and bacteria remove toxic substances from air, water, and soil and thus help in pollution control.

In view of its diverse uses, it is necessary to preserve biodiversity and prevent its loss. This aspect is dealt with in a subsequent section.

Biodiversity has social, ethical, moral, and aesthetic values. Traditional societies were aware that biodiversity is a life-supporting resource. In fact, traditional societies preserved biodiversity in contrast to affluent modern-day societies which have utilized biodiversity resources indiscriminately, leading to their large-scale depletion. Biodiversity must also be preserved, considering the ethical and moral values associated with it.

## 4.4   THREATS TO BIODIVERSITY

The enormous growth of human population and industrialization are among the major threats to biodiversity. In fact, humans are responsible for massive destruction of forests and hunting of wild animals, and this has severely affected biodiversity. Deforestation is mainly caused by anthropogenic activities such as shifting cultivation, development projects, cutting of trees for fuel requirements (fuelwood), overgrazing, agriculture, mining, and urbanization. Industries that manufacture drugs, scents and perfumes, resins, gums, waxes, turpentine, latex and rubber, tannins, alkaloids, bees wax, and so on procure their raw materials from plants, which ultimately leads to the destruction of plants. The use of forest land for housing, industries, and construction of roads and dams causes considerable deforestation.

Deforestation, combined with human hunting activities, threatens the survival of wildlife species, for example, pitcher plants, several orchids and rhododendrons species, rhinoceroses, and the Indian pangolins are counted among the endangered species of the wild. The great Indian bustard—due to habitat destruction and hunting—has been placed in the category of critically endangered species. Similar is the case with the Bengal tiger whose survival has become a question mark because of increased deforestation for timber procurement and the development of farmlands. Presently, some of the wildlife species are endangered while some have become extinct. Some species that became extinct due to human activities include the Carolina parakeets, Heath hens, Labrador ducks, passenger pigeons, dodos, and the great auks. Conservation experts have warned that if deforestation, desertification, and destruction of wetlands and coral reefs will continue at the present rate, as many as 500,000 to 1 million species are likely to become extinct. According to the International Union for the Conservation of Nature (IUCN), an estimated 50,000 plant species will become extinct or endangered by 2050.

## 4.5 ENDEMIC SPECIES IN INDIA

A large variety of species are endemic to India. It means they are native to India and are not found in any other part of the globe. About 3.3% of the recorded flora of India is endemic to the country (see Tables 4.2 and 4.3). They mainly occur in the North-East, Western Ghats, north-west Himalayas, and the Andaman and Nicobar Islands.

There are about 42,219 total plant species, out of which 5150 are endemic. These species are distributed over 141 genera under 47 families. These endemic species amount to about 30% of the world's recorded flora. According to the Botanical Survey of India and the Zoological Survey of India, there are 47,000 plant species and 81,000 animal species. Tables 4.3 and 4.4 give the details of plant and animal species recorded in India and the world.

**Table 4.2** Endemic plant and animal species of India

| Group | No. of species |
|---|---|
| Pteridophyta | 200 |
| Angiosperms | 4,950 |
| Mollusca (land) | 878 |
| Mollusca (freshwater) | 89 |
| Insects | 16,214 |
| Amphibians | 110 |
| Reptiles | 214 |
| Aves | 69 |
| Mammalians | 38 |

**Table 4.3**   Endemic plant species in India

|  | Species | | |
|---|---|---|---|
|  | India | World | Percentage in India |
| Bacteria | 850 | 4,000 | 21.25 |
| Viruses | Not known | 4,000 | 21 |
| Algae | 6,500 | 40,000 | 16.25 |
| Fungi | 14,500 | 72,000 | 20.14 |
| Lichens | 2,000 | 17,000 | 11.80 |
| Bryophyta | 2,850 | 16,000 | 17.80 |
| Pteridophyta | 1,100 | 13,000 | 8.46 |
| Gymnosperms | 64 | 750 | 8.53 |
| Angiosperms | 17,500 | 25,000 | 7 |

The crop diversity of India is quite rich. It includes 167 cultivated species and 320 wild relatives of crop plants. India ranks seventh in terms of contribution to world agriculture. It is also considered as the centre of origin of 30,000–50,000 varieties of rice, pigeon pea, mango, ginger, turmeric, sugar cane.

## 4.6   WETLANDS, MANGROVES, AND CORAL REEFS

India has a wealth of wetland ecosystems which are directly or indirectly connected to the river systems. Wetlands are the lands transitional between terrestrial and aquatic systems. In wetlands, the water table is usually near the surface and the land is covered with shallow water. Wetlands are effective in flood control, wastewater treatment, reducing sediments, and recharging of aquifers. In

**Table 4.4**   Animal species endemic to India and the world

|  | In India | In the world | Percentage in India |
|---|---|---|---|
| Protista | 2,577 | 31,259 | 8.24 |
| Mollusca | 5,070 | 66,525 | 7.62 |
| Arthropoda | 68,389 | 987,949 | 6.90 |
| Other invertebrates | 8,329 | 87,121 | 9.56 |
| Protochordata | 119 | 2,106 | 5.65 |
| Pisces | 2,546 | 21,723 | 11.72 |
| Amphibia | 209 | 5,150 | 4.06 |
| Reptilia | 456 | 5,817 | 7.84 |
| Aves | 1,232 | 9,026 | 13.66 |
| Mammalia | 390 | 4,629 | 8.42 |

winters, a variety of birds take shelter in wetlands and breed there. They are also a suitable habitat for flora and fauna. They act as a buffer against the effects of hurricanes and cyclones. They also stabilize shoreline and check soil erosion by sea. In addition, they are a source of durable timber, fuelwood, fruits, vegetables, traditional medicines, and protein-rich fodder for cattle. Thus, wetlands are of great economic, aesthetic, and scientific values. In India, there are 27 wetlands which are present in 15 states. There are 19 sites which have been designated as Ramsar sites and 6 more have been proposed for the designation.

Mangroves are salt-tolerant forest ecosystems and can survive in high salinity, tidal extremes and storms, and help control soil erosion. They provide medicines and fuelwood. They are a habitat for a variety of flora (such as *heritiera fomes*) and fauna (such as saltwater crocodiles and royal Bengal tigers).

India has nearly 7% of the world's total mangrove area. The Sundarbans in West Bengal is the world's largest mangrove forest. It has also been included in the World List of Biosphere Reserves by the United Nations Educational, Scientific, and Cultural Organization (UNESCO).

Mangrove forests are shrinking continuously as they have been subjected to unsustainable exploitation. The mangrove area is shrinking due to various activities such as surface run-off, siltation, encroachment, and discharge of wastewater and industrial effluents. In India, the National Committee on Mangroves and Coral Reefs (NCMCR) is dedicated to the protection and preservation of the mangrove forests. Presently, the mangrove conservation is being actively carried out in five cyclone-prone coastal states of India—West Bengal, Odisha, Andhra Pradesh, Tamil Nadu, and Gujarat. At present, there are 35 mangrove areas which have been identified by the Ministry of Environment and Forests (MOEF) for intensive conservation and management. These mangroves contain 69 species under 42 genera and 28 families. Out of these, two species are endemic to India.

Coral reef areas in India are mainly spread in the Gulf of Mannar, the Gulf of Kutch, the Lakshadweep Islands, and the Andaman and Nicobar Islands. These areas are under conservation and management since 1987. In addition, there is a National Coral Reef Research Centre in Port Blair.

A large number of species are under the threat of extinction. According to the International Union for the Conservation of Nature (IUCN), a worldwide organization and headquartered in Switzerland, globally the number of species under various categories such as endangered, vulnerable, and rare is increasing gradually.

According to the 2000 IUCN Red List, the number of critically endangered primates has increased to 19 from 13 in 1996. Similarly, there is an increase in the number of critically endangered and endangered species (see Table 4.5).

**Table 4.5**   Increase in the number of critically endangered and endangered species from 1996 to 2000

| | Critically endangered | | Endangered species | |
|---|---|---|---|---|
| | 1996 | 2000 | 1996 | 2000 |
| Mammals | 169 | 180 | 315 | 340 |
| Birds | 168 | 182 | 235 | 312 |
| Reptiles | 10 | 24 | 28 | 47 |
| Turtles (freshwater) | 10 | 24 | | |

Madagascar has the most number of critically endangered and endangered primates and has already lost nearly 90% of its original vegetation. The Philippines also has lost almost 97% of its original vegetation and, thus, has the highest number of critically endangered and endangered bird species.

Indonesia has the highest number of species of threatened mammals. The number of species threatened in India is 80, while Brazil and China have 75 and 72 threatened mammal species, respectively. The number of threatened bird species in various countries is listed in Table 4.6.

The number of plant species is also declining in South and Central America, Central and West Africa, and South East Asia. Worldwide, the total number of threatened plant species is 5611. Since only 4% of the world's plant species is known, the actual number could be far greater.

Malaysia has the largest number of plant species (681). For Indonesia, Brazil, and Sri Lanka, the corresponding numbers are 384, 338, and 280, respectively. Table 4.6 lists the threatened bird species of the world. Table 4.7 lists the threatened plant and animal species in India, as per the 2000 IUCN Red List.

According to IUCN (2000), India is second in terms of the number of threatened mammal and bird species. The number of threatened species by taxonomic group is listed in Table 4.8.

**Table 4.6**   Threatened bird species of the world

| Country | Number |
|---|---|
| Indonesia | 115 |
| Brazil | 113 |
| Colombia | 78 |
| China | 76 |
| Peru | 75 |
| India | 74 |

**Table 4.7** Threatened species (plants and animals) in India

| Category | Plants | Animals |
|---|---|---|
| Extinct | 7 | 0 |
| Extinct in the wild | 2 | 0 |
| Critically endangered | 44 | 18 |
| Endangered | 113 | 54 |
| Vulnerable | 87 | 143 |
| Lower risk–conservation dependent | 1 | 10 |
| Lower risk–near threatened | 72 | 99 |
| Data deficient | 14 | 31 |

There are many reasons for the extinction of species that finally lead to the biodiversity loss. The most notable reasons are biological, environmental, and anthropogenic activities. Out of these, the anthropogenic activities deserve serious consideration as the ecosystem loss caused by the first two factors is less severe.

The different causes of extinction are as follows:

(i) **Random variation in population:** If a species has low abundance, the variations in its (low) birth and death rates can lead to its extinction. This is called population risk.

(ii) **Environmental factors:** The variation in physical or biological environment and changes in predator, prey, competitor, or symbiotic species may lead to their extinction, especially, if the species are rare and isolated.

(iii) **Natural catastrophe:** A sudden change introduced in the environment as a result of natural activities such as earthquakes, floods, fires, and storms can greatly affect the survival of the area's biodiversity.

**Table 4.8** Threatened species by taxonomic group

| Taxonomic group | Number |
|---|---|
| Mammals | 86 |
| Birds | 79 |
| Reptiles | 25 |
| Amphibians | 3 |
| Fish | 3 |
| Molluscs | 2 |
| Other invertebrates | 21 |
| Plants | 244 |
| Total | 459 |

**Table 4.9**  India's ranking in some species

|  | *World ranking* | *Number of species* |
|---|---|---|
| Mammals | Eighth | 350 |
| Birds | Eighth | 1200 |
| Reptiles | Fifth | 453 |

   **(iv) Genetic risk:** The small population of a species has less genetic variability. Such a population is more vulnerable to various factors (including environmental) causing extinction as compared to large populations which have enough genetic variability to withstand such risks.

   **(v) Human activities:** Although human beings have affected the extinction of species since ancient times by their activities such as clearing of forests and land for settlement, the rate of extinction has increased tremendously in the recent past only.

India is among the top mega-diverse nations in the world. This is evident from the data on mammals, birds, and reptiles in which India occupies a high position in the global rating (Table 4.9). In addition, India ranks 15th in the world in terms of plant diversity. It hosts about 45,000 plant species, most of which are angiosperms (182 species). These plant species include ferns (1022 species) and orchids (1002 species). India has nearly 50,000 insect species, including 13,000 species of butterflies and moths. It is believed that numerous unknown species exist in India. Among plants, 18% of Indian plants are endemic to the country. The flowering plants have a much higher degree of endemism. Among the amphibians found in India, about 62% are endemic. In fact, high endemism has also been recorded for various groups of insects, marine worms, mayflies, and freshwater sponges. This proves that India is a mega-diverse nation.

According to the IUCN estimates, since 1600, humans have a high degree of involvement in the extinction of more than 75% bird and mammal species. Hunting alone is responsible for the extinction of about 42% of birds and 33% of mammals.

The introduction of exotic species (species introduced into a new geographic area) can have both positive and negative consequences on biodiversity. For example, some inadvertently introduced species can cause the spread of diseases or become pests or parasites. In the 19th century, the introduction of cats, rats, goats, dogs, and insects to new geographic regions led to dramatic extinctions. For example, the dodo birds faced extinction because their eggs were easy prey for dogs.

Many species face an additional risk of extinction because they are killed for their fur, skin, horns, ivory, and other products. The illegal trade in horns of rhinoceroses which are in the list of endangered species, puts them at risk in spite of the legal restrictions in such trade.

Human activities cause the alteration and destruction of habitats of species by introducing changes in land patterns, that is, deforestation, clearing of land for agriculture and urbanization, and industrial activities. With the increasing pressure of human population and requirements, plants and animals are being overexploited.

The recent origin of biotechnological techniques has led to the development of many genetically modified organisms (GMOs). The impacts of such proliferation are yet to be observed; however, they would definitely affect biodiversity as the introduction of GMOs would have serious effects on the existing species and other varieties with which they may have to compete for their existence.

## 4.7   CONSERVATION OF BIODIVERSITY

The survival of human beings depends on biodiversity. It should be noted that the loss of biodiversity is not reversible. Once a species is lost, it will not come into existence again. In view of this, it is essential that biodiversity should be preserved. One way to achieve this is to declare some areas as protected areas. They should consist of a network of national parks and wildlife sanctuaries to preserve major wildlife species such as tigers, lions, elephants, and deer.

Crocodiles are threatened species as their skin is used for making leather goods. A crocodile breeding and conservation programme was initiated in 1975 to protect the remaining crocodile population in its natural habitat by setting up breeding centres. This is probably the most successful conservation project in India.

When particular species are very close to extinction, they are generally conserved outside their natural habitat, in a controlled condition, such as a botanical garden for plants or a zoological park for animals, where there is expertise to multiply the species under artificially managed conditions. For the conservation of biodiversity, a number of conventions, protocols, and acts have been formulated. At the national level, various legislative and regulatory mechanisms have been initiated to protect biodiversity.

**(i) Convention on Biological Diversity, 1992:** The Convention on Biological Diversity or CBD (1992) was held in the Earth Summit, organized by the United Nations Conference on Environment and Development (UNCED). The main objectives of the convention are as follows:

(a) Conservation of biological diversity

(b) Sustainable use of its components

(c) Fair and equitable sharing of benefits

So far, 180 countries have become party to this convention.

**(ii) Convention on International Trade in Endangered Species of Wild Fauna and Flora (CITES), 1973:** This convention aims at the prevention of international commercial trade in endangered species or products derived from them. The trade in the following two categories of species are prohibited.

(a) Species in danger of extinction

(b) Species that may become endangered if their trade is not controlled

**(iii) Wildlife (Protection) Act, 1972, and Amendments:** The Wildlife (Protection) Act, 1971, was adopted to protect the endangered species of flora and fauna. It empowers the central and state governments to declare any area as a wildlife sanctuary, national park, or closed area where no industrial activity is allowed. This Act prohibits hunting completely.

**(iv) Biodiversity Act, 2000:** The Biodiversity Act, 2000, was adopted in 2002 to establish state-level boards and local-level biodiversity management committees to deal with matters concerning the conservation of biodiversity, its sustainable use, and equitable sharing of benefits.

**(v) Forest (Conservation) Act, 1980:** The Forest (Conservation) Act, 1980, was adopted to protect and conserve forests. As per this Act, unauthorized felling of trees, grazing, and hunting are punishable with a fine or imprisonment or both.

## 4.8 HOTSPOTS OF BIODIVERSITY

As already stated, hotspots of biodiversity are regions rich in various species. On a global scale, there are as many as 34 hotspots. These are listed in Table 4.10.

**Table 4.10** Hotspots of biodiversity

| S. No. | Hotspot | Region | Remarks |
| --- | --- | --- | --- |
| 1 | California Floristic Province | North America | • Mediterranean-type climate<br>• Tall trees such as Douglas, teak, and oak |
| 2 | Caribbean Islands hotspot | West Indies Islands | • Montane cloud forests to cactus shrubs<br>• Deforestation mainly occurs as a result of agriculture and grazing |
| 3 | Madrean pine-oak woodlands | The USA–Mexico Border | Hot and dry regions |
| 4 | Mesoamerican forests | Central America | • Third-largest hotspot of the world with more than 17,000 species of plants<br>• Endemic species include quetzals, howlers, and monkeys |
| 5 | Atlantic forests of Brazil | South America | • Richest biodiversity hotspot of the world<br>• Evergreen forests |

*Contd...*

**Table 4.10** *Contd...*

| S. No. | Hotspot | Region | Remarks |
|---|---|---|---|
| 6 | Brazil's Cerrado | Brazil | Contains a large number of endemic species of plants and animals |
| 7 | Chilean Winter Rainfall-Valdivian Forests | Stretch over Andes mountains and coast of Pacific Ocean | Contain rich endemic species of flora and fauna |
| 8 | Tumbes-Choco-Magdalena | Bordered by Mesoamerica and tropical Andes | Has diversity in both fauna and flora |
| 9 | Tropical Andes | Equatorial Andes, Ecuador, Peru, and Brazil | A small biodiversity hotspot but has rich endemic plants and animals |
| 10 | Caucasus region | Mountainous region of Armenia Georgia and Azerbaijan | Contains a large number of endemic plant species, which have been threatened by human interference |
| 11 | Iran-Anatolia region | Anatolia Plateau (Turkey), Kurdistan (North Iraq), and Iran | Has numerous endemic species of plants and animals |
| 12 | Mediterranean region | Europe and Central Asia | Contains more than 22,500 endemic plant species and animals |
| 13 | Mountains of Central Asia | Central Asia | Have great diversity in species of fauna and flora |
| 14 | Cape Floristic Hotspot | South Africa | Has great diversity of endemic plants and animals |
| 15 | Coastal Forests of Eastern Africa | Eastern Africa | Rich in endemic plants |
| 16 | Eastern Afromontane | Eastern mountains of Africa | Has several species of plants and animals |
| 17 | Guinean forests | Western Africa | Home of more than 25% of African mammals including more than 20 species of primates |
| 18 | Horn of Africa | Africa | Rich in endemic plants and animals |
| 19 | Madagascar and Indian Ocean islands | Madagascar and neighbouring island groups | Has 8 plant, 4 bird, and 5 primate families |

*Contd...*

**Table 4.10** *Contd...*

| S. No. | Hotspot | Region | Remarks |
|---|---|---|---|
| 20 | Maputaland-Pondol-and-Albany Hotspot | Africa | Is an important centre of plant endemism |
| 21 | Succulent Karoo | Namibia, South Africa | Has great diversity in endemic plants and animals |
| 22 | East Melanesian Islands | New Guinea in Southeast Africa (has 16,000 islands) | Rich in endemic plants and animals |
| 23 | Himalayan hotspot | Himalayas covering India, Pakistan, Nepal, and Bhutan | Mostly affected by growing population deforestation, industrialization, urbanization, and agricultural activities. A number of species of plants and animals are endangered or threatened |
| 24 | Eastern Himalayas | North-East India (Sikkim, Bhutan, and western Myanmar) | • Higher rainfall; trees such as oaks<br>• Characterized by swamps and mangroves<br>• Has 163 globally threatened species |
| 25 | Japan biodiversity hotspot | Japan | Has considerable biodiversity in ecosystems |
| 26 | Mountains of South-West China | China | Has great diversity in endemic plants and animals |
| 27 | New Caledonia | South Pacific Ocean | Has more than five endemic plant families |
| 28 | New Zealand biodiversity hotspot | New Zealand | Has great biodiversity in endemic plants |
| 29 | Philippine biodiversity hotspot | Philippines (700 Islands) | One of the world's richest biodiversity hotspots |
| 30 | Polynesia and Micronesian Islands including Hawaii | Polynesia (4500 islands) | Epicentre of the current global extinction crisis |
| 31 | Southwest Australia | Australia | High endemism among plants and animals |
| 32 | Western sundae | Indonesian, Malay and Brunei | Rich in endemic plants and animals |
| 33 | Wallace | Eastern Indonesia | Varied fauna and flora |

*Contd...*

**Table 4.10** *Contd...*

| S. No. | Hotspot | Region | Remarks |
|---|---|---|---|
| 34 | Western Ghats of India and islands of Sri Lanka | India and Sri Lanka | Home to 1100 animal species (20 are endemic), 450 bird species (35 are endemic), 6000 vascular plant species (3000 are endemic), and 15,000 flowering plants |

## SUMMARY

- Biodiversity or biological diversity refers to that part of nature which includes all forms of life such as plants, animals, and microorganisms.
- Biodiversity is measured by the number of species found in an area.
- Genetic diversity arises because of the combination of a large number of different genes.
- Species diversity refers to the number of plant and animal species present in a region.
- Ecosystem diversity arises because of differences in species and their habitats across different ecosystems.
- Biodiversity is of enormous value to human beings. The survival of humankind depends on biodiversity.
- Threats to biodiversity mainly occurs due to the destruction of forests which may lead to the extinction or endangering of various plant and animal species.
- Wetlands are the lands transitional between terrestrial and aquatic systems.
- Mangroves are salt-tolerant forest ecosystems.
- The extinction of species leads to the loss of biodiversity.
- Biodiversity loss is irreversible; therefore, it must be preserved.
- Biodiversity hotspots of the regions rich in various species. On a global scale, there are about 34 hotspots.

## EXERCISE

## [A] Multiple-choice questions

1. Which of the following statements are correct about biodiversity?

   (a) Biodiversity refers to that part of nature which includes all forms of life.

(b) It is measured by the number of species found in an area.

(c) Biodiversity is of three types: (i) genetic diversity, (ii) species diversity, and (iii) ecosystem diversity

(d) All are correct

2. The number of plant and animal species present in a region is referred to as

(a) Species diversity

(b) Genetic diversity

(c) Ecosystem diversity

(d) All of the above

3. Photosynthesis by green plants helps in

(a) Reducing the amount of $CO_2$ in the atmosphere

(b) Releasing oxygen into the atmosphere

(c) Both (a) and (b)

(d) None of the above

4. Deforestation contributes to

(a) Shortage of oxygen

(b) Abundance at $CO_2$

(c) Both (a) and (b)

(d) None of the above

5. Deforestation is caused by

(a) Felling of trees

(b) Shifting cultivation

(c) Overgrazing

(d) Urbanization

(e) All of the above

**ANSWERS**

1. (d)      2. (a)      3. (c)      4. (c)      5. (e)

## [B] Fill in the blanks.

1. Biodiversity refers to that part of nature which includes ______.

2. Biological wealth includes ______.

3. The combination of a large number of different genes is called ______ biodiversity.

4. Photosynthesis reduces the amount of ______ in the atmosphere.

5. Development of better varieties of plants and animals has become possible due to ______.

6. A number of species went extinct because of ______.

7. Deforestation leads to the shortage of ______.

8. Species which are native to a particular region are called ______.

9. Lands transitional between terrestrial and aquatic systems are called ______.

10. The loss of biodiversity is not ______.

11. The United Nations Conference on Environment and Development is known as the ______.

12. Regions that are rich in various species are called ______ of biodiversity.

**ANSWERS**

| | |
|---|---|
| 1. All forms of life | 2. All forms of life |
| 3. Genetic | 4. $CO_2$ |
| 5. Genetic engineering | 6. Human activities |
| 7. $O_2$ | 8. Endemic species |
| 9. Wetlands | 10. Reversible |
| 11. Earth Summit | 12. Hotspots |

## [C] Short-answers questions

1. What is biodiversity?
2. What are the different types of biodiversity?
3. What do you understand by the value of biodiversity?
4. What are the uses of biodiversity?
5. Write notes on:
   (a) Hotspots of biodiversity
   (b) Threats to biodiversity
   (c) Endemic species
   (d) Threatened species
   (e) Conservation of biodiversity

# Environmental Degradation, Pollution, and Conservation

## 5.1 INTRODUCTION

The term 'environment' means surroundings. It is defined as the sum total of all biotic and abiotic components constituting the environment. The earth's environment has been considerably degraded as a result of the pollution. In view of the harmful effects of environmental pollution, it is essential to conserve the environment (for details refer to Chapter 1).

## 5.2 ENVIRONMENT DEGRADATION

The degradation of the quality of environmental segments is called environmental degradation. It is caused by both natural processes and anthropogenic activities. Most of the environmental degradation is the result of human activities. Some of these are discussed here.

**(i) Deforestation:** It is primarily caused by cutting trees for wood and using forestland for cultivation to support the ever-increasing population. The land resulting from deforestation is mainly used for urbanization and industrialization.

Deforestation is also responsible for soil erosion. In fact, deforestation is the main cause of floods, droughts, and loss of valuable wildlife. There has been extinction of a number of species including insects, vertebrates, plants, fungi, and microorganisms. All this has led to environmental degradation.

The most important negative effect of deforestation is the reduction in photosynthetic activities. This implies that the $CO_2$ concentration in the atmosphere increases, which can lead to an increase in the 'greenhouse effect' and contributes immensely to global warming. This in turn results in the melting of ice caps that causes sea levels to rise, leading to floods. Global warming is also responsible for causing major atmospheric changes. In addition, a decrease in photosynthetic activities is accompanied by the reduction of oxygen levels in the atmosphere, which is essential for the survival of the earth's inhabitants. Tree cutting should be a planned process, keeping in  mind the fatal consequences of indiscriminate deforestation. For example, new saplings should be planted in between trees so that when a tree is cut, a new tree can replace the old one. In this way, deforestation can be prevented.

**(ii) Hunting activities:** Since time immemorial, gentle animals have been killed for food and fierce animals for security reasons. Hunting is also undertaken as a sport. This has led to the extinction of a large number of animal species.

**(iii) Urbanization:** Environmental degradation is caused by urbanization in a number of ways. Some of these are discussed below.

*(a) Loss of forestland:* As development of urban areas involves clearing of productive forestland, it is lost permanently.

*(b) Depletion of water resources:* Owing to the rapid increase in population, it becomes rather impossible for the municipal water supply to meet the growing demand for water. Also, the local groundwater gradually declines and water has to be taken from other sources.

*(c) Building materials:* The construction of residential areas needs large quantities of building materials such as bricks and wood. These materials, generally, are arranged from the adjoining areas comprising fertile lands, which results in further damage.

*(d) Industries:* Industries established in urban areas need large quantities of materials and water.

*(e) Slums:* According to an estimate by the United Nations, more than 1 billion people live in slums, which are crowded and have unsanitary conditions. In general, these slums are located in the outskirts of cities and towns. In fact, slums represent one of the worst types of environmental degradation.

*(f) Water pollution:* Pollution of fresh waterbodies such as urban lakes and rivers as a result of urbanization and industrialization is enormous. Human wastes and discharge of industrial effluents are responsible for the massive pollution of fresh waterbodies.

*(g) Air pollution:* Industries that use coal or oil for energy generation pollute the air by emitting pollutants such as sulphur dioxide, oxides of nitrogen, hydrogen sulphide, and suspended particles (fly ash and many more). These gases and pollutants are also discharged by poorly maintained vehicles. These pollutants are harmful to plants, animals, and humans.

*(h) Waste production:* A considerable amount of solid waste is produced by households, industries, hospitals, and so on. Solid waste disposal is a major problem in urban areas.

**(iv) Industrialization:** Industrialization has a very severe effect on the environment. Various industries are responsible for atmospheric pollution because they discharge a large number of harmful and poisonous gases. Industrial effluents are responsible for polluting soil and various waterbodies, including groundwater.

Various pollutants are also responsible for adverse effects on human health. In fact, the discharged effluents in waterbodies are responsible for various diseases such as Minamata, *Itai-Itai,* and methaemoglobinaemia. The last two centuries witnessed great advancements in technologies that led to the rapid expansion of the industrial sector. New industrial setups were labour-intensive, resulting in the migration of millions of people from rural to urban areas. More land was needed for the settlement of the migrated population in towns and cities; this considerably reduced the availability of land. This rapid growth gave way to urban, economic, and social problems. The result was that the cities became overcrowded and unmanageable.

Urbanization and industrialization are interrelated. This is a worldwide phenomenon and has resulted in environmental degradation. As the population increased in urban areas, people needed land for settlement. So productive farmlands and rich forests were cleared, leading to the irrecoverable loss of land and its biological resources. A greater concentration of people in urban areas led to unplanned developments in these areas. This resulted in the non-availability of drinking water, clean air, transportation, and recreational space. Another problem that added to people's misery was the disposal of waste.

**(v) Effect of environmental disasters on environment:** A number of environmental episodes have adversely affected the environment. Some notable examples include the Great Smog of London (which killed about 4000 people) and many nuclear catastrophes such as the nuclear bombing of the two towns of Japan, Hiroshima and Nagasaki, during World War II (responsible for the death of thousands of people and the permanent disability of millions). The Bhopal gas tragedy, caused by the leakage of methyl isocyanate (MIC) gas from the Union Carbide factory in Bhopal, India, on 2 December 1984, is the world's worst-ever industrial disaster.

In view of the above discussion, it can be stated that environmental protection (a matter of primary importance for humans and their future) must be kept as the top priority.

## 5.3  ENVIRONMENTAL POLLUTION

Pollution is defined as an undesirable change in the physical, chemical, or biological characteristics of the environmental components such as air, water, and soil, which adversely affects the life-support system of the biosphere. Pollution is caused by the addition of harmful constituents or substances to water, air, or land, which adversely alter the natural quality of the environment. Therefore, it can be said that pollution is an unfavourable alteration of the environment. Agents that contaminate (or pollute) the environmental components are called pollutants. Even a normal constituent of the atmosphere becomes a pollutant if its concentration increases beyond a certain limit. A typical example is that of carbon dioxide. Normally, carbon dioxide is not considered a pollutant. However, the presence of excessive carbon dioxide in the atmosphere contributes to global warming. This aspect will be discussed subsequently (for details, refer to Chapter 1, Section 1.4).

Pollutants are of two types—non-degradable and biodegradable pollutants. Non-degradable pollutants such as pesticides, heavy metals, rubber, plastic, and nuclear waste remain unchanged in the environment for a very long time. These pollutants cannot be decomposed or broken down by bacteria. Hence, they persist for a very long time in nature, get accumulated, and often biomagnify to a dangerous level. On the other hand, pollutants such as paper, domestic sewage, garden wastes, and fertilizers break down into simple products by bacterial decomposition. Such products are referred to as biodegradable pollutants.

As already stated, environmental pollution includes air pollution, water pollution, and soil pollution. Besides these, we come across other pollution types such as thermal pollution, noise pollution, and pollution by radioactivity (for details, refer to Chapter 1, Section 1.4).

## 5.4 CONSERVATION AND MANAGEMENT OF THE ENVIRONMENT

Conservation and management of the environment are very important for the survival of humankind. In this regard, the United Nations has identified five challenges for the world community: (i) loss of biodiversity, (ii) climatic changes, (iii) water pollution, (iv) ozone-layer depletion, and (v) land degradation.

The loss of biodiversity is not reversible. Once a species becomes extinct, it is gone forever. For the conservation of biodiversity, a number of conventions, protocols, and acts have been formulated by various countries (discussed in Chapter 4).

The climate of any region is never constant; it keeps on changing. A number of factors are responsible for bringing changes in climate. These include solar energy, waterbodies (such as oceans, seas, and rivers), altitude, land breeze, and human activities. In fact, human activities change the climate in a drastic way and at a much faster rate. This includes air pollution, which is also due to the release of greenhouse gases (GHGs) and the subsequent greenhouse effect. This results in global warming, which in turn causes fast melting of glaciers and flooding of low-lying areas.

Water pollution can occur in freshwater, marine water, and groundwater due to the contamination of various pollutants in waterbodies. Polluted water is hazardous to human health. Water pollution has caused irreversible environmental changes, hardship for the poor, and economic losses. The stratospheric ozone layer provides a protective shield by absorbing most of the ultraviolet (UV) radiations that can harm living organisms on earth. Stratospheric ozone is constantly being created and destroyed by natural photochemical processes in dynamic equilibrium. This equilibrium is disrupted by various human activities by releasing anthropogenic chemicals—especially chlorine and bromine compounds such as chlorofluorocarbons (CFCs)—halons, and a broad range of industrial chemicals used as refrigerants, foaming agents, aerosols, retardants, and fumigants. All these chemicals can deplete the ozone layer. This permits more UV-B radiation to reach the earth, resulting in skin cancer, cataract, and irreversible eye damage, and could also suppress the immune system.

Land degradation is attributed to various human activities among which desertification and deforestation are prominent. It is also central to the global environmental progress. The environmental and economic consequences of land degradation are not only confined to countries where it occurs. It also leads to the loss of biodiversity and pollution of international waters.

Most of the countries are adopting a variety of policies and measures to conserve biodiversity, prevent climate change, and degradation of international waters. These include improved farming and grazing practices; afforestation, reforestation, and forest management; and upgraded water management as policy reforms for better land-use policies.

An important aspect of conservation and management of the environment is the management of solid wastes generated by various processes, especially industrial.

Solid waste comprises food scraps, used paper and cardboards, plastic, and metal. Solid wastage is collectively referred to as garbage. The term 'municipal solid waste' (MSW) is generally used to describe most of the non-hazardous solid wastes disposed in a city, town, or village. Sources of MSW include residential buildings, commercial establishments (such as offices), institutions, and industrial facilities. However, MSW does not include industrial effluents, agricultural run-offs, debris from construction and demolition activities, and sewage and mining wastes.

Solid waste disposal in India, as in many Western countries, has traditionally been given low priority by the civil authorities. The basic attitude of the authorities is that solid waste management does not yield adequate returns and so can be neglected without endangering public health. However, the adverse environmental effects of this approach are now becoming visible.

It is desirable that remedial steps be taken before the problem becomes acute. India's urban population is estimated to generate about 50 million tonnes of solid waste per year, and the approximate cost of its collection and disposal is about ₹400 million. The earlier disposal methods were very crude. Solid wastes were dumped in open pits outside the city. With the increase in population, solid waste disposal became more problematic. Until recently, the dumping of solid wastes, and occasionally burning, were the only methods of solid waste disposal.

The strategy for waste management includes the following three components:

(1) Reduction at the source

(2) Recycling

(3) Disposal

Reduction of waste at its source is the most effective approach towards waste management and can be achieved by using less material. Using glass containers that can be reused in place of plastic and metal containers, we can reduce the waste generated by throwing away of plastic and metal containers. In a similar way, we can reduce the amount of paper waste if we use both sides of the paper for writing and printing.

Recycling is another way of reducing solid waste generation. For example, paper, cardboard, newspaper, aluminium, iron, and glass wastes can be recycled. Plastics are difficult to recycle because different types of resins are used for their production. However, the same type of plastic can be recycled.

The best method for  solid waste disposal is by sanitary landfills or by incineration (Figure 5.1). In the sanitary landfill procedure, a site of suitable size is dug (of $50 \times 50 \times 10$ m$^3$). The sides of the site are lined with an impermeable material such as plastic membrane. Solid waste is placed in the landfill site in a careful manner. The waste is spread out and compacted with heavy machinery. Each day, the waste is covered with a layer of compacted soil. When the landfill site is full, it is closed by cement concrete. In such a procedure, there is no possibility of groundwater pollution as had been the case with the older landfills in which groundwater pollution occurred due to percolation of the waste during rains.

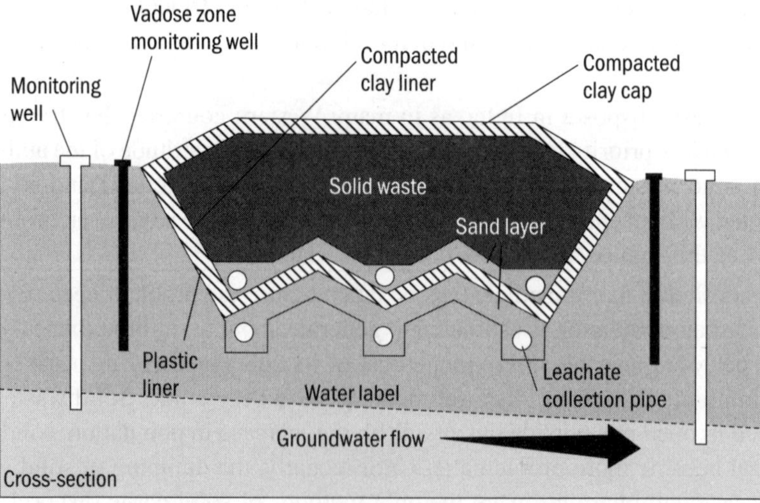


**Fig. 5.1**  Various layers of a sanitary landfill

The landfill method for solid waste disposal is an economic procedure; however, selection of an economically suitable site is very difficult. An alternative procedure for the disposal of MSWs is incineration. In this procedure, wastes are burnt in a suitably designed furnace. Heating is carried out at about 85°C for about an hour. Incineration is basically an oxidation procedure that converts wastes into carbon dioxide and water. The advantage of this procedure is that the solid waste is reduced by about 90% in volume and 75% in weight. However, any toxic gas that is evolved during this procedure pollutes the atmosphere. The remains, which may contain some toxic materials, are disposed of in sanitary landfills.

It is always advisable to separate the vegetable and perishable waste from MSW and convert it into manure. The process is called vermicomposting and is carried out as described here.

A pit of about $1 \times 1 \times 1$ m$^3$ in size is dug. It is lined with straw or dried leaves and grass. All organic wastes are put in the pit as and when generated. A culture of worms (now commercially available) is introduced into the pit. The pit is covered with twigs and dried leaves every day and watered twice a week to keep it moist. After 15 days, the contents of the pit are turned over to ensure complete vermicomposting. In about 40–45 days, the wastes will be decomposed by microorganisms. The final product is obtained in the form of soil rich in nutrients and can be used as manure in place of chemical fertilizers.

## 5.4.1  Control Measures for Industrial Waste

A large number of chemical manufacturing companies such as petroleum refining, paper mills, smelters, and metallurgical operations produce large quantities of hazardous waste. A waste is considered hazardous if it has one of the following characteristics:

Vermicomposting is a common practice
for farmers in India

   (i) Ignitability: catches fire easily

  (ii) Corrosiveness: wears away other materials

 (iii) Reactivity: reacts with water or explodes on reaction with other chemicals

 (iv) Radioactivity: releases ionizing radiation

  (v) Toxicity: produces symptoms of metabolic disorder, poisoning, or malformations

Toxic waste has the capacity to cause damage after entering the metabolic system of the consumer—an animal, a plant, or a human being. These wastes are poisonous even in small or trace amounts and affect humans or animals immediately, causing various illnesses and even death. All hazardous wastes are not toxic, but all toxic wastes are hazardous.

A hazardous waste, because of its quantity or concentration or its physical, chemical, or biological characteristics, may cause or significantly contribute to an increase in mortality or in serious, irreversible or incapacitating reversible illnesses or may pose a potential threat to the environment.

Today all countries are facing the problem of management of hazardous waste as the amount of waste to be managed is enormous. The control measures or the management of waste involves the following four approaches:

   (i) Waste minimization or producing less waste

  (ii) Recycling of industrial waste

 (iii) Treatment of hazardous waste

 (iv) Disposal of hazardous waste

## 5.4.2   Waste Minimization

Waste minimization is the most important aspect of waste management. It can be achieved by adopting the following three procedures:

**(i) Process modification:** The industrial processes can be modified or altered in such a way that the amount of hazardous waste is reduced to the barest minimum. This can be achieved in a way such that most of the starting materials are incorporated into the final product and thus no waste is generated.

**(ii) Concentration of waste:** Using the techniques of evaporation and precipitation, the amount of hazardous waste can be reduced considerably.

**(iii) Segregation of waste:** It is useful to separate non-hazardous waste from its hazardous counterpart. This can be done at the source of waste generation. By this method, the volume of hazardous waste can be decreased substantially, making it easier to handle and treat.

### 5.4.3  Recycling of Industrial Waste

Recycling and reuse also eliminate hazardous waste generation. Certain solvents and acids can be recovered and recycled; for example, baghouse dust from scrap steel processors, containing up to 25% zinc oxide, can be reacted with waste sulphuric acid to make galvanizer's pickle acid. The spent pickle liquor, containing up to 10% zinc sulphate and some iron salt, can be used as fertilizer. Also, certain industries can mutually benefit by taking wastes from one industry and using them as raw materials in another industry.

### 5.4.4  Treatment of Hazardous Waste

The toxicity of hazardous waste can be reduced by physical, chemical, and biological methods.

Physical methods such as phase separation (including the steps of lagooning, prolonged storage in tanks, and sludge drying in beds), absorption by charcoal, or resin filters for absorbing toxins can be used. Distillation is also helpful. Precipitation and immobilization are useful in making wastes suitable for long-term storage.

Chemical methods such as neutralization, oxidization, reduction, and ion-exchange are useful for breaking down hazardous wastes and detoxifying them.

Biological methods involve the use of bacteria and soil microorganisms to reduce the hazardous characteristics of the waste. Biodegradation can be accomplished by aerobic and anaerobic procedures.

In addition to the above procedures, incineration is also a method of detoxification. In this process, the oxidation of waste detoxifies it. Incineration is also a good procedure of waste minimization. It is also an effective method of waste disposal.

### 5.4.5  Disposal of Hazardous Waste

Prior to the disposal of wastes, their physical characteristics must be known. Their characteristics must be assessed from the place where the waste is generated (point source). Also, the physical characteristics must be kept in mind during different stages of waste management such as collection, interim storage, transport, and disposal of waste. Waste is a complex mixture. Mixing of non-compatible wastes for convenience in transit could create an acute hazard, either immediately or on treatment and disposal. For example, a mixture of ether waste containing sodium residues with aqueous ether will explode. Therefore, proper collection, transport, and storage are very important for the safe disposal of hazardous waste. The non-compatible wastes should be dealt with separately.

The final disposal of hazardous wastes must be carried out very carefully using the following procedures.

**(i) Landfill disposal:** Open dumps are a poor method of waste disposal because they cause environmental problems. Hazardous waste should be disposed of in properly operated sanitary landfills, which causes the least damage to the environment. The area or the site to be filled with wastes must be lined with a non-porous substance such as clay or high-density polyethylene (HDPE)—plastic membrane to prevent wastes from leaking into the surrounding area or polluting the groundwater. The waste should be packed and dumped at the site and covered with soil (this prevents insects from getting into the refuse). After the site is full, it should be covered for the final time in such a way so that land can be used for recreational purposes.

Dumping of the hazardous waste in landfill sites constructed on a structure made up of concrete walls is a new and successful concept of waste dumping.

**(ii) Incineration:** In this process, the waste is burnt, which detoxifies it. This is also a very good method of waste reduction. Flue gases are released into the atmosphere, and the slag or ash produced is deposited in a landfill.

Generally, wastes having inflammable characteristics are incinerated. Such wastes include solvent waste and sludge; waste mineral oil; varnish and paint wastes and sludge; plastic, rubber, and latex waste sludge and emulsions; oil, emulsions, and oil/water mixtures; phenolic wastes; resin wastes; grease and wax wastes; pesticide wastes; and organic wastes containing halogen, sulphur, or phosphorus compounds.

Wastes that contain high chlorine, sulphur, and phosphorus contents, polychlorinated biphenyls (PCBs), and heavy metals and carcinogenic substances need special incineration technologies and precautions.

**(iii) Dumping at the sea:** The notion that the enormous volume of water in the seas will have so much dilution effect and so can be used for dumping anything is an erroneous conviction. Hazardous waste has to be put in sealed containers before dumping into deep seas. All precautions must be taken to prevent the contamination of water.

Disposal of waste at sea is governed by international legislation and by national legislation required for ratification. Accordingly, direct dumping into sea is prohibited, particularly waste containing chemicals such as organo-silicon compounds, halogenated organics, mercury and its compounds, cadmium, carcinogenic waste, and plastics.

The methods/procedures described above are used for the disposal of hazardous wastes. In addition, nuclear waste (a dangerous type of hazardous waste) is disposed of by the underground disposal method. Nuclear wastes are generated in all operations that use nuclear energy and other processes involving testing of nuclear weapons. For such wastes, salt mines are used because of the excellent properties of salt deposits to prevent the interaction of waste with other geological formations. Also, salt absorbs moisture, reducing the risk of metallic containers from rusting.

### *5.4.5.1  Effects of Improper Disposal of Hazardous Waste*

Improper disposal of waste causes adverse effects on the environment and, consequently, on human health. The usual practice of waste disposal on land or the insanitary open dumping leads to the contamination of groundwater by leaching from the wastes, thus causing one of the most serious environmental effects. It is impossible to reverse the damage once the groundwater gets polluted with hazardous waste.

Pesticides have been used to destroy harmful organisms with a view to increase food production. These pesticides are not biodegradable and keep on accumulating, and during rain, find their way into the groundwater or other waterbodies. Pesticides are responsible for a number of health hazards.

There is a worldwide awareness among people against the improper and uncontrolled practices of dumping of hazardous wastes. Such practices have led to a number of environmental problems, death of livestock, and ill health in humans. The most important ill effects of dumping heavy metals, especially mercury (Minamata disease) and cadmium (Itai-Itai disease), are always talked about.

In India, one of the most alarming episodes was noted in 1988 in the Bichhri village of Udaipur District. Wastes from a silver cyanide factory were discharged on to the land and waterbodies. The water acquired a red colour due to the use of a dye. Drinking this water caused vomiting. The water became so polluted that it was unfit even for irrigation purposes.

Discharge of wastewater from electroplating and heat treatment operations of metals, which use cyanide as one of the raw materials, is another cause of generation of hazardous waste. Discharge of cyanide (a deadly poison) into waterbodies has led to serious problems.

## 5.4.6  Individual Role in Prevention of Pollution

Before discussing the role of an individual in preventing pollution, we must understand that human activities are solely responsible for maximum damage to the environment. According to Peter J. Bryant, about 50% of the land surface (agricultural and urban) has been degraded. Some of the environmental concerns are as follows:

  (i) Human beings are responsible for increasing the atmospheric concentration of carbon dioxide by about 30%.

 (ii) We use more than half of the accessible freshwater resources.

(iii) Over 50% of terrestrial nitrogen fixation is due to human activities.

(iv) About 20% of the bird species have become extinct in the past 200 years, mainly due to human activities.

(v) About 22% of marine fisheries have been over-exploited or depleted. About 44% more are at the limit of exploitation.

Although these problems seem too difficult to be solved, there should be some attempts or initiation on our behalf to eradicate some of the problems. As human activities are responsible for most of the environmental problems, it is the responsibility of each and every individual to get involved in improving the environment. People may sometimes get confused as to which of the environmental issues one should try to solve. The best option is to attend to the problem that has the maximum effect on people and then try to find solution. People should help themselves rather than waiting for the authorities to take care of the problems.

Following are some of the guidelines which can help individuals to cope up with the problem of pollution.

(i) **Plants reduce air pollution:** We need to plant trees and, more importantly, take care of the existing plants.

(ii) **Protection of forests:** Forests can be conserved by reducing the use of wood and paper products whenever possible. The manufacturing of wooden and paper products leads to the loss of forests (deforestation). Forests help maintain the balance of oxygen in the atmosphere. Therefore, we should try to save forests by using recycled paper products to the extent possible. Use both sides of the paper for writing and printing. Joining an afforestation programme will help one become aware and also generate awareness among others about the ill effects of deforestation.

(iii) Use of plastic or paper plates should be discouraged in a get together. Instead, crockery that can be washed, cleaned, and reused should be preferred.

(iv) **Kitchen gardens:** If one has a kitchen garden, use of pesticides should be reduced to a bare minimum. It is best to use biological pest control measures. Watering plants with water used for washing vegetables can help prevent water wastage. Setting up a compost bin in the kitchen garden will cater to the need of fertilizers. Vegetable wastes and garden wastes can be converted into manure.

(v) **Conserve fossil fuels: The** use of automobiles for covering small distances should be avoided (because they consume fossil fuels). Instead, walk short distances or use a cycle. For office commuting, a car pool or use of public transport will prove environment-friendly. The idea is to use the available resources for getting the maximum benefits. Personal vehicles should be kept in excellent condition by getting them regularly serviced to maximize the use of gasoline. It is best to change the vehicle if it is more than 15 years old.

**(vi) Conserve resources:** Switch off lights, fans, air conditioners, and heaters when not in use. Avoid using artificial light when a sufficient amount of natural light is present. Water should not be wasted. Do not keep the tap running while brushing. In the washroom, low-flush toilets instead of full-flush toilets should be installed to save water. Remember that saving each drop of water is important.

**(vii) Avoid smoking:** At least one research shows that smoking is a major contributor to atmospheric pollution. Therefore, one should try to avoid it. It is estimated that smoking is a major cause of cancer. Cigarette smoke contains a large number of organic chemicals, some of which are potential carcinogens. Even non-smokers face the risk of developing cancer if they become passive smokers.

**(viii) Say no to plastics:** Plastics are one of the major causes of environmental pollution. Whenever we go shopping, we should not accept goods in plastic bags. Instead, making our own cloth bag for carrying goods can help minimize the use of plastic bags. It is best to buy consumer goods in refillable glass containers instead of cans or throwaway bottles.

**(ix) Recycle:** Recycling of newspapers; paper products; cardboards; and products made of metals such as aluminium, copper, and iron should be encouraged.

**(x) Population control:** Most of the environmental problems are caused by human activities, and the increase in human population compounds the problems. The population growth can be brought within control if each family has only one or two children. The Government of India has adopted a number of programmes to control the country's population.

On the basis of the above discussion, it can be stated that the environment we live in has deteriorated very fast, particularly in the past 30 years or so. The air we breathe and the water we drink are getting polluted (both air and water are essential for our life). Rains are becoming irregular. The scarcity of rains leads to famines, while excessive rains lead to floods. Forests are getting depleted. A large number of plant and animal species are becoming extinct (all due to human activities). The topsoil is getting eroded, and the ozone layer is depleting. There is definite danger of global warming, which may lead to the melting of glaciers and consequent flooding of low-lying areas. This environmental degradation threatens the very existence of human beings who are directly or indirectly responsible for all these problems.

The environment provides all life-supporting materials; hence, it should be properly managed. There is an urgent need to educate people to develop a positive attitude towards the environment. In a positive development, the Supreme

Court of India has asked the Government of India to implement environmental education in the curriculum of schools and colleges.

## 5.4.7  Public Awareness

Public awareness plays a vital role in the management of the environment. In fact, most of the environmental problems are due to the lack of public awareness. Environmental damage is caused by the activities of individuals who are not conscious and do not have adequate knowledge of the environment. As an example, when trees in a forest are cut to obtain timber and firewood or land for agriculture, the environment is damaged. In a similar way, air and water get polluted when pollutants are allowed to enter the atmosphere or waterbodies in large quantities. While agriculture is essential, grazing by animals is unavoidable. Forests have to be harvested for their produce, dams have to be built, automobiles have to be run for transportation, and electricity has to be produced; however, we can perform all these activities in a scientific and planned manner so that the ecosystem's balance is not disturbed. Every natural system has a limited capacity to absorb shock. If these shocks exceed the limit, repair becomes difficult. As an illustration, if trees are harvested from forests and young trees are left to grow, the forests will continue to grow and provide products. In a similar way, if a waterbody receives biodegradable wastes in a controlled way, its water quality is not affected much and the water remains unpolluted. However, in case the same waterbody is used for dumping unlimited quantities of all kinds of waste, it gets polluted, resulting in the death of its aquatic life. Another example is grazing of pastures by animals. If pastures are used in a scientific and planned way, they can remain useful for an indefinite period of time. On the other hand, overgrazing of pastures will result in the disappearance of greenery. If that happens, the fertile soil will be displaced by wind and water erosion, rendering the area barren.

Natural resources and the environment can be utilized in two ways. The first way is to use the natural resources in a planned manner so that the environment is not endangered and we can benefit from it indefinitely. In the second, resources and the environment can be utilized in an unscrupulous manner. In this case, the benefits can be obtained only initially, while in the long run, we become losers. People normally adopt the second route due to ignorance and lack of information. The most important point is to make people aware of the consequences of such an approach. Hence, environmental awareness is essential.

Governments are making efforts in a number of ways for creating environmental awareness among people. The Ministry of Environment and Forests (MoEF), Government of India, has created a division known as Education and Information Division. Its role is to create awareness among all classes of people and provide information about the environment. One of the activities of this division is the National Environmental Awareness Campaign, which is organized every year (since 1986) for creating awareness about environment at the national level. Funds are also provided to voluntary organizations, universities, schools, colleges, and government agencies to conduct programmes for environmental awareness. These agencies generate  awareness through rallies, exhibitions, *padyatras*, drama, dance, film shows, seminars, and workshops. Funds are also provided by the government to establish eco-clubs in educational institutions and for conducting seminars and workshops.

The main obstacle in spreading environmental awareness is illiteracy among the masses. It is obvious that a literate person can be made aware of any problem, but an illiterate person has to be persuaded.

## 5.5  MANAGEMENT OF ENVIRONMENTAL QUALITY

In most of the cases, it is rather impossible to eliminate pollution completely. However, it is possible to minimize it.

### 5.5.1  Management of Air Pollution

Air pollution is responsible for grave health hazards (for details, refer to Chapter 1). The main pollutants of air include oxides of carbon, sulphur, nitrogen, hydrocarbons, and particulates. There are two main approaches for controlling air pollution—effluent control and techniques for prevention. A number of procedures have been used for controlling air pollution. In addition, pollutants from automobile exhaust (sulphur dioxide and oxides of nitrogen) can be controlled by using catalytic converters. Finally, the quality of air should be ascertained by estimating the amount of various pollutants in the air as per the prescribed air-quality standards.

### 5.5.2  Management of Water Pollution

The two main sources of pollution of waterbodies are industrial and household discharges, including human wastes. It should be made mandatory for various industries to eliminate pollutants before discharging wastes into waterbodies. It is, however, best to reuse the same purified water in the same industry repeatedly. MSW, which basically contains human wastes, must be treated before it is discharged into waterbodies or before it is purified further for drinking purposes.

The effect of water pollutants on health is discussed in Chapter 1.

### 5.5.3  Management of Soil Pollution

Soil pollution can have a number of harmful effects on human health. Land is polluted mainly by industrial wastes and the use of pesticides and herbicides for agricultural purposes. It should be made mandatory for all industries to deal with their own wastes and dispose them as per rules. In other words, industries must treat their waste prior to its disposal. The use of agrochemicals such as pesticides and herbicides should be regulated. There is no doubt that switching to organic farming is the most sustainable method of agriculture. Unlike conventional farming which uses chemical fertilizers for increasing crop produce, organic farming is based on the use of organic fertilizers in the form of biomass. Radioactive wastes are another genre of soil pollutants and should be disposed of following the standard procedure. In addition, the management of environment also involves preventing the degradation of ecosystems. Various acts have been passed—both nationally and internationally—for the prevention and protection of various segments of the environment. Some of these acts passed by the Government of India are discussed next.

## 5.6   ENVIRONMENT PROTECTION ACTS

With the progress of civilization, humans began altering the natural environment to meet their own needs. This resulted in the depletion of natural resources and degradation of the environment. A lot of strain on natural resources and, consequently, on the environment resulted mainly because of the increase in human population, industrialization, urbanization, and numerous development projects. The problem is further compounded by the pollution of air, water, and land. The situation has deteriorated to such an extent that the environmental problems pose a threat not only to the health of humans but also to their very existence. To protect the environment from deterioration, a number of legislations have been enacted at the national and international levels. Various acts enacted for the protection of the environment at the national level are discussed next.

### 5.6.1   Water (Prevention and Control of Pollution) Act, 1974, Amended in 1988

This act was passed by Parliament in 1974 under Article 252 of the Constitution of India. The administrative machinery for the act is called the Water Pollution Board at the central and state levels. Its objective is to control and prevent the pollution of water, including that of streams, river water courses, inland waters, subterranean water, seawater, and tidal water. The Water Pollution Boards are given powers to advice, coordinate, and provide technical assistance for the prevention and control or abatement of water pollution. The Water Act prohibits the dumping of poisonous, noxious, or polluting matter into waterbodies. Some problems in the administration of the act led to its amendment in 1988. According to the amendment, the Water Pollution Boards are empowered to issue directions and order closures, prohibition, or regulation of any industry or its operation and stop its water, electricity, or any other services. Strict penalties and punishments are imposed for not complying with the procedures of the act.

## 5.6.2  Air (Prevention and Control of Pollution) Act, 1981, Amended in 1987

This act was passed for the prevention and control of air pollution under Article 235 of the Constitution of India. Its objective is to control and abate air pollution from automobiles and industrial plants. The act defines various terms such as air pollution and air pollutants. The Central Board for the Prevention and Control of Air Pollution is authorized to implement and enforce the act. This body prescribes standards for air quality. The Amendment of 1987 was enacted to empower the boards for meeting emergencies, wherein they  were authorized to take immediate measures and also to impose penalties on the offenders. According to the amendment, the boards were also given powers to cancel the permission in case the industry does not comply with the prescribed standards. Air pollution also includes pollution created by noise.

Some other measures to control air pollution were also taken. These measures include the Atomic Energy Act of 1988 (dealing with radioactive waste) and the Motor Vehicles Act of 1988 (for regulating vehicular traffic and transportation of hazardous wastes).

The emission standards for motor vehicles were notified in 1990, made stricter in 1996, and subsequently revised in 2000. The Supreme Court also notified Euro I and Euro II emission norms for Delhi in April 1999.

## 5.6.3  Wildlife (Protection) Act, 1972, Amended in 1982 and 1991

Enacted by Parliament in 1972, this act empowers the state wildlife advisory boards to regulate the hunting of wild animals and birds, establish sanctuaries and national parks, regulate trade in wild animals and animal products, and to judicially impose penalties for violating the rules laid by the act. Any harm to the regulated species, listed in Schedule 1 of the act, is prohibited throughout India. This act is administered by wildlife wardens and their staff. Amendment to the act was made in 1982 that permitted the capture and transportation of wild animals for the scientific management of animal population. A further amendment in 1991 makes the near-total prohibition on hunting of animals more effective.

## 5.6.4  Forest (Conservation) Act, 1980, Amendment in 1988

According to this act, a state may declare its forestlands as reserved forests. Unauthorized felling of trees, quarrying, grazing, and hunting in reserved forests are punishable with a fine or an imprisonment or both. The preservation of protected forests is enforced through rules, licences, and criminal prosecutions. The act is administered by forest officers and their staff. The 1988 amendment makes the provisions more stringent for the violators of the act. The amendment includes cultivation of tea, coffee, rubber, palm, oil-bearing plants, and medicinal plants under non-forest purposes.

## 5.6.5 Environment (Protection) Act, 1986

This act, passed by Parliament on 23 May 1986, refers to the Stockholm Conference of 1972 and is based on Article 253 of the Constitution. With this act, the Government of India has armed itself with significant powers considered necessary for the prevention, control, and abatement of environmental pollution. The powers include coordination of action by states, planning and execution of nationwide programmes, and deciding on environmental quality standards, particularly with respect to emission or discharge of environmental pollution. The powers also include handling of hazardous substances and prevention of environmental accidents. In fact, manufacturing units have to take environmental clearance from the MoEF. This is also applicable for the construction of multistorey buildings.

## 5.6.6 Biodiversity Act, 2000

This act enables the establishment of state-level boards and local-level biodiversity management committees to deal with matters concerning the conservation of biodiversity, its sustainable use, and fair and equitable sharing of biological resources. The National Biodiversity Authority was set up in Chennai on 1 October 2003 under this act.

## 5.6.7 Issues Involved in Enforcement of Environmental Legislation

The aim of environmental legislation is to protect the environment, including the health of the people and the earth's resources. The enactment of environmental legislation does not mean that the problems are solved. Once legislation is brought about at the global, national, or state level, it has to be implemented. This is possible only by having an effective agency that can collect all the relevant data, process it, and pass it on to the law enforcement agency. The people who do not follow the rules must be punished by a legal process. In case, cognizance is not given, individuals can file a public interest litigation (PIL) to protect the environment. Non-governmental organizations (NGOs) can also take these matters to court in the interest of conserving the environment. A number of legal experts (for example, M.C. Mehta) have successfully defended such cases in the court of law. One of the major issues involved in such cases is illegal gratification in order to get the necessary clearance from the enforcement agency. The public should act a watchdog so that the concerned authorities are informed and offenders are suitably punished.

## 5.6.8  Environment Impact Assessment

Before any development project can be initiated, the MoEF's permission is necessary. The MoEF, in order to consider such requests, needs an environment impact assessment (EIA), which should be carried out by a competent organization. The EIA should reflect the likely impact of the proposal on waterbodies, soil, and air (if it is accepted). The EIA must also specify if the project is likely to have adverse effects on the habitat of any endangered species. The MoEF has listed 30 different industries that need clearance before they are set up. The projects are not to be passed in case the anticipated impacts are likely to be severe for the environment.

# SUMMARY

- The environment meaning surroundings, is defined as the sum total of all biotic and abiotic components.
- Environmental degradation is the degradation of the quality of environmental segments.
- Deforestation is caused mostly by cutting trees and is largely responsible for soil erosion.
- Deforestation reduces plants' photosynthetic activity and is accompanied with an increase in $CO_2$ concentration and decrease in $O_2$ concentration in the atmosphere.
- Environmental degradation is caused by urbanization, which includes the loss of forestland, depletion of water resources, creation of slums, and generation of wastes.
- The environment is adversely affected by a number of environmental pollution episodes including the Great Smog of London and the Bhopal gas tragedy.
- The survival of humankind is dependent on the conservation and management of the environment, which includes reduction (at source), recycling, and disposal of waste.
- Various methods of hazardous waste disposal include landfill dumping, incineration, and dumping at sea.
- Individuals can play an instrumental role in the prevention of pollution.
- Public awareness can play a key role in the management of the environment.
- Environmental quality can be maintained by the management of air, water, and soil pollution.

- Environment protection acts authorize the central government to protect and improve environment quality by imposing restrictions on hunting of wild animals, declaring forest areas as reserved areas, making decisions about the industrial setup of an area, and many more. However, a number of issues jeopardize the enforcement of these acts.

# EXERCISE

## [A] Multiple-choice questions

1. Environmental degradation is caused mostly by human activities including
   - (a) Deforestation
   - (b) Hunting activities
   - (c) Urbanization
   - (d) Industrialization
   - (e) All of the above

2. The conservation and management of the environment is effected by
   - (a) Preventing loss at biodiversity
   - (b) Climatic changes
   - (c) Water pollution
   - (d) Depletion of the ozone layer and land degradation
   - (e) All of the above

3. The strategy for waste management includes
   - (a) Source reduction
   - (b) Recycling
   - (c) Disposal
   - (d) All of the above

4. A waste is considered hazardous if it
   - (a) Catches fire easily
   - (b) Is corrosive
   - (c) Releases ionizing radiation
   - (d) Is toxic
   - (e) All of the above

5. The most important method for the disposing hazardous waste is
   - (a) Landfill disposal
   - (b) Incineration
   - (c) Dumping at sea
   - (d) All of the above

6. Environmental quality can be managed by minimizing
   - (a) Air pollution
   - (b) Water pollution
   - (c) Land pollution
   - (d) All of the above

### ANSWERS

| | | | | |
|---|---|---|---|---|
| 1. (e) | 2. (e) | 3. (d) | 4. (e) | 5. (a) |
| 6. (d) | | | | |

## [B]  Fill in the blanks.

1. The environment is the sum total of _____ and _____ components.
2. The degradation of environmental quality is caused by _____
3. Deforested land is used for _____, _____, and _____.
4. The most important effect of deforestation is the cutting down of _____.
5. Photosynthesis involves using the _____ of the atmosphere and generating _____.
6. Urbanization is caused basically by _____.
7. The most devastating environmental pollution episode is the _____.
8. The best way for the management of solid waste is by _____.
9. The most important way of waste management is by using _____.
10. A waste which catches fire easily is called _____ waste.

### ANSWERS

| | |
|---|---|
| 1. Biotic, abiotic | 2. Human activities |
| 3. Cultivation, industrialization, urbanization | 4. Photosynthetic activities |
| 5. $CO_2$, $O_2$ | 6. Loss of forestland |
| 7. Bhopal gas tragedy | 8. Landfill disposal |
| 9. Gas material | 10. Hazardous |

## [C]  Short-answer questions

1. What do you understand by the term 'environment'?
2. How does environmental degradation occur?
3. How is the environment managed?
4. Write a note on the management of solid waste.
5. How can industrial waste be controlled?
6. How is hazardous waste disposed?
7. Discuss the role of an individual in pollution prevention?
8. How is environmental quality managed?
9. Write a note on environment protection acts.

# Environmental Disasters and Their Management

## 6.1 INTRODUCTION

A disaster is a sudden calamity or natural catastrophe that causes a large number of people to be displaced, injured, or killed. The harm caused depends on the nature of the event and its intensity. Disasters can be either man-made or due to natural activities. Human-made disasters include chemical, industrial, and nuclear accidents, the most common examples being the Bhopal gas tragedy and the Chernobyl nuclear episode.

Natural disasters, for example, floods, earthquakes, cyclones, and landslides, arise due to natural causes that cannot be controlled by humans and are generally unavoidable. In most of the cases, we have to deal with the after-effects of the event. In such cases, appropriate steps can be taken to minimize the harm. The most important aspect of disasters is that they drastically imbalance the ecosystem by polluting waterbodies and introducing pollutants in all segments of the environment.

## 6.2 HUMAN-MADE DISASTERS

Man-made disasters can be defined as the hazards caused primarily due to human error or negligence, resulting in significant injuries or deaths. As already stated, the most common examples of man-made disasters are the Bhopal gas tragedy and the Chernobyl nuclear episode.

### 6.2.1 Bhopal Gas Disaster

On the night of 2 December 1984, the world's worst-ever industrial disaster took place in Bhopal, India. It is also known as the Hiroshima of the chemical industry because of the death toll and the suffering it caused, as a result of leaking of 27 tonnes of methyl isocyanate (MIC) and other deadly gases from the Union Carbide's pesticide manufacturing factory in Bhopal. The MIC was used in the manufacturing of the insecticide carbaryl which was marketed under the commercial name Sevin. The sequence of the reactions involved is as follows:

$$CH_3NH_2 + COCl_2 \longrightarrow CH_3\text{—}N{=}C{=}O + 2HCl$$

Methyl amine   Phosgene            Methyl isocyanate

$$CH_3\text{—}N{=}C{=}O + \underset{\text{(naphthol)}}{\text{OH}} \longrightarrow \underset{\text{Carbaryl}}{O\text{—}C\text{—}N\text{—}CH_3}$$

Methyl isocyanate, which was stored in the tanks, leaked and escaped into the surrounding environment. A cloud of the poisonous gases was formed over a large area of the city, killing about 4000 people and affecting thousands of others. Approximately, half-a-million people were exposed to the leaked gases and at least 22,000 have died so far because of the effects of the exposure. It is estimated that about 120,000 people are suffering from serious long-term health effects. The number of deaths as reported at that time is much lower than the actual number because the deaths continued to occur due to the long-term effects of the exposure to the gas. In fact, on an average, one person died per hour because of these long-term effects of exposure.

The gas leakage caused irritation in the eyes, nose, and mouth. The affected people felt burning sensations as that of frying chillies. They started coughing and froth streaking up with blood from their mouths. They started running here and there. Some had convulsions and died while the others lost control over their senses.

Water had probably entered into the largest MIC tank. Unfortunately, none of the six safety systems was operational and the plant siren was also not working. The vent gas scrubber was also turned off; otherwise, the leaking gas could have been detoxified. The pipe connecting to the flare tower had also been removed for maintenance. The refrigeration system for cooling liquid MIC was shut down to save expenses on electricity. Out of the three storage tanks, tank E 619 was empty while tank E 610 contained 40 tonnes and tank E 611 contained 15 tonnes of the gas. On that disastrous night, water entered into the tank E 610 and a deadly cloud comprising MIC, hydrogen cyanide, monomethyl amine, and other poisonous chemicals spread out over the city of Bhopal.

Methyl isocyanate is always associated with unreacted phosgence ($COCl_2$) to the extent of about 2%. The threshold limiting value (TLV) for MIC is 0.02 parts per million (ppm) and for $COCl_2$, it is 0.1 ppm. Exposure to MIC results in tightness in the chest and breathing troubles due to irritation of the respiratory tract. As MIC is invariably accompanied by $COCl_2$, the combined effect becomes fatal within a span of 24 hours. $COCl_2$ is known to be a deadly, poisonous gas and was used as a poison gas during World War I. The immediate symptoms of

MIC–COCl$_2$ poisoning include bronchospasms, coughing, constriction, and chest pain. The majority of the victims (about 80%) died within 24 hours of the tragedy while those who survived died of bronchopneumonia or became disabled for the rest of their lives.

It is appropriate to mention here that Du Pont has developed a process (the reaction is given below) for producing MIC on demand so that it need not be stored as was the case with Union Carbide.

$$\text{CH}_3\text{NH}_2 + \text{CO} \rightarrow \text{CH}_3\,\text{NHCHO} \xrightarrow{\text{O}_2 > 240^\circ\text{C}} \text{CH}_3\,\text{NCO}$$

MIC 84–89% yield

Using the above procedures, disasters such as the Bhopal gas tragedy could be avoided.

## 6.2.2  Chernobyl Nuclear Disaster

The explosion at the Chernobyl nuclear plant in USSR (now Ukraine) is the worst nuclear disaster known till date. On 26 April 1986, the control rods of the fourth reactor were pulled out during the night shift as a part of a deliberate but unauthorized experiment. The temperature of the core shot up. The graphite in the core caught fire and melted the fuel. The pressure of the hydrogen build-up led to the cracks in the ceiling and the explosions were so severe that the 1000-tonne concrete lid of the reactor blew off. The fire produced a cloud of radioactive particles which went about 5000 ft up in the atmosphere. The radioactive cloud spread north-westwards and affected a large area of Ukraine, Byelorussia, Russia, and North Europe. The accident became known to the public only when high levels of radioactivity were recorded by the workers of another nuclear power plant in Sweden.

It was reported that about 237 people suffered from acute radiation sickness, of which 31 died. In the 30-km zone, about 115,000 people were evacuated and about 24,000 people were affected by an average radiation of 0.43 sievert (Sv). A total of about 3 billion people in the Northern Hemisphere were affected by radiation. It was found that people suffered from diseases such as leukaemia, thyroid, and cancer due to radiation exposure.

The vegetation within a 7-km area of the power plant was considerably damaged. The pine trees showed the presence of radioactivity even after four years of the accident. The area was uninhabitable due to the contamination of soil and water.

## 6.3  NATURAL DISASTERS

Natural disasters arise due to natural causes and, unlike human-made disasters, cannot be controlled by humans and are mostly unavoidable. These include floods, earthquakes, tsunamis, volcanoes, droughts, landslides, and avalanches.

### 6.3.1  Floods

Floods are the most frequently occurring natural disaster. Normally, floods are caused by overflowing of rivers, usually because of heavy rainfall. Floods are likely to occur if the rainfall is much heavier than usual, continues for a longer period, is unseasonal or occurs in unexpected places. When more water flows into a river than can be drained out, overflowing occurs, leading to floods.

Floods are the most frequently occurring
natural disasters

Floods may occur in any season of the year, depending on the climate and rainfall of a region. In tropical countries, rivers are flooded during the rainy season, whereas there is hardly any flow during the rest of the year. Some rivers have originated from the mountains and are fed by the melting glaciers. Such rivers often flood during the spring and summer seasons because of the speedy melting of snow and ice. The discharge of unusually large amounts of carbon dioxide in the atmosphere by human activities leads to the greenhouse effect, increasing the global temperature. An increase in the global temperature will increase the rate of glacier melting, which will consequently flood the rivers.

In India, the lower plains, particularly Gujarat, North-East states, Bihar, Uttar Pradesh, and West Bengal (through which the river Ganga flows), and Assam (through which the river Brahmaputra flows), suffer from the adverse effects of floods every year. Only a small fraction (10%–15%) of the river water can be stored in dams and reservoirs. The remaining 85%–90% of the rainwater flows through rivers and ultimately into the sea. Floods, therefore, will remain a recurrent phenomenon in India. The recent floods in Mumbai, Tamil Nadu, Gujarat, and Assam proved devastating. These were attributed to excessive rainfall. The level of water in these flooded places reached so high that it choked the drainage system of houses. This resulted in the accumulation of filth, not only on the streets but also in the houses. This filth contained bacteria that caused health hazards. The occurrence of diseases including cholera, dysentery, influenza, and typhoid is the outcome of such floods. In addition, the standing water did not drain out for weeks, resulting in the loss of vegetation and crops.

An important step to reduce the devastation caused by floods is to have flood forecasting and warning services. This is available in most of the countries across the globe. If there is a forecast of the likelihood of floods in a particular zone, people in the low-lying areas can be evacuated and taken to safer places. This measure may substantially reduce the loss of life and property due to floods. Some of the possible mitigation measures are as follows:

(i) The excess flow of water during the monsoons should be stored in underground tanks, from where it can be pumped into overhead tanks and used whenever required.

(ii) Embankments can be constructed on the river to prevent or minimize the overflow of water.

(iii) Once a place has been flooded, arrangements should be made to pump out the excess water.

(iv) The loss due to floods should be insured.

(v) Authorities should make sure that relief reaches the victims within the shortest possible time.

## 6.3.2  Earthquakes

Earthquakes are one of the most destructive natural disasters. There is absolutely no warning system which can forecast the occurrence of an earthquake. Thus, it is rather impossible to make preparations against damage, collapse of buildings, and loss of life and property caused by this natural calamity.

An earthquake is a sudden violent shaking of the earth's surface. It is usually caused by the faults in the rocks of the earth's surface—a break along which one rock mass has rubbed on another with great force and friction. The large amount of energy generated due to this rubbing creates vibrations. These vibrations may travel thousands of kilometres. An earthquake is the strongest along the fault line made by the shifting of earth blocks. After an earthquake, most of the changes or destruction on the earth may be seen along this fault. The part of the fault line where the vibration is felt most strongly is called the epicentre of the earthquake. The earth's trembling may cause cracks in buildings or their collapse. A large number of people may be injured or killed. An earthquake with a great destructive capacity may change the earth's surface a little. In some places, the ground on one side of the fault may rise higher or go down lower than it was before.

In some regions of the world, for example, Japan, earthquakes occur frequently. Fortunately, they are not always severe and do not cause much damage. However, in the famous Japanese earthquake of 1923, more than 100,000 people died. Such a massive loss of life is usually due to falling of buildings and fires caused due to broken electrical and gas lines.

The study of earthquakes is known as seismology. The intensity of earthquake is determined by instruments called seismographs. A scale for measuring the

Gujarat earthquake, 2001

intensity of an earthquake was developed by Charles F. Richter in 1935. The strength of an earthquake is indicated by a number called the Richter magnitude, which is obtained from seismographs. Studies found that earthquakes measuring up to 5 or 6 on the Richter scale are not very harmful. However, earthquakes above 7 (7–12) can be disastrous. Table 6.1 lists the details of the earthquakes which occurred in different parts of the globe.

**Table 6.1**   Major earthquakes of the world

| Year | Location | Deaths | Intensity (Richter Scale) |
|---|---|---|---|
| 1905 | Kangra (HP), India | Large number | 8.0 |
| 1906 | San Francisco, USA | 3,000 | NA |
| 1905 | Avezzano, Italy | 32,610 | NA |
| 1920 | Gansu, China | 235,000 | NA |
| 1923 | Tokyo, Japan | 142,800 | NA |
| 1934 | India–Nepal border at Bihar | Large number | 8.3 |
| 1939 | Ezican, Turkey | 32,740 | NA |
| 1941 | Andaman Islands, India | Large number | 8.1 |
| 1950 | Assam, India | Large number | 8.5 |
| 1960 | Agadin, Morocco | 12,000 | NA |
| 1970 | Chimbote, Peru | 67,000 | NA |
| 1975 | Lahul Spiti (J & K), India | Large number | 6.2 |
| 1976 | Guatemala city, Guatemala | 67,000 | NA |
| 1976 | Tangshan, China | 290,000 | NA |
| 1985 | Mexico City, Mexico | 10,000 | NA |
| 1988 | India–Nepal border at Bihar | 900 | 6.5 |
| 1988 | Spilak, Armenia | 25,000 | NA |
| 1989 | San Francisco, USA | 68 | NA |

*Contd...*

**Table 6.1** *Contd...*

| Year | Location | Deaths | Intensity (Richter Scale) |
|------|----------|--------|---------------------------|
| 1991 | Uttarkashi (UP), India | 10,000 | 6.6 |
| 1993 | Latur (Maharashtra), India | 40 | 6.3 |
| 1995 | Kote, Japan | 100,000 | NA |
| 1997 | Jabalpur (MP), India | 40 | 6.0 |
| 1999 | Chamoli (UP), India | Extensive | 6.8 |
| 1999 | Izmit, Turkey | 17,000 | NA |
| 1999 | Taichung, Taiwan | 2,400 | NA |
| 2001 | Bhuj (Gujarat), India | 20,000 | 6.9 |

NA – Not available

The best mitigation measure for earthquakes is basically the construction of earthquake-resistant shelters (houses). Disaster-linked insurance should cover not only life but also household goods, cattle, structures, crops, and so on.

An important aspect associated with an earthquake is what to do after one strikes. This requires a large amount of work including rescuing trapped people, providing medical help, and taking out dead bodies from the debris. Dead bodies have to be disposed of (by cremation or other means) before they start decomposing and lead to epidemics.

As already discussed, about 50%–60% land area of India is vulnerable to seismic activities of varying intensities. Most of the vulnerable areas are located in the Himalayas and sub-Himalayan regions. In India, earthquakes occurred in 1934 (about 6000 casualties), 1935 (about 40,000 casualties), and 1950 (574 casualties). The most disastrous earthquake in the history of India struck Gujarat on 26 January 2001, claimed more than 20,000 lives, and injured about 167,000. The earthquake of North America that occurred in 1966 in San Francisco, California, killed about 700 people. On 11 March 2011, an earthquake having a magnitude of 9 occurred along the northeastern coast of Honshu Island in Japan. The death toll was close to 20,000 and over 3000 people went missing in this catastrophe.

## 6.3.3  Tsunami

'Tsunami' is a Japanese word, meaning harbour (*tsu*) and wave (*nami*). Tsunamis are caused by the earth's sudden vertical movement along faults (these are the same forces that cause earthquakes).

Earthquakes that occur below the surface of the oceans are referred to as submarine earthquakes which can form huge waves that can be up to 40 feet high and 350 km long (from crest to crest). These huge waves cross the oceans at a great speed and can bring about massive destruction and loss of life. These long and high waves are known as tsunamis. Besides undersea earthquakes, tsunamis can also be generated by any disturbance that rapidly displaces a large mass of water, such as volcanic eruptions or submarine landslides. In India, a tsunami occurred on 26 December 2004 in Nicobar Islands, causing havoc and killing about 310,000 people. This was the deadliest tsunami recorded in the history of the humankind. Tsunamis are also responsible for a number of environmental problems. Table 6.2 lists the details of some of the worst tsunamis in history.

The most destructive tsunami occurred in Japan on 11 March 2011. It was triggered by an earthquake. Waves as high as 10 m struck Japan, minutes after the earthquake. About 7348 deaths, 2603 injured people, and 10,947 missing cases were reported. About 100,000 buildings were damaged or destroyed. At least three nuclear reactors suffered explosions due to the hydrogen gas that had built up. According to Japanese Prime Minister Naoto Kan, this tsunami was the most difficult crisis for Japan after World War II.

A warning system operates continuously around the seismically active areas of the Pacific Ocean to alert coastal residents for the possible occurrence of a tsunami. This system has been responsible for averting the loss of a number of lives. In India, such a system has not been installed so far.

### 6.3.4  Volcanoes

Volcanoes are openings in the earth's surface through which extremely hot lava, gases, and rock fragments are ejected, sometimes with explosive force. Volcanic activity, caused by a build-up of pressure as a result of the earth's movements, forces magma out through a weak region on the earth's surface. The pressure usually builds up over a long period of time (Figure 6.1).

Any further increase in pressure causes the magma to melt or blast a channel in a fractured part of the rock. Finally, the magma rushes up through the channel and comes out by blasting an opening. The molten lava coming out of the opening gradually piles up around the vent, forming a conical hill or mountain that is

**Table 6.2**  Some major tsunamis of the world

| Date | Place | Maximum height of seismic waves (in m) | Deaths |
|---|---|---|---|
| 2 September 1992 | Nicaragua | 10 | > 170 |
| 12 December 1992 | Flores Island | 20 | > 110 |
| 12 July 1993 | Papua (New Guinea) | 15 | > 2,500 |
| 12 July 1993 | Okushiri (Japan) | 15 | > 2,500 |
| 26 December 2004 | Sumatra (Indonesia) | 15 | > 200,000 |
| 17 July 2006 | S.W. Java (Indonesia) | > 26 | > 600 |
| 11 March 2011 | Tohoku (Japan) | > 15 | > 10,000 |

commonly called a volcano. After eruption stops, a bowl-like crater forms at the top.

It is normally not possible to predict the eruption of volcanoes. The only remedy involves evacuation of people from the region of volcanic eruption. The speedy flow of an immense volume of hot and liquid lava down the slope of the volcanic eruption site causes all objects such as vegetation, crops, houses, buildings, animals, and people (if not evacuated in time) to burn and get destroyed. A timely evacuation can avert a severe loss of life and property. Volcanoes are found only in certain well-defined areas of the earth where continental plates collide. It is appropriate to mention here that the most severe volcanic eruption occurred on 14 April 2010 at Eyjafjallajökull. In fact, a series of volcanic eruptions occurred. These eruptions resulted in the suspension of dust particles to such an extent that the visibility was reduced to nil, resulting in the cancellation of a number of flights. For this reason, airline companies incurred a large amount of financial losses.

Volcanic eruptions contribute to environmental pollution. The atmosphere is polluted by oxides of carbon, nitrogen, sulphur, and particulate matter. The leftover solid magma pollutes the land. When it rains, magma particles are washed down and mix with waterbodies. There are no warning signs for volcanic eruptions. One has to deal only with the after-effects.

## 6.3.5  Cyclones

A cyclone is a circular, whirling mass of cloud and air centred on an area of low atmosphere pressure. A cyclone is generally accompanied by winds of high

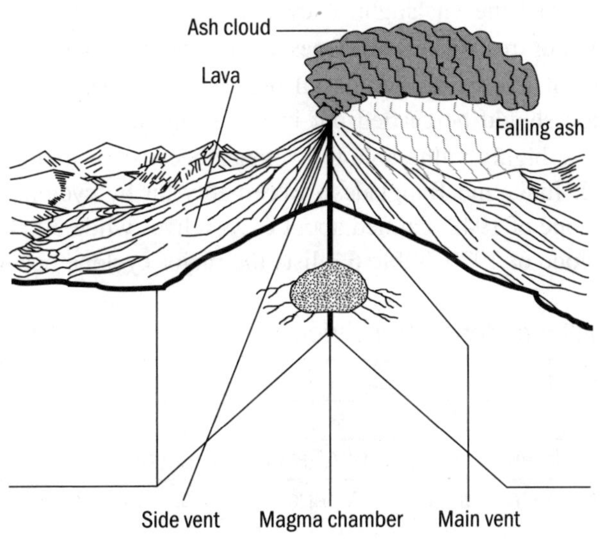


**Fig. 6.1**  Schematic diagram of a volcano

speed and heavy rainfall. The centre of the cyclone is called the 'eye' and it has unusually quiet conditions, that is, the eye has calm weather conditions.

A hurricane is a tropical cyclone. It is a powerful whirling tropical storm that measures 320–480 km in diameter. The wind near the centre of a hurricane blows at a high speed. Hurricane winds rotate around the eye, a calm area in the centre of the storm. It occurs as a result of low air pressure over oceans in tropical regions. It is usually accompanied by heavy rain.

India has a long coastline of about 5700 km, which is exposed to tropical cyclones arising in the Bay of Bengal and the Arabian Sea. The Indian Ocean is one of the six major cyclone-prone regions of the world. In India, cyclones usually occur in April and December. The eastern coastline is more prone to cyclones as it is hit by about 80% of the total cyclones that occur in the region. A cyclone occurred in the area around the University of Delhi in 1978 and caused severe damage to life and property.

The occurrence of cyclones is a natural process and thus cannot be controlled. However, its effects can be decreased by taking appropriate measures, some of which are as follows:

(i) Early warning systems can be installed along the coastlines to forecast any expected cyclone so that people in the area can be evacuated to safer areas.

(ii) It is best to develop permanent shelters (which should be cyclone resident) for the affected people. In other times, these shelters can be used for recreational purposes.

(iii) Concrete houses should be built in cyclone-prone areas as such houses can withstand the onslaught of cyclones.

(iv) Plantation of trees is helpful. Trees act as effective wind and tide breakers.

(v) Building of houses in the coastal regions is not permitted. Instead, tree plantation should be carried out in these regions.

Bangladesh is highly vulnerable to cyclones because of its location near the Bay of Bengal. India and Bangladesh were badly hit by cyclones in 1942 and 1970. The cyclone of 1942 claimed about 61,000 lives while 300,000 lives were lost in the cyclone of 1970. Table 6.3 lists the major cyclone occurrences.

**Table 6.3** Major cyclones of the world

| Year | Country | Deaths |
|------|---------|--------|
| 1961 | USA | 600 |
| 1965 | Florida and Louisiana, USA (Hurricane Betsy) | 75 |
| 1988 | Caribbean and Central America (Hurricane Gilbert) | 355 |
| 1991 | Bangladesh | 139,000 |
| 1992 | Florida and Louisiana, USA (Hurricane Andrew) | 62 |

### 6.3.6  Drought

Drought is a significant environmental problem and is mainly caused by a lower-than-average rainfall over a long period of time. Droughts are perennial features in some states of India. About 16% of the country's population is drought-prone. Most of the drought-prone areas lie in arid and semi-arid regions of the country. In drought-hit areas, the land becomes dry, develops cracks, and consequently becomes so barren that it can no longer support vegetation. As a result, people have to depend on the government for food and other basic facilities. Even cattle perish due to the non-availability of water and food.

### 6.3.7  Landslides

The descent of earth and rock down a mountain is called a landslide. It can be caused by either rains or by melting of glaciers on mountains, or earthquakes. During a landslide, there may be destruction across a wide area of habitable or agricultural land. It is difficult to forecast a landslide. However, appropriate rescue operations could be undertaken to minimize human and property loss.

### 6.3.8  Avalanches

Avalanches are similar to landslides but occur in snow-covered areas of high mountains. A massive amount of ice becomes loose and slides down the mountain slopes at a great speed. They increase in size as they collect more snow and ice while sliding down the mountains. Avalanches can be so destructive that sometimes in the course of their movement, they bury the entire village. Avalanches damage the roads and destroy the houses which lie in their path.

A timely prediction and forecasting, followed by safety measures can considerably reduce the life and property loss in an avalanche-hit area. Avalanches in India mainly occur in the mountain ranges of Jammu and Kashmir, Himachal Pradesh, and Uttarakhand. A major cause of avalanches and landslides is the lack of vegetation in the mountains.

## 6.4  DISASTER MANAGEMENT

In the cases of all types of disasters, post-disaster management, that is, dealing with the aftermaths of a disaster, is very important. It involves the following:

  (i) Evacuation of the people

 (ii) Rescue of the trapped

(iii) Providing medical aid to the injured

(iv) Firefighting in the case of fires

 (v) Shifting the injured to hospitals

(vi) Providing relief and shelter to the disaster victims

(vii) Caring for casualties

## 6.5   IMPACT OF DISASTERS ON THE ENVIRONMENT

Disasters have the following effects on the environment:

(i) **Destruction of property:** The property or houses destroyed in a disaster have to be repaired or rebuilt. The construction activities as well as cleaning up of the debris affect the environment substantially.

(ii) **Destruction of crops:** Standing crops are destroyed by natural disasters, such as floods, cyclones, and earthquakes.

(iii) **Environmental pollution:** The release of gases and particulate matter in the atmosphere by volcanic eruptions causes environmental pollution.

(iv) **Dead bodies:** Dead bodies have to be disposed of as soon as possible. It generally takes a couple of days for the bodies to start decomposing, which causes foul smell and at times has resulted in the spread of epidemics.

(v) **Floods:** Floods, if not controlled in time, can also cause epidemics.

The impact of disasters on the environment varies, depending on the nature and type of disaster.

# SUMMARY

- A disaster is a sudden calamity or natural catastrophe, responsible for displacing, injuring, or killing a large number of people.
- A disaster can either be man-made or natural.
- Examples of man-made disasters include the Bhopal gas disaster and the Chernobyl nuclear disaster.
- Natural disasters arise due to natural causes and are unavoidable. Examples include floods, earthquakes, tsunamis, volcanoes, droughts, landslides, and avalanches.
- Floods are mostly caused by the overflowing of rivers, usually due to heavy rains.
- An earthquake is one of the most destructive natural disasters and primarily involves a violent trembling of the earth's surface.
- The study of earthquakes is known as seismology.
- Earthquakes that occur below the surface of oceans are called submarine earthquakes.
- The long and high waves, created due to the occurrence of submarine earthquakes, are known as tsunamis.
- Volcanoes are openings in the earth's surface through which hot lava, gases, and rock fragments are ejected.

- A cyclone is a circular, whirling of cloud and air centred on an area of low atmospheric pressure.
- A drought is caused by a lower-than-average rainfall over a long period of time.
- The descent of earth and rock down a mountain in called a landslide.
- Avalanches are similar to landslides but occur in snow-covered areas of high mountains.
- In all types of disasters, the most important aspect is the post-disaster management.
- Disasters—both natural and man-made—are extremely harmful to the environment.

# EXERCISE

## [A] Multiple-choice questions

1. The most important aspect of disasters is
   - (a) Damage to the ecosystems
   - (b) Pollution of waterbodies
   - (c) Discharge of pollutants into all segments of the environment
   - (d) All are equally important

2. Which of the following statements are correct about natural disasters?
   - (a) Natural disasters arise due to natural causes.
   - (b) These are unavoidable.
   - (c) These cannot be controlled by humans.
   - (d) All are correct

3. Which of the following in your opinion is the most harmful natural disaster?
   - (a) Earthquakes
   - (b) Floods
   - (c) Both (a) and (b)
   - (d) None of the above

4. The most devastating floods were reported in India from
   - (a) Gujarat
   - (b) Assam
   - (c) Mumbai
   - (d) Both (a) and (b)

5. The 2011 earthquake in Japan claimed about _____ lives.
   - (a) 10,000
   - (b) 5,000
   - (c) 20,000
   - (d) 1,000

6. The most destructive tsunami in history occurred in
    (a) Japan                                  (b) Indonesia
    (c) India                                  (d) All were equally destructive
7. Post-disaster management includes
    (a) Evacuation of the people        (b) Rescue of the trapped
    (c) Shifting the injured to hospitals (d) Caring for casualties
    (e) All of the above

### ANSWERS

| | | | | |
|---|---|---|---|---|
| 1. (d) | 2. (d) | 3. (c) | 4. (d) | 5. (c) |
| 6. (a) | 7. (e) | | | |

## [B] Fill in the blanks.

1. The Bhopal gas disaster is a ______ disaster.
2. The most frequently occurring natural disaster is the ______.
3. The most destructive natural disaster is an ______.
4. In India, the most devastating earthquake occurred in ______.
5. Earthquakes occurring below the surface of the oceans are called ______ earthquakes.
6. The most destructive tsunami occurred in ______.
7. The most severe volcanic eruption occurred in ______.
8. A circular, whirling mass of cloud and air centred on an area of low atmospheric pressure is called ______.
9. The most important aspect of any disaster is ______ management.

### ANSWERS

| | |
|---|---|
| 1. Man-made | 2. Flood |
| 3. Earthquake | 4. Bhuj (Gujarat) |
| 5. Submarine | 6. Japan |
| 7. Eyjafjallajökull | 8. Cyclone |
| 9. Post-disaster | |

## [C] Short-answer questions

1. Explain the term 'disaster'.
2. The Bhopal gas disaster was caused due to the leakage of MIC from storage tanks. How can the occurrence of such a disaster be prevented?
3. How does the discharge of large amounts of $CO_2$ cause floods?

4. How is a tsunami caused?
5. What is a volcano? How does it affect the environment?
6. Write notes on:
   (a) Cyclones
   (b) Droughts
   (c) Avalanches
7. How can a disaster be managed?
8. What is the impact of disasters on the environment?

# Natural Resources

## 7.1   INTRODUCTION

The term 'environment', as we know, means the 'surroundings' of an object. In fact, everything around us is a part of our environment. While all living beings interact intimately with their environment, the interaction of human beings with the environment is the maximum.

The environment provides various essential resources that are necessary for the sustenance of life. The three primary natural resources of the environment, available to living beings, include air, water, and land. In addition, sunlight provides energy while plants and soil nutrients and minerals are found in plants and soil. Another important natural resource is the forest which is the storehouse of a large number of important minerals. Through natural resources, humans meet most of their requirements of food, clothing, accommodation, and transportation.

Human beings have exploited natural resources since the dawn of civilization. Globally, these natural resources have been expolited at rates that are much higher than the rates at which these resources can be naturally replenished. Phenomena, such as population explosion, considerable increase in per capita resource demand, and continuous industrial developments are widening the gap between exploitation and replenishment. All these have led to the disruption of the functioning of the natural environment substantially.

The natural environment, which includes forests, grasslands, deserts, rivers, lakes, oceans, and so on is the habitat for different communities of plants and animals. The interaction between the abiotic and biotic components of nature is the basis for the formation of various types of ecosystems (for more details, refer to Chapter 2, Section 2.2).

## 7.2   TYPES OF NATURAL RESOURCES

Natural resources can be categorized into renewable and non-renewable. Renewable resources get replenished in a human's lifetime and are not likely to be completely exhausted by human consumption. Air, sunlight, water, oxygen, and nitrogen are examples of renewable resources. The oxygen present in the air is replenished by photosynthesis; in a similar way, nitrogen gets constantly renewed.

Non-renewable resources cannot be easily replenished by the environment and are used up much faster than they are produced. Examples of such resources include fossil fuels which are formed in millions of years. Figure 7.1 lists some renewable and non-renewable natural resources.

## 7.3   EARTH RESOURCES

Earth resources comprise atmosphere, hydrosphere, lithosphere, and biosphere. Living beings including humans are dependent on all these resources for their sustenance.

### 7.3.1   Atmosphere

The region of air above the earth's surface is called the atmosphere. It extends up to a height of about 500 km from the earth's surface. The atmosphere consists of a number of gases (for details, refer to Chapter 1, Table 1.1).

Out of the various gases present in the atmosphere, the most prominent are oxygen and carbon dioxide. Carbon dioxide is needed by plants for photosynthes. It is also responsible for the greenhouse gas effect. Oxygen is used by living beings for respiration (metabolic requirement).

In fact, no life can survive without oxygen. It is produced by the reaction between carbon dioxide and water in the presence of sunlight and chlorophyll (during photosynthesis, chlorophyll in plants absorb light to convert carbon dioxide and water into glucose, and release oxygen as a by-product).

The temperature of the atmosphere varies from $-92°C$ to $1200°C$, depending on its height from the earth's surface. The atmosphere is divided into four regions: (i) troposphere, (ii) stratosphere, (iii) mesosphere, and (iv) thermosphere (for more details, refer to Chapter 1, Table 1.1). Among these regions of the

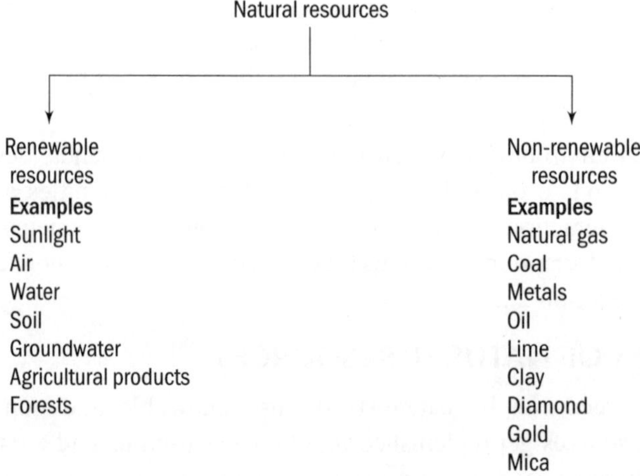


**Fig. 7.1**   Various types of renewable and non-renewable natural resources

atmosphere, the stratosphere is the most important (Chapter 2, Figure 2.2). It contains a layer of ozone which absorbs harmful ultraviolet (UV) radiation from the sun. The UV radiation is known to cause cancer. The solar energy reaching the earth is absorbed by the earth's surface, resultantly increasing its temperature. The rest of the heat radiates back to the atmosphere. Some amount of the heat is trapped by greenhouse gases (GHGs), such as carbon dioxide and methane, which are responsible for global warming.

Living beings cannot survive without air, even for a few seconds. As air is essential for survival, it must be kept clean and free of pollutants. Various pollutants, such as oxides of carbon, sulphur, and nitrogen, are discharged into the atmosphere by industrial waste units and by burning of fuels in automobiles and power-generating units. In fact, the growing number of automobiles, such as scooters, motorcycles, cars, buses, and trucks, that run on fossil fuels (petrol and diesel) is the major cause of air pollution in cities. Air pollution severely affects human health; it is responsible for acute and chronic respiratory problems, such as lung infections, asthma, and even cancer. It is also responsible for acid rain.

## 7.3.2  Hydrosphere

The hydrosphere covers about two-thirds of the earth's surface. This may imply that the supply of water on our planet is inexhaustible. However, oceans alone account for 97% of the earth's total water supply. The ocean water has high-salt content and cannot be used for human consumption and other activities, such as agriculture. Of the remaining 3%, about 2% is blocked in the polar ice caps and glaciers, and only about 1% is available as freshwater in the form of rivers, lakes, reservoirs, and groundwater. In fact, only this 1% of freshwater is suitable for human consumption, agriculture, and industrial uses.

Clean water is needed for drinking which is a metabolic requirement for all living processes. In addition, water is used for washing, cooking, agriculture, and industry. Electricity or hydro energy is harnessed from falling water or water falling very fast.

If existing supplies are not properly harnessed, wastage is not avoided, and pollution is not checked, then a serious water crisis is looming all over the world. Water pollution, as a result of the presence of dissolved or suspended chemical substances, changes the physical properties of water, such as its colour, taste, temperature, and makes it acidic, alkaline, or saline. Contamination of water with toxic substances such as arsenic, cyanide, ammonia, mercury, lead, phenol, pesticide makes it harmful for human use. These substances are also the cause of many diseases, such as cholera, typhoid, and dysentery. Millions of people all over the world, particularly in developing countries, die every year from water-borne diseases. Water gets polluted when industrial wastes, sewage, domestic wastes, and agrochemicals are discharged into waterbodies. Oil spills which mainly happen as a result of oil tanker accidents are another major cause of water pollution, particularly marine pollution.

### 7.3.3 Lithosphere

The earth, the third planet in the solar system, is the only planet that supports life. The lithosphere includes the crust and uppermost mantle of the earth's surface. Rocks in the lithosphere are subjected to continuous processes of physical, chemical, and biological weathering. The resulting primitive soil is colonized by higher plants. Soil (topsoil) plays a very important role in the lives of human beings and animals as it produces food for them. However, human activities cause soil pollution. Some of the pollutants include pesticides, fertilizers, particulate matter, industrial wastes, sewage, and domestic wastes.

The uppermost layer of the soil is essential because all nutrients required by plants are present in this layer. Removal of the topsoil, that is soil erosion, is a natural process and is evoked by wind, water, and ocean waves. Activities such as felling of trees, overgrazing, overcropping, and improper tilting accelerate soil erosion.

### 7.3.4 Biosphere

The biosphere is composed of water, atmosphere, and many small coexisting ecosystems. It consists of three main subdivisions: (i) lithosphere (land), (ii) hydrosphere (water), and (iii) atmosphere (air) or the gaseous envelope of the earth that extends up to a height of 22.5 km. The graphical representation of the biosphere is given in Chapter 1, Figure 1.3.

The biosphere is the area of contact and interaction between the lithosphere, hydrosphere, and atmosphere. For the continouous funtioning of the biosphere, it is extremely important that different life forms not only interact in the local communities but also all species and communities interact globally (Figure 2.4). Living organisms are mostly confined to those parts of the biosphere that receive solar radiation during the day. The sun is the source of energy for life within the biosphere and without it the biosphere will collapse. Air, water, and soil supply the necessary nutrients to living organisms and are recycled over and over again for the life to continue.

The biosphere provides food to all forms of life and maintains various food chains in nature. Human beings rely on these food chains for their survival. Biomass fuelwood from forests, along with other forms of organic matter, is used as an energy source. Timber from forests is used for construction purposes.

The atmosphere, hydrosphere, lithosphere, and biosphere interact physically and chemically. Thes interactions are mainly in the form of various cycles, such as water cycle, oxygen cycle, nitrogen cycle, and energy cycle (for details, refer to Chapter 3).

In the hydrological or water cycle, water evaporates from the hydrosphere and forms clouds in the atmosphere. These clouds condense and fall in the form of rain. Rain provides moisture to the lithosphere, which is essential for life processes. Also, the action of air on rocks results in the weathering of rocks, which leads ultimately to the formation of soil in which plants grow.

## 7.4  RENEWABLE AND NON-RENEWABLE RESOURCES

As discussed earlier, there are two types of natural resources—renewable and non-renewable. The ecosystems in the biosphere function as resource producers. The driving force of the earth's ecological systems is solar energy which helps in the growth of plants in forests, grasslands, and aquatic ecosystems. The forest ecosystem recycles the dead plant materials and returns nutrients to the soil. In grasslands, the recycling of material is much faster because grass dries up every year after the rains. Solar energy also regulates life in aquatic ecosystems and is responsible for the maintenance of the hydrological cycle.

Our food requirement is met mostly by agricultural ecosystems. Although such ecosystems are dependent on rainfall, the use of agrochemicals, such as fertilizers and pesticides, help in increasing production. However, modern agricultural methods which make use of agrochemicals are largely responsible for a variety of environmental problems, such as the formation of unproductive land. Modern irrigation procedures are responsible for increasing salinity in the soil. In addition, the use of chemical-based pesticides pose health problems for humans.

Various industrial units that produce consumer products need raw materials, including water, minerals, and power. Industrial processes release large amounts of gases and waste products into the environment, which lead to environmental degradation. This can be avoided if the industries are properly managed and their effluents checked and treated before being discharged.

### 7.4.1  Problems Associated with Natural Resources

The overexploitation of natural resources is posing a problem. A major part of the natural resources is consumed by technologically advanced or developed countries. Some countries, such as India and China, also overuse many natural resources because of their huge population. A good indicator of a country's energy consumption is the per capita consumption of natural resources. The per capita consumption of natural resources in developed countries is more than 50 times to that of developing countries. For example, the USA alone, with only about 4% of the world population, consumes about 25% of the total earth resources. Same is the case with waste generation. The developed countries alone generate more than 75% of global industrial wastes and greenhouse gases.

Raising animals for food puts exteme pressure on natural resources than growing crops and vegetables. Thus, countries dependent on meat-based diet use more land, as pastureland, than countries dependent on all-vegetarian diet. However, such a problem does not exist for nations that depend on seafood.

Land as a resource is becoming scarce with increased substantial demands placed on it. Land is needed for food production, animal husbandry, industrial units, and for the ever-growing human settlements. A rational land policy needs to be developed to find a balance among different requirements. Deforestation is the most alarming problem; depletion of forests reduces the oxygen level in the atmosphere, which in turn increases the carbon dioxide concentration. Deforestation leads to decreased supply of food, fuel, timber, fodder, medicinal plants. This loss is beyond repair. Thus, a well-planned forest policy needs to be developed. If required, the trees in forests should be felled in phases so that the place from where the trees are cut can be redeveloped by plantation. Pollution originating from industrial wastes and rural and urban sewage is also acutely affecting land.

## 7.4.2  Non-renewable Resources

Fossil fuels such as coal, oil, and natural gas are the most important non-renewable resources. Another important non-renewable resources are minerals.

### 7.4.2.1  Coal

Coal reserves have been derived from prehistoric forests through the processes of decaying and transformation. Coal was formed from the remains of trees and ferns that grew in swamps some 500 million years ago. Initially, bacterial decomposition and chemical action on such plant debris produced peat (dead plant material) as an intermediate product. Peat is composed of dead leaves, stems, and roots of plants; it mainly consists of cellulose. As a result of high pressure and temperature during geological changes under the earth's surface, peat was transformed into coal. The sequence of changes that results in the formation of coal is depicted in Figure 7.2.

Dead plant material or peat

Coal has been a major contributor to the world's energy needs. India's dependency on coal is very high. About 30% of its energy needs are met through coal. The major consumers of coal are the power, steel, cement, railways, fertilizer, and household sectors. In India, coal reserves are substantial, constituting about 5.7% of the total coal reserves of the world. Direct combustion of coal causes major air pollution. Gases produced from combustion of coal such as oxides of carbon, nitrogen, and sulphur are toxic and potential air pollutants. Besides, the coal industry is responsible for several health hazards, especially, for those working in such plants. With the present rate of coal consumption, soon the coal reserves will be completely exhausted.

### 7.4.2.2  Petroleum

At present, petroleum is the world's most important source of energy. Petroleum is an oily, thick, and generally dark-coloured liquid. It is found deep below the earth's crust, trapped within the rock structure. The origin of the word 'petroleum' lies in two Latin words—*petra* (meaning rocks) and *oleum* (meaning oil). Petroleum is believed to have been formed by the decay of the remains of ancient microscopic marine plants and animals which were buried under the layers of rock and clay over millions of years. As petroleum occurs at a depth of 500–600 km below the surface of the earth, it is obtained by the drilling process. The most important aspect is to locate the oilfields for which scientific methods are now available. Once the drill strikes the oil, the underground pressure of the gas (known as petroleum gas or natural gas) forces the oil to come out to the surface.

Nowadays, petroleum is also obtained by drilling into the seabed. In India, the procedure is used for producing crude oil from Bombay High. The petroleum thus obtained is separated into various fractions at different stages of fractional distillation. The various fractions obtained are given in Table 7.1.

Crude oil if continued to be used at the present rate, will not last too long. So, it must be used judiciously and alternative fuels should be used for the same purpose.

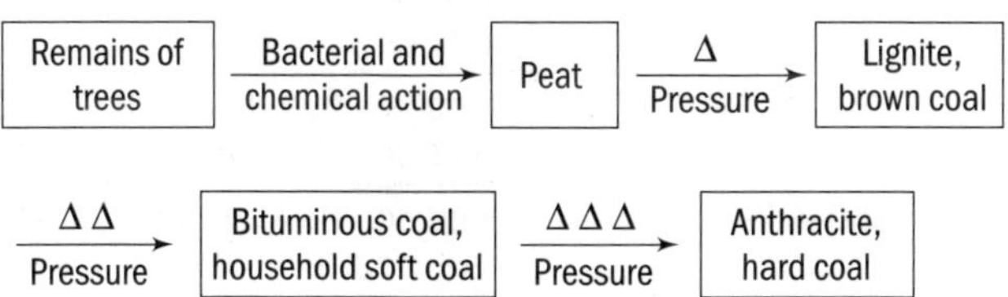


**Fig. 7.2**  Process of coal formation

Offshore drilling of petroleum

### 7.4.2.3  Natural Gas

Natural gas is a mixture of combustible gases and found in naturally occurring oil wells. There are many underground reservoirs of natural gas where petroleum oil is absent. Natural gas, like petroleum, was formed from the decomposition of organic matter trapped in the layers of sedimentary rocks.

In India, the natural gas industry is in its infancy and is largely derived from the cracking units of petroleum refineries. It occurs in large amounts in Bombay High, the Gulf of Cambay, and Ankleshwar in Gujarat. New gas fields have been found in Tripura, Jaisalmer, and the Krishna–Godavari delta.

About 7% of India's total natural gas stock is used in power generation and in the production of fertilizers and petroleum. Natural gas can reduce dependency

**Table 7.1**  Fractions obtained from petroleum refining

| Fraction | Temperature range | Uses |
|---|---|---|
| Petroleum gas | Up to 25°C | Used as fuel. Liquefied petroleum gas (LPG) is used as domestic gas and also for running automobiles. |
| Petroleum | 30–80°C | Used as solvent for the extraction of oils and fats in the industry |
| Gasoline or petrol | 80–170°C | Used as motor fuel, aviation spirit, and also for dry-cleaning |
| Kerosene oil | 170–250°C | Used as a fuel for stoves, for lamps as an illuminant, and as fuel for jet aircraft engines |
| Diesel oil | 250–350°C | Used as fuel for high-speed diesel engines in trains, buses, and cars |
| Fuel oil | 350–400°C | Used for making lubricating oil, paraffin wax, and asphalt |
| Petroleum coke | Residue | Used for heating purposes |

An autorickshaw running on
compressed natural gas

on foreign oil. Nowadays, natural gas is used in the form of compressed natural gas (CNG) for running automobiles, particularly taxis and buses.

### 7.4.2.4  Pollution Caused by Burning of Fossil Fuels

Fuels such as coal, wood, petrol, diesel, and kerosene are used in homes, industries, and transport. Although these fuels meet our energy needs, the products of their combustion cause severe air pollution. Table 7.2 lists the various pollutants, their sources, and harmful effects.

### 7.4.2.5  Minerals

Minerals are natural substances obtained from the earth by mining. They are found to occur in the earth as their salts. A number of metals are necessary for maintaining numerous biological life processes. These are absorbed by plants and used in metabolism. These metals find their way into animals when they consume plants. When animals die, their remains contain the metals that can be used again. This is commonly known as mineral cycle.

For centuries, a number of minerals (both metals and non-metals) have been exploited by human beings. These are mostly used for industrial purposes.They are the backbone of our industries and are of commercial and economic use. Nowadays, minerals such as uranium are used for generating energy; thus, they can be considered an alternative source of energy. A number of minerals such as iron, copper, aluminium are indispensable to meet our day-to-day requirements. India is self-sufficient in about 35 minerals, which are used as raw materials for basic industries. Iron, aluminium, and phosphates, which are available here, are used for making phosphate fertilizers. Some important non-ferrous metals such as copper, zinc, and lead, are imported.

During mining, the particles of the minerals enter the environment, pollute it, and are responsible for numerous health hazards. Some metals are also deposited

**Table 7.2** Pollutants obtained from burning of fossil fuels

| Pollutants | Source | Effects |
| --- | --- | --- |
| Carbon monoxide[*] | Combustion of coal and petrol | Toxic gas |
| Carbon dioxide | Combustion of coal and petrol | Carbon dioxide is a non-toxic gas. However, excess of carbon dioxide in the atmosphere is considered a pollutant as it produces greenhouse effect and is also responsible for global warming. |
| Sulphur dioxide[#] | Combustion of coal and petrol | Causes suffocation and affects lungs |
| Oxides of nitrogen[#] Nitric oxide and nitrogen dioxide | Combustion of coal and petrol | Both are toxic, but nitrogen dioxide is more harmful. It is harmful for both humans and plants. |
| Particulate matter[x] | Combustion of both coal and petrol | Affects lungs |

Notes:

[*]Carbon monoxide is a deadly, poisonous gas. On inhaling, it combines with haemoglobin in blood and restricts transport of oxygen by blood to other parts of body tissues. This leads to respiratory problems, suffocation, and even death.

[#]Both sulphur dioxide and oxides of nitrogen react with air and moisture in the atmosphere to produce sulphuric acid and nitric acid. These are responsible for acid rain.

[x]Particulate matter gets deposited in the lungs and is responsible for a number of health problems, including tuberculosis.

as polymetallic nodules at the oceanic floor. If the current rate of exploitation of minerals continues, then mining activities are not likely to last beyond 2020. Minerals are found in limited quantities and with the present rate of consumption, a number of minerals may not last for long. Conservation means that there should be judicious use with minimum wastage. Therefore, it is best to conserve mineral resources. One way to conserve metals is to extract these minerals from old discarded objects. The recovered materials can be reused after processing. The scraps of used metals can be recycled or used again. This will reduce the demand of many mineral reserves.

The alloys of magnesium are fast replacing steel and reducing the demand for metals such as copper, lead, and tin, which are already in short supply. Substitutes for metals such as mercury, gold, silver, platinum and also for minerals including asbestos are urgently needed.

Mining minerals makes the area after mining useless. The area becomes barren and does not permit growth of any vegetation. Such lands can be covered with fresh topsoil; use of fertilizers, sewage waste, domestic or municipal waste, farmyard manure can help restore the fertility of these degraded and barren lands.

Elements such as arsenic, cadmium, beryllium, chromium, lead, manganese, mercury, selenium, and zinc are extremely toxic in nature. Industrial units that utilize metals in their production processes discharge poisonous metallic wastes into waterbodies. This results in the pollution of waterbodies, which contaminate aquatic organisms and affect humans who consume these organisms. It is best for industries to treat their wastes at the site of generation and discharge only the harmless effluents onto land or waterbodies.

## 7.4.3 Renewable Resources

Natural resources that can be replenished from time to time by natural processes are called renewable resources. The most common renewable resources include air, water, land, forest, food, and energy.

### 7.4.3.1 Air

Air (or the atmosphere) is present in abundance. As we do not use air (except in some chemical processes), there is no question of its replacement. It is mot important to maintain its quality (purity) and composition. The ratio of oxygen to nitrogen in air is 1:4. The percentage of carbon dioxide in the atmosphere is low, about 0.032% by volume. If there is a shortage of carbon dioxide, then there will be a shortage of oxygen too because oxygen is produced from carbon dioxide by photosynthesis. On the other hand, the presence of excess carbon dioxide causes the greenhouse effect and global warming.

It is most important that air should be free of pollutants, especially the oxides of carbon, nitrogen, and sulphur that are discharged into the atmosphere by industrial units. Automobiles are a major contributor of these oxides. Necessary precautions should be taken so as to restrict the amount of various pollutants in the air to a bare minimum.

### 7.4.3.2 Water

The most essential requirement of life is water. Although water is available in appreciable amounts (particularly in oceans and seas), only a small percentage can be used by humans. The importance of water is evident from the fact that many early civilizations had flourished on riverbanks. Freshwater is one of the most important components for sustaining human life.

Less than 3% of the total water available on earth is freshwater and only one-fifth of this is in usable liquid form. More than 90% of the freshwater is in the form of groundwater while only 1% is available in lakes and ponds. India is fortunate in terms of the total annual rainfall it receives, which is another resource of freshwater.

Industralization and mismanagement of water resources, particularly over the past two decades have resulted in significant water shortage. For a large number of human population, shortage of water means epidemic, hunger, despair, and death. The world's population has crossed the 6 billion mark and, therefore, the demand for freshwater has increased. This increased requirement cannot be met in many parts of the world. In fact, overutilization of water occurs at various levels. A large number of people use more water than required while taking a bath, using a shower, or washing clothes. On the basis of various studies conducted, it is estimated that a person needs a minimum of 20–40 L of water per day for drinking and sanitation. It has been found that more than 1 billion people worldwide have virtually no access to clean water. The scarcity of clean water has led to many conflicts. For example, Karnataka and Tamil Nadu are fighting over the Cauvery River water while Karnataka and Andhra Pradesh are fighting over the Krishna River water. Hence, it is essential that the world rethinks about the overall water resource management.

Some agriculturists also use more water than necessary to grow crops. A number of procedures exist by which farmers can use less water without any reduction in crop yield, such as by using sprinklers for watering plants and grass. The use of drip farming method is also very advantageous. In this procedure, water is allowed to fall in the form of drops near the roots of the plants (Figure 7.3).

Industries use enormous amounts of water for various stages. Untreated wastewater is discharged by them into waterbodies. This is done to maximize short-term gains as processing wastewater for reuse involves costs.

In most of the arid regions of the world, rains are unpredictable. This results in periods when there is acute scarcity of drinking water. Although it is not possible to prevent monsoon failure, its ill effects can be reduced by proper environmental management. Drought conditions also lead to food shortages and malnutrition, especially, in children.

It is necessary that people become aware of 'save water' campaigns. In fact, not a drop of water should be used unless it is necessary. The following points can be helpful in saving water:

**Fig. 7.3**   Drip farming method helps conserve water

(i) Effective rainwater harvesting, especially in the urban environment (Figure 7.4).

(ii) Reduction of water wastage in agriculture by using drip irrigation.

(iii) Prevention of leakage of water from taps and municipal pipelines.

(iv) Pricing of water at its real value so that people use it judiciously and reduce wastage.

(v) Prevention of water pollution.

The sources of water pollution caused by anthropogenic activities include the following:

(i) Domestic effluents

(ii) Industrial effluents

(iii) Surface run-offs

(iv) Waste heat

Necessary precautions should be taken to ensure that the rivers, ponds, and lakes are not polluted. An important source of potable water is groundwater and is commonly used in a number of countries. In the USA, 50% of the groundwater is used as potable water. It is generally believed that groundwater is chemically and microbiologically non-polluted and is safe for drinking and cooking. However, groundwater gets polluted due to leaching of pollutants from toxic waste dumps. Even agrochemicals get leached into upper aquifers, thus, contaminating the groundwater. These contaminants are responsible for serious health hazards in humans in the long run.

Dams are large water reservoirs which are constructed on the course of rivers at a height. Dams are useful in generating hydro energy; they also help in improving and increasing irrigation, and controlling floods. They also serve as a source of water for principal and industrial purposes. However, large dams may have adverse ecological and socio-economic implications which include the following:

**Fig. 7.4**  Rainwater harvesting prevents wastage of water

- Deforestation, soil erosion, and landslides (due to the clearance of site for the dams).
- Increase in seismic activity, which may result in more susceptibility to earthquakes.
- Water logging and salination of the water.
- Displacement of inhabitants who lose their main occupation.

The five major dams of India are Sardar Sarovar, Nagarjuna Sagar, Bhakhra, Hirakud, and Tehri. The Three Gorges Dam in China is the world's largest dam. In the USA, the Oroville Dam is the tallest dam.

Rains are water droplets formed due to condensation of water vapour in the atmosphere. In the atmosphere, water vapours are formed when water from various sources (particularly, rivers and oceans) gets evaporated by the sun's heat. However, when torrential rain occurs, it leads to flooding. When rivers swell because of extensive rainfall, the excessive water drains out and results in the occurrence of floods. The existence of some rivers depends on glacier melting. Devastating floods have occurred because of excessive melting of glaciers due to global warming and the greenhouse effect. In 1931, floods in the Yangtze Kiang River of China claimed around 140,000 lives. Nearly 40,000 people died in the Dongting area of China as a result of a catastrophic flood. In recent times, India faced devastating floods due to excessive rainfall in Kedarnath (Uttarakhand), Mumbai (Maharashtra), and Chennai (Tamil Nadu). Floods can also lead to outbreak of water-borne diseases such as cholera, dysentery. An important step to reduce the devastation caused by floods is to have flood forecasting and warning services. These measures may reduce the loss of life due to floods.

However, when rainfalls are lower-than-average over a period of time, it is responsible for drought, another significant environmental problem. In drought-hit areas, the land becomes dry and cracks develop and, consequently, no vegetation is possible. This leads to starvation and other related problems.

### 7.4.3.3  Land

Land is the basic resource and foundation on which the entire ecological system rests. It is the living ground (habitat) for all terrestrial plants and animals. Land is considered a renewable resource if it is properly utilized or managed. However, if it is loaded continuously with highly toxic pollutants, mainly from industrial and nuclear wastes, it becomes a non-renewable resource.

The efficiency of land to support life and other activities of human and animals is dependent on its biological productivity and the load-bearing capacity of soil and rocks. Due to population increase, land is under great pressure. Mismanagement of land resource due to indiscriminate deforestation has caused considerable damage to the soil quality. As on date, the per capita land resource

Forests, grasslands, wetlands, and mountains are biodiverse natural hobitats

available in India is less than 0.27 hectares, which is likely to go down to 0.18–0.16 hectares by 2025.

As any other natural resource, land is also a limited resource. Human beings use land for building homes, cultivating food, maintaining pastures for domestic animals, and developing industries. It is equally important that humans protect forests, grasslands, wetlands, and mountains, and maintain valuable biodiversity. In view of all this, it is necessary to adopt a rational land policy that maintains protected areas (national parks and wildlife sanctuaries).

Soil forms the uppermost layer of land. It is the most precious of all reserves as it supports all terrestrial life system, provides food and fodder in the form of vegetation, and stores water. Soil contains sand, silt, and clay mixed with air and moisture. It is also rich in organic and mineral nutrients. It takes nature around 50 years to build a centimetre of topsoil. Annually, about 6000 million tonnes of soil, all over the world, is lost as a result of soil erosion. This involves loss of about 2.6 million tonnes of nitrogen and 3.3 million tonnes of phosphorus. The best way to prevent soil erosion is adequate tree and grass cover. Alternatively, we should resort to counter building and gully-plugging on scientific lines, followed by growing green manure shrubs and trees on field bunds. In India, the commonly used green manure crops are sunn hemp, dhaincha, cluster beans, senji, cowpea, horse gram, berseem, and lentil.

In arid and semi-arid regions, too little or too much irrigation can lead to the formation of saline or alkaline soil. The alkalinity is due to the increase in the concentration of soluble salts. The most effective method of reducing the alkalinity of soils is treatment with gypsum. A good drainage system must also be provided to assist in the washing out of sodium from saline salts. Such salts are useful for growing most salt-tolerant species. The use of excess fertilizers or improper use of pesticides can pollute the soil, thereby inhibiting plant growth.

The Ernakulum National Park, Kerala

Also, the run-offs from agricultural fields lead to discharge of pesticides and fertilizers into waterbodies and cause severe environmental problems.

Soil erosion occurs when the rate of removal of soil by water and/or wind exceeds the rate of soil formation. As already stated, the rate of soil formation is exceedingly low. Soil erosion renders the land unproductive and can be controlled by the following methods:

(i) **Contouring:** It involves ploughing, planting, and cultivation across a slope following elevation contour lines. This practice reduces loss of soil from sloping lands, compared to cultivating up and down slopes.

(ii) **Contour bunds:** These are earth banks (1.5–2.0 m wide) thrown across the slope. These act as barriers to run-off, to form a water storage area on their upslope side.

(iii) **Terraces:** These are earth embankments constructed across the slope in order to intercept surface run-off.

The Namdapha National Park,
Arunachal Pradesh

Degradation of productive land creates wastelands. These are formed by deforestation, overgrazing, over-cultivation, and wrong practices of irrigation. Mining is another anthropogenic activity that causes deforestation and land degradation. Deserts are natural wastelands. These wastelands can be reclaimed by improving the physical structure and the quality of soil, improving both availability and quality of water, preventing shifting of soil, and conserving biological resources of the land. The process by which productive land gets converted into unproductive land is called desertification. The major causes of desertification are as follows:

- Following inappropriate land-use practices is a major contribution to desertification. This involves cultivation on marginal lands, affecting the adjacent fertile land.
- Overexploitation of water and land resources by intensive farming.
- Uncontrolled grazing and indiscriminate cutting down of trees.

### 7.4.3.4  Forests

Forests are our national treasures. They provide us with a wide variety of commodities, such as timber, fuelwood, fodder, fibre, fruits, herbal drugs, cosmetics, and many types of raw materials used by industries. Forests provide shelter for wildlife, check air pollution, and play a vital role in the economy of a nation. In fact, forests are indispensable for human beings.

Forests are being depleted rapidly due to increased population and human activities. Deforestation apart from diminishing the natural beauty of a place also disturbs its ecological balance. It has been estimated that an area of tropical forest four times the size of Switzerland disappears every year. In India, about 12% of total land has been estimated to be under forest cover. Ideally, it should have been 33% of the land. Moreover, the country has lost a substantial portion of its vegetation cover in the Himalayas; this is a major cause of avalanches and landslides.

Deforestation is a global problem that involves destruction of forests. Some of the causes of deforestation include the following:

- Explosion in human and livestock population
- Cutting down of trees for timber and fuel as the demand has become acute owing to population explosion
- Use of forest areas for farming and cattle grazing
- Use of forestland for construction of power stations, dams, roads, and railways
- Urbanization
- Industrialization

Deforestation is also responsible for soil erosion. It is believed to be the main cause of floods, droughts, and loss of valuable wildlife part from changing the landscape, wind direction, temperature, and humidity in nearby areas.

An important effect of deforestation is loss of rainwater due to surface run-off which results in the occurrence of floods. It leads to excessive washing away of topsoil, resulting in low fertility of the soil. Deforestation is the main cause for lowering groundwater level and also for reduced rainfall. Through transpiration, forests help in recycling moisture back into the atmosphere. Due to deforestation, the natural recycling of moisture gets disturbed which in turn leads to low rainfall. To prevent deforestation, plants should be grown in between trees so that when a tree is cut, the newly grown plants can bloom to full size in a much shorter time.

### 7.4.3.5  Food

Humans are dependent on their food resources which are primarily based on agriculture, animal husbandry, and seafood. The most important crops are wheat, rice, maize (corn), potatoes, barley, and oats. Other less important foods include sweet potato, sugar cane and beet, pulses (legumes), sorghum and millet, vegetables and fruits, and milk products.

The three primary crops on which the majority of humankind depends on for its nutrients and calorie requirements are wheat, rice, and maize. Wheat and rice are the global staple food. Potatoes, barley, oats, and rice are staple food for the people of mountainous regions and high altitudes, as they grow well in cool and moist climates. Cassava, sweet potatoes, and other roots and tubers need warm and wet areas for their growth. Sorghum and millet are drought-resistant crops and used as staple food in dry regions of Africa.

Although meat and milk are very nutritious, their distribution is unequal across the globe. Fish and seafood are good sources of high-quality proteins and account for about 75% of the world's protein consumption as compared to land animals.

On the basis of various studies, it has been found that we have already surpassed the sustainable harvest of fish from most oceans. There is a danger of seafood being contaminated by poisonous heavy metals such as cadmium, lead, and mercury which are discharged into waterbodies as industrial wastes. Consumption of such seafood leads to a number of health hazards in humans (for example, Minamata and Itai-itai diseases). Farming of fish and crustaceans in ponds under controlled conditions can offset this problem. Even environmentally sensitive fish such as trout can be farmed in high-density ponds. Genetic engineering techniques are being applied in fish breeding to develop special types of fish. The idea is to revolutionize fish breeding through genetic engineering as was done in the case of crop yield through the Green Revolution.

India is self-sufficient in food production. This is the result of the Green Revolution of the 1960s which involved extensive use of inorganic and organic fertilizers and genetically engineered crops. Though the Green Revolution considerably reduced the problem of starvation in the country, many of the techniques adopted are now being questioned from environmental perspectives. Some of these are as follows:

(i) Fertile soils exploited at a rate faster than they can recuperate.

(ii) Forests, grasslands, and wetlands have been converted into agricultural lands which led to serious ecological problems.

(iii) Most farmers grow single crops (monoculture) which if infested by pest, will be destroyed completely.

If traditional varieties of crops are used and several types are grown, the chances of complete failure decreases considerably. The use of harmless alternatives to inorganic pesticides and fertilizers has proved to be the best. This is known as integrated crop management. As far as possible, agriculture should be sustainable. According to the Food and Agricultural Organization (FAO), sustainable agriculture conserves land, water, plant, and animal genetic resources, does not degrade the environment, and is economically viable.

It is a well-known fact that crop yield considerably increases because of fertilizers. However, excessive use of fertilizers or repeated use of the same fertilizer pollutes the soil. For example, when ammonium sulphate is repeatedly used as a soil fertilizer, ammonium ions are used by crops but sulphate ($SO_4^{2-}$) ions get accumulated in the soil. Sulphate ions, being acidic, render the soil acidic and make it unfit for further plant growth. However, acidic soil can be reclaimed or improved by liming, that is, by the addition of lime (calcium carbonate). In highly acidic soils, the bacterial population decreases, resulting in an increase in fungi population. The net result is excessive growth of weeds.

When sodium nitrate or potassium nitrate is used as a fertilizer repeatedly or in excessive amounts, nitrate ions are used by crops but sodium and potassium ions get accumulated in the soil, thereby rendering the soil alkaline and making it unfit for subsequent crop cultivation. Alkaline soils can be reclaimed or improved by treating the soil with aluminium sulphate or ferrous sulphate, which sets acids free on hydrolysis. Alkaline soil can also be improved by the addition of sulphur, which is oxidized in the soil by bacterially mediated reactions to sulphuric acid.

Due to excessive amount of nitrogen fertilizer, the concentration of nitrate ions increases in leafy vegetables. When humans consume these leafy vegetables, it results in bioaccumulation of nitrates in their body. By itself nitrate is not harmful, but in a human body, it is reduced to nitrite, which is a probable factor for cancer. Excessive amounts of nitrates may also lead to blue baby syndrome or methaemoglobinaemia in small children. Nitrates in the body are reduced to nitrites, which in turn react with haemoglobin (in the bloodstream) and reduce the oxygen-carrying capacity of the blood. This condition is referred to as blue baby syndrome. The symptoms of this fatal disease include diarrhoea, vomiting, and the child's complexion becoming stale blue.

Problems associated with the use of nitrogen-based fertilizers can be overcome by the rotation of crops on a scientific basis and by using fertilizers in accordance with professional advice. It is safer to use less amount of fertilizer than required. However, it is best to use organic manures as far as possible. Vermicompost is the best natural fertilizer for plants.

Whenever fertilizers are being used for improving crop yield, the agricultural fields must be well irrigated. In case there is no outlet for unused water, salts get accumulated in the soil and the soil becomes saline. This salinity is responsible for creating wastelands. Reclamation of saline soil requires removal of salts. This can be achieved by mixing soil with gypsum, followed by leaching, which helps in removing the salts. Moreover, instead of using agrochemicals such as pesticides, herbicides, and fungicides, biopesticides or biofungicides can be added to improve crop yield.

## 7.5  ENERGY

Principally, energy resources are of two types—renewable energy sources (also known as non-conventional energy sources) and non-renewable energy sources (also known as conventional sources of energy). Renewable energy sources include solar energy, hydro energy, tidal energy, wind energy, and biomass energy (Figure 7.5). Non-renewable energy sources include fossil fuels, such as coal, petroleum, and natural gas. Another important energy resource includes radioactive minerals, particularly uranium ($^{235}$U). Radioactive minerals produce nuclear energy or atomic energy.

The demand for energy approximately doubles in every 14 years. Energy consumed by a country is considered as one of the indicators of development. India, which supports about 16% of the world's population, consumes only 2% of the total energy produced in the world. This is in total contrast with the USA that has only 6.25% of the world's population but utilizes 33% of the energy produced in the world. This gives us an idea about the low level of our development and should be an incentive for generation of more energy to meet our growing energy demand. Even today, about 80% of our population continues to depend on conventional sources of energy, such as fuelwood, dung, and agricultural wastes for their energy needs. It is well known that non-renewable sources of energy, such as coal, petroleum, and natural gas may not last for long. Forests are also being depleted at a fast rate due to indiscriminate felling of trees. In view of all this, it has become necessary to think about alternative, non-conventional sources of energy as described in Figure 2.2 of Chapter 2.

## 7.5.1  Non-renewable Energy Resources

Non-renewable energy resources are natural resources that exist in fixed amounts and are formed in the environment over long periods of time (even millions of years). The time gap between their generation and consumption is very high. In other words, they are consumed at a much faster rate as compared to the rate at which they are formed. With the rapid increase in human population and industrialization, these resources are likely to be exhausted before long. In view of this, efforts must be made to develop renewable sources of energy. Fossil fuels (coal, natural gas, and petroleum), metals, and minerals are examples of such resources.

## 7.5.2  Renewable Energy Resources

We have plentiful supply of renewable energy resources in nature that can be reproduced and harvested continuously. Solar energy, wind energy, water energy (in the form of hydroelectric and tidal energy) are being harnessed more efficiently nowadays. Renewable resources also include firewood or fuelwood obtained from forests and agricultural wastes such as biogas and animal dung. Firewood or fuelwood cannot be harnessed in short time intervals, the reason being that once trees are cut, it takes a long time for new trees to grow. However, with proper planning of the forest system, a more or less continuous supply of fuelwood (in reasonable quantities) can be maintained.

**(i) Solar energy:** Solar energy is the most readily available and abundant source of energy. It is a free and non-polluting source of energy. Solar energy has the greatest potential of all sources of renewable energy. Until now, only a small amount of this form of energy could be used. However, it can become one of the most important supplies of energy, especially as other sources in the country are being rapidly depleted. It has been estimated that the sun gives 1000 times

Uranium is an abundant source of
nuclear energy

more power than required. If we can utilize even 5% of this energy, it will be 50 times what the world will require.

Solar cookers that use solar energy are being used in many parts of India for cooking. Solar energy can be also used directly to heat water during winter. This procedure is used in hotels and industrial establishments to get hot water. Refrigerators that run on solar energy have been developed for rural areas. They keep vegetables and fruits fresh for long period. There is great potential for using solar energy for cold storages. It can be also used to heat rooms in colder regions. These days, high-rise and multi-storey buildings are constructed with glass surfaces to trap the sun's heat. This has the potential to utilize solar energy even in less sunny climates.

Solar energy can be used to produce electricity. The plant for the production of electricity consists of four main parts as shown in Figure 7.6. The plant should have a sunlit rooftop with no tall building or trees around. Around 100 square feet is required for each kilo-watt of capacity. However an investment between ₹5 lakh and 15 lakh is required to install a photo-voltaic system that can run fans, LED lights, television, fridge and even air conditioners. A plant usually costs ₹1 lakh for every kW. It usually comes with a warranty of 15-25 year. The central government provides some subsidy while banks grant low-

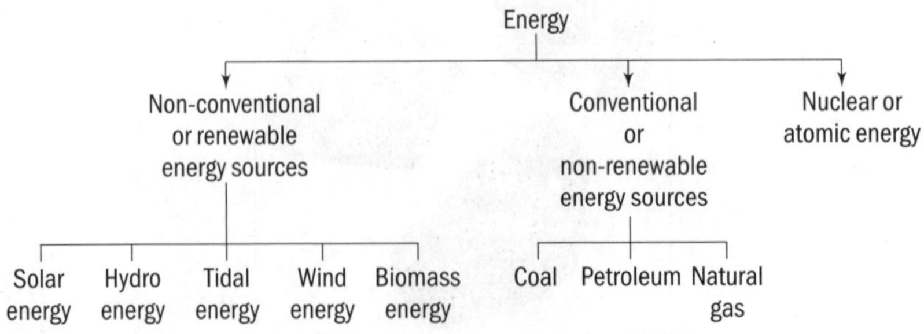



**Fig. 7.5**  Types of energy sources

interest loans. Professionals will be doing the installation and maintenance of a solar plant. There are many new firms in the market besides older enterprises that offer solar technology.

Installing a plant for electricity production leads to reduction in the demand on the grid. Users of solar power find their electricity bills to have halved. Moreover, costs are recovered within three to six years. The plant can be installed in online as well as offline mode. Offline mode helps in storing solar power which can be used at night or during a power cut. Surplus power can be given to the grid. It will be adjusted with the amount due to the DISCOM. A number of such solar plants have been installed in New Delhi. In fact in some parts of the country even metros are run on solar electricity.

**(ii) Hydro energy:** Hydro energy is one of the cheapest, cleanest sources of energy. Water power is developed by allowing water to fall under the force of gravity and is used almost exclusively for generation of electric power. Potential energy of water is converted into mechanical energy by using prime movers known as hydraulic turbines. Hydro energy is inexpensive at places where water is available in abundance. Although the capital costs of hydroelectric power plants are higher compared to other types of power plants, their operating costs are quite low, as no fuel is required (Figure 7.7).

However, the construction of mega dams has given rise to many controversies in recent times. In this regard, small hydropower plants are emerging as viable alternatives. These plants serve the energy needs of remote and rural areas where the grid supply is not available. In these plants, a natural or artificial waterfall is made to turn a modern type of pedal wheel, called a turbine, which generates electricity upon rotation.

**(iii) Tidal energy:** Tides in the sea occur due to universal gravitational effect of heavenly bodies such as the sun and moon. Tides can be used to produce electric power, which is known as tidal power. The use of tidal energy for the generation of electric power is possible only in a few favourably situated sites where the geography of an inlet or bay favours the construction of a hydroelectric plant.

In 1960, a 240 MW-capacity tidal plant was constructed in France. In India, the first tidal energy project with a capacity of 150 MW was set up at Vizhinjam near Thiruvananthapuram. A major tidal wave power project costing ₹ 50,000 million is proposed to be set up in the Gulf of Kachchh in Gujarat. Other suggested sites for tidal power plants are the Gulf of Cambay and the Sundarbans areas of West Bengal. Figure 7.8 provides the structure and functioning of a tidal power station. Both incoming and outgoing tides are held back by a dam. The difference in water levels generates electricity in both directions as water runs through reversible turbogenerators.

**(iv) Wind energy:** Wind energy has been used for sailing, grinding grains, and irrigation for hundreds of years. The energy present in wind can be economically used for generation of electrical energy and has great potential as a clean energy

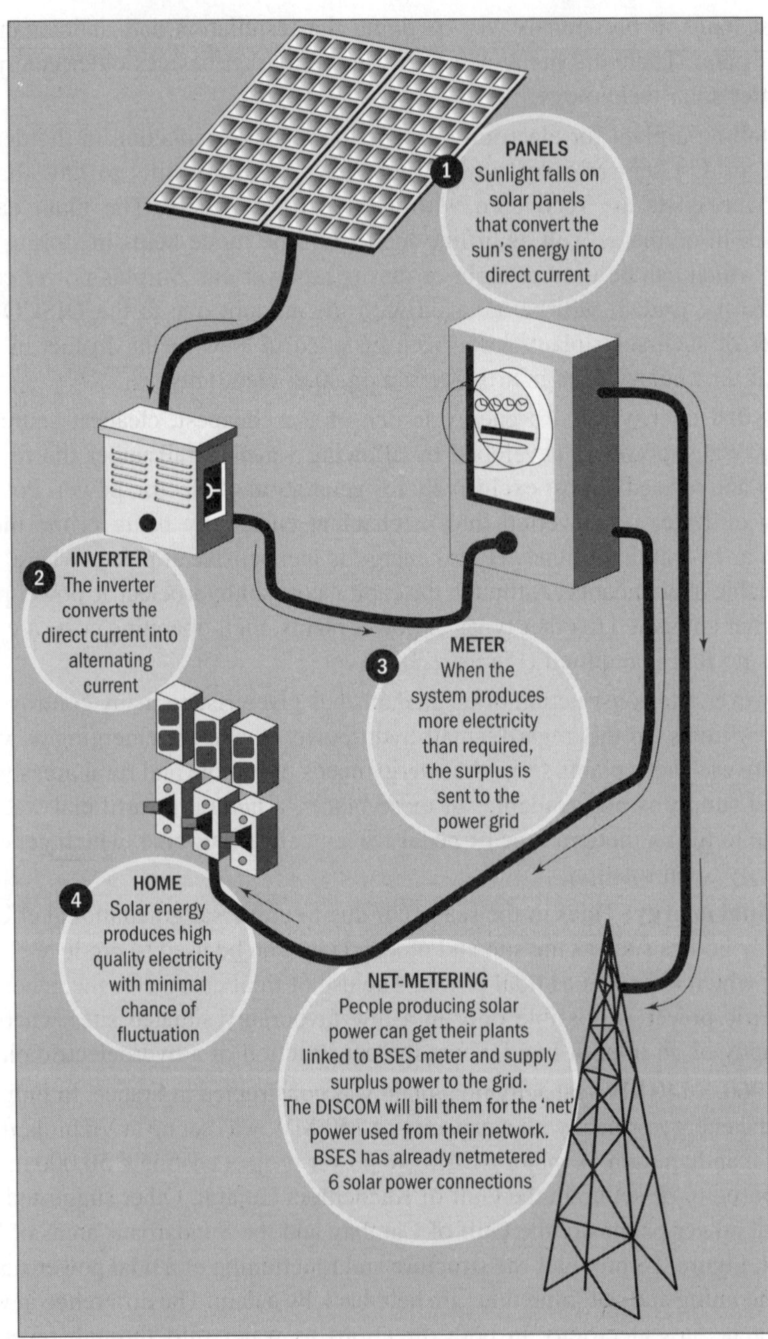


**Fig. 7.6**   Plant for the conversion of solar energy into electricity
*Source:* The Hindustan Times (8 May 2015)

source. The total amount of wind energy available over the earth's surface is estimated to be $1.6 \times 10^7$ MW, which is equivalent to the present energy consumption of the world. Wind is harnessed to run windmills, which in turn drive generators to produce electricity. Wind can also be used to generate mechanical power, such as pumping water. Windmills for water pumping have been installed in many countries, particularly in rural areas.

In India, generally, wind speeds are in the lower ranges. Attempts are being made to develop low-cost, low-speed windmills for irrigation of small and marginal farms and for providing drinking water in rural areas. Wind speeds are high in coastal areas of Saurashtra, Western Rajasthan, and Central India. In these areas, medium- or large-sized windmills could be set up for generation of electricity.

Wind energy is an eco-friendly power source. It is a non-polluting renewable source of energy and does not need any fuel to work. It can generate a few kilowatts of electricity and is less costly than the other sources of renewable energy on a small scale.

**(v) Biomass energy:** Biomass is a renewable energy source derived from plant resources, animal wastes, and the waste of various human activities. It can be also produced from the by-products of the timber industry, agricultural crops, raw materials from forests, major parts of household wastes, and wood. Biomass is an important source of energy and the most important fuel worldwide after coal, oil, and natural gas (Figure 7.9). Biomass can be used to generate electricity with the same equipment or power plants that are now being used to burn fossil fuels.

In India, biomass fuels account for about one-third of the total fuels used in the country. At present, over 90% of rural households and 15% of urban households use biomass fuels (wood, cow dung cakes, crop residue, saw dust). However, inefficient burning of such fuels in traditional *chullahs* leads to the

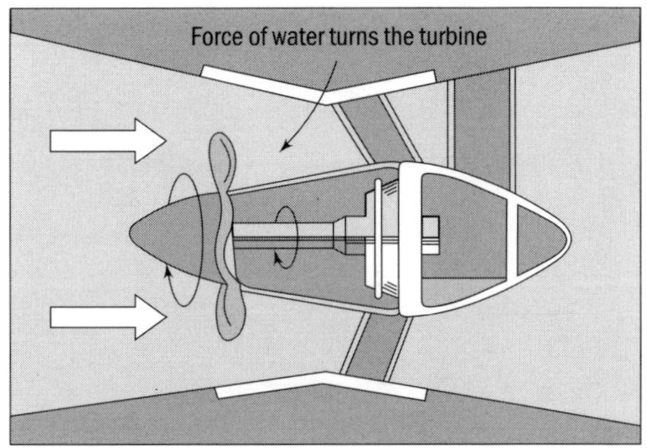


**Fig. 7.7**  Schematic of a turbine engine

serious problem of indoor air pollution and its consequent health hazards. Also, unsustainable consumption of fuelwood leads to deforestation, which is responsible for environmental degradation. Biomass resources can be divided into the following categories:

    **(a) Traditional solid biomass:** Such biomass is burned directly to obtain energy. Some examples are wood and agricultural residue.

    **(b) Non-traditional biomass:** Such biomass is first converted into ethanol and methanol, which are then used as liquid fuels in engines.

**(vi) Biogas:** Biogas is a source of energy that is largely used for cooking. Using a simple process, a gas (called biogas) is produced from cattle dung. Biogas contains nearly 55%–70% of inflammable methane gas. It is a clean and an efficient fuel for rural areas. Waterweeds such as water hyacinth, water lettuce, salvinia, hydrilla, duckweeds, and algae have been found to be useful supplements to cattle dung (Figure 7.10). Biogas can also be used to raise steam, which in turn may be used for running engines or machines in factories or for running turbines to generate electricity. Biogas plants can meet energy needs of a number of families or even small villages. The residual dung or digested slug left after generating biogas can be used as manure for agricultural purposes. This is an

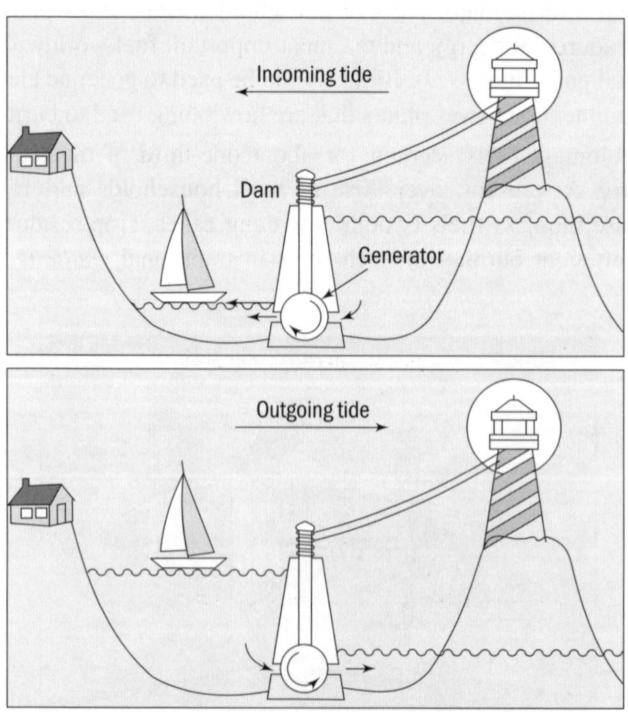


**Fig. 7.8** Representation of a tidal power station

economical way of obtaining energy from organic wastes. In India, efforts are being made to install thousands of biogas plants in rural areas. Figure 7.11 shows the production of biogas by anaerobic fermentation.

## 7.6  NUCLEAR ENERGY

To overcome the problems associated with coal and petroleum, nuclear energy could become an important source of energy. It is projected as the fuel to replace fossil fuel energy. Nuclear energy resources are believed to be about 10 times more than fossil fuels. Nuclear energy is the heat energy released when large atoms split into two or more lighter atoms (fission) or when two or more lighter atoms are fused into a large atom (fusion). Uranium, a mineral found in the earth's crust, is the main fuel used to produce nuclear energy through fission process. It has been estimated that fission of 1 kg of $^{235}$U will release energy equal to that obtained by burning 3 million tonnes of coal.

In India, uranium is found in Rajasthan, Bihar, and Andhra Pradesh. For nuclear energy generation, $^{235}$U, a radioisotope of uranium, is used. The element uranium occurs in nature as uranite, a mineral form of uranium oxide.

Presently, nuclear energy is used for various purposes, such as generating electricity, propelling ships and aircrafts, and making radioactive isotopes that can be used in medical diagnosis and in the treatment of diseases. However, this source of energy has certain drawbacks. The cost and maintenance of atomic power plants are astronomically high. Also, the effects of nuclear wastes on human life are extremely hazardous. The dumping of nuclear wastes has become a global environmental problem.

The advantage of nuclear energy is that there is no emission of oxides of carbon, nitrogen, or sulphur. The major risk to human health and the environment arises from improper management and accidents in nuclear reactors. The Chernobyl disaster in 1986 is a glaring example of such accidents in which many people and thousands of miles of land were exposed to nuclear radiations. Nuclear waste can be dumped deep into the sea. However, this procedure is no longer used. The best way is to bury it underground in strong vaults.

Windmills were first employed for producing energy in 1973

**Fig. 7.9** Biomass fuels such as wood and cow dung are primary sources of energy in most households

## 7.7 STATUS OF POWER GENERATION IN INDIA FROM RENEWABLE RESOURCES

Table 7.3 gives the status of renewable resources used in India. From the data, it can be concluded that India has to make substantial efforts in order to achieve success in the field of renewable energy sources.

## 7.8 ROLE OF AN INDIVIDUAL IN CONSERVATION OF NATURAL RESOURCES

We have learnt about the depletion of natural resources, degradation of land, deforestation, and pollution of air, water, and land. With the progress of civilization, human beings started altering the natural environment in pursuit of creating an economic, a social, and a cultural environment of their own choice. This slowly resulted in depletion of natural resources and degradation of the environment. Further, with increase in human population, rapid industrialization, and urbanization, the strain on natural resources and the environment has grown. Now the situation is deteriorating so fast, especially over the last few decades, that environmental problems are posing threats not only to human health, but also humankind's existence.

**Fig. 7.10** Water weeds such as water hyacinth and water lettuce are used in biogas production

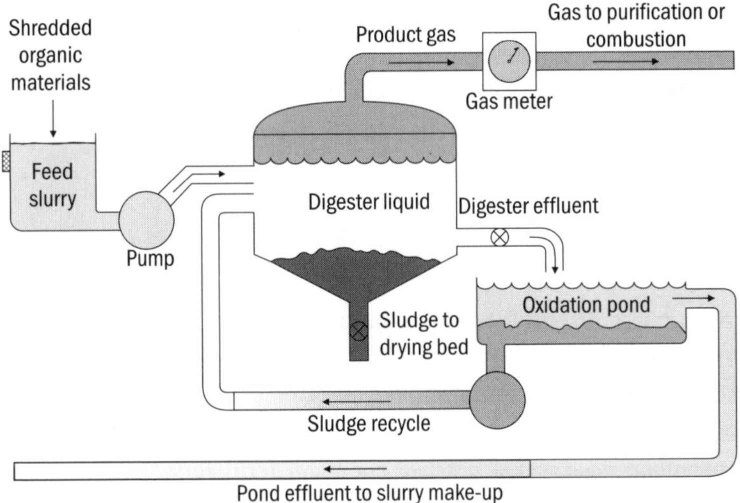


**Fig. 7.11**   Biogas production by anaerobic fermentation

We must understand that each one of us is individually responsible for maintaining the environment quality. Actions of individuals, to a large extent, have a direct influence on the environment. It is extremely necessary that each individual should not only be aware of the various environmental issues and the consequences of their actions, but also make a firm resolve to develop an environmentally ethical lifestyle. Following are guidelines that individuals should observe:

- Develop respect for all forms of life.
- Try to plant trees wherever you can and, more importantly, take care of them. Trees help reduce atmospheric pollution.
- Wherever possible, reduce the use of wood and paper products. Both wood and paper are derived from forests. Overuse of these lead to defor-estation. Try to recycle paper products and use recycled paper wherever possible.
- Reuse as the envelopes you receive.
- Join an afforestation programme.
- Advocate organic farming by asking your grocery store to stock organi-cally grown vegetables and fruits. This will considerably reduce the risk of pesticide exposure.
- Reduce the use of fossil fuels, either by walking short distances or by using carpool service or public transport. This practice will also help in reducing air pollution.

- Switch off lights and fans when not needed.
- Do not pour pesticides, paints, solvents, oil, or other products that contain harmful chemicals down the drain or on the ground.
- Buy consumer goods in reusable glass containers instead of in cans or throw-away bottles.
- Use rechargeable batteries.
- Say no to plastic carry bags. Buy your vegetables and groceries in cloth bags.
- Do not use disposable papers or plastic plates when reusable versions are available.
- Recycle newspapers, aluminium, and other items.
- Set up a compost bin in your garden and use it to produce manure from plant wastes. Do not use chemical fertilizers.
- Join any of the several non-governmental organizations (NGOs) that work towards environmental conservation.
- Do not use leaded petrol in your vehicles.
- Install catalytic converter in the exhaust system of your vehicle.
- Discard vehicles that are more than 15 years old. New vehicles are equipped with better technologies.
- Do not burn garbage. The smoke emitted by burning wood, paper, and leaves pollutes the air. Plastic wastes emit dangerous toxic fumes on burning. It is best to recycle plastic wastes whenever possible.
- Do not discharge municipal waste on land or into waterbodies.
- Conserve water and avoid wastage. It is precious and should be used carefully.
- Use pressure cooker for cooking. Pressure cooking is faster and can save up to 75% of the energy you would have spent otherwise.
- Soak lentils before cooking. This consumes less energy.

**Table 7.3**   Renewable energy resources—potential and current status

| Resource | Proposed gross potential in GW (till 2022) | Achieved in MW (December 2016) |
|---|---|---|
| Wind | 60 | 28,700 |
| Solar | 100 | 9,013 |
| Biopower | 10 | 8,021 |
| Small hydro | 5 | 4,334 |

*Source:* Ministry of New and Renewable Energy (MNRE), Government of India

- Covering a vessel with a lid during cooking helps to cook faster, thus saving energy.
- Switch off the television and radio as soon as the programme of interest is over.
- Keep bulbs and tube lights clean. The dust on tube lights and bulbs decreases lightening level by 20%–25%.
- Use tube lights and energy-efficient bulbs that save energy. A 40 W tube light or a 15 W fluorescent bulb gives as much light as a 100 W bulb.

## 7.9   MANAGEMENT OF RESOURCES FOR A SUSTAINABLE LIFESTYLE

We have studied about various natural resources such as land, water, soil, and minerals. Most of these resources are scarce and should be used more efficiently. However, the most important challenge is the unsustainable and unequal use of resources. In fact, population control is essential for the survival of our nation and of humankind everywhere. Even the most important resources, such as solar energy that we derive from nature, are not distributed evenly throughout the world. There is discrimination with respect to the availability of some vital resources, even within the country. One glaring example is that of water. In rural areas, drinking water has to be brought from long distances. All towns do not have municipal water supply systems either. On the other hand, a lot of water is misused or wasted.

As has been mentioned earlier, the per capita consumption of resources of developed countries is about 50 times greater than in most developing or underdeveloped countries. Even within our country, there is disparity in the use of resources. One such example is that of the Sardar Sarovar Project. This dam on the Narmada River in Gujarat has displaced thousands of tribal folk whose lives and livelihood were linked to the river and its surrounding forests and agricultural land. While the local residents and fishermen lost their homeland, rich farmers downstream get water for agriculture. The most important issue is that local tribes are being rendered homeless at the cost of other people who will benefit. Why should the poor and less fortunate be made to bear the cost of development for wealthier farmers? It is the duty of the government to see that this disparity is removed and the people are amply compensated.

It is for the various nations of the world to formulate policies for equitable distribution of natural resources. At the individual level, each one of us can contribute to bring about sustainable lifestyles. This can basically come from caring for Mother Nature in all respects.

Respecting nature and loving it is the best way to enhance our thinking regarding how to use our natural resources in a sustained way.

# SUMMARY

- The environment provides various essential resources.
- Natural resources are of two types—renewable and non-renewable.
- Renewable natural resources include sunlight, air, water, soil, and forests.
- Non-renewable natural resources include natural gas, coal, metals, oil, and petroleum.
- The atmosphere contains a number of gases out of which the most prominent are $O_2$ and $CO_2$.
- The presence of excess $CO_2$ causes the greenhouse effect and global warming.
- Photosynthesis uses $CO_2$ from the atmosphere and produces oxygen.
- Water is the most essential requirement of life.
- The demand for potable water has increased considerably, primarily due to the increase in human population.
- Forests are storehouses of resources and provide a variety of commodities. They play an integral role in the formation of soil, conservation of water, and regeneration of oxygen, and are important for the climate.
- Deforestation is a global problem and involves destruction of forests.
- Renewable energy resources include solar energy, hydro energy, tidal energy, wind energy, biomass energy, and nuclear energy.
- Use of solar energy for the generation of electricity is becoming more popular.
- The role of individuals is important for the conservation of natural resources.
- For a sustainable lifestyle, it is necessary to manage resources.

# EXERCISE

## [A]  Multiple-choice questions

1. Which of the following is a non-renewable resource?
   - (a) Petroleum
   - (b) Water
   - (c) Forests
   - (d) Wildlife

2. The most severe impact of deforestation is
   - (a) Climate change
   - (b) Changes in rainfall pattern
   - (c) Loss of biodiversity
   - (d) All of the above

3. Deforestation causes
    (a) Drought
    (b) Soil erosion
    (c) Flood
    (d) Global warming
4. Forests are
    (a) Renewable resources
    (b) Non-renewable resources
    (c) Inexhaustible
    (d) None of the above
5. Fossil fuels are
    (a) Renewable resources
    (b) Non-renewable resources
    (c) Inexhaustible
    (d) None of the above
6. Energy and fuel are generated by
    (a) Hydroelectric plants
    (b) Thermal plants
    (c) Nuclear plants
    (d) Biogas plants
7. The resources of the earth are
    (a) Atmosphere
    (b) Hydrosphere
    (c) Lithosphere
    (d) Biosphere
    (e) All of the above
8. The most important region of the atmosphere is
    (a) Troposphere
    (b) Stratosphere
    (c) Mesosphere
    (d) Thermosphere
9. The most harmful air pollutant is
    (a) CO
    (b) $CO_2$
    (c) $SO_2$
    (d) Particulate matter
10. Which of the following is a renewable energy source?
    (a) Coal
    (b) Petroleum
    (c) Natural gas
    (d) The sun

### ANSWERS

| | | | | |
|---|---|---|---|---|
| 1. (a) | 2. (c) | 3. (d) | 4. (a) | 5. (b) |
| 6. (d) | 7. (e) | 8. (b) | 9. (a) | 10. (d) |

## [B] Fill in the blanks.

1. The oxygen present in air is replenished by _______.
2. Ozone is mostly present in the _______ region of the atmosphere.
3. Too much of carbon dioxide in the atmosphere leads to _______.
4. The main problem associated with natural resources is their _______ consumption.

5. In agriculture, water wastage can be minimized by _______.

6. The three primary crops on which the majority of human beings depend are _______, _______, and _______.

7. The most important renewable source of energy is the _______.

**ANSWERS**

1. Photosynthesis        2. Stratosphere
3. Global warming        4. Unequal
5. Drip irrigation        6. Wheat, rice, maize
7. Sun

## [C] Short-answer questions

1. What are the types of resources?

2. What are the resources of the earth?

3. Why is the stratospheric region of the atmosphere considered to be the most important?

4. Lithosphere is the only _______ that supports life. Comment.

5. What in your opinion are the problems associated with natural resources?

6. How can water be saved?

7. Write a note on forests.

8. What are the different types of energy sources?

9. How can solar energy be converted into electricity?

# Major Crops and Cropping Patterns in India

## 8.1  INTRODUCTION

India is an agricultural country. A large proportion of India's population depends on agricultural crops, such as wheat, barley, peas, grains, pulses, maize, and millets. In fact, in India agriculture provides livelihood to about 70% of the population. Though agriculture is necessary for the sustenance of life, it is responsible for a number of environmental problems. In order to cater to the food requirements of the growing human population, more and more agricultural land is required. For this, forests are being cleared (deforestation) at a rapid pace. Consequently, a wide range of environmental issues has emerged. Besides this, a number of agrochemicals such as fertilizers, insecticides, and herbicides are used for increasing the yield. However, the extensive use of agrochemicals also leads to environmental degradation.

Apart from agrochemicals, agriculture needs a large amount of water for various purposes, with irrigation being the most important water-consuming activity. For this, water should be conserved and made free from impurities such as total dissolved solids (TDS), sodium ions, sulphate, chloride, and boron. In addition, the water's pH must not be unusually high or low. The surface irrigation methods used traditionally require large amounts of water. Instead, it is advantageous to use sprinkler irrigation or drip irrigation methods (see Chapter 9).

In India, the production of cereals has considerably improved not only by using forestland for cultivation but also due to the utilization of efficient technologies. In fact, India has become self-sufficient in the production of cereals, fruits, vegetables, fish, and milk.

It was in the mid-1960s that an interdisciplinary team of scientists working in Mexico and the Philippines developed new and better varieties of wheat and rice, which could be cultivated in tropical climate as well. This resulted in much higher yields of wheat and rice crops. This was referred to as the Green Revolution. The following three steps formed the basis for the success of the Green Revolution:

(i) Development and monoculture farming of selectively bred or genetically engineered high-yielding varieties of crops such as rice, wheat, and corn.

(ii) Excessive use of fertilizers, pesticides, and water on crops to produce higher yields.

(iii) Increase in the frequency of cropping.

In India, the Green Revolution came in the 1960s and considerably reduced the starvation of the people. However, many of the techniques that were employed for enhancing the crop yield are now being questioned by environmentalists. These include:

- Fertile lands have been exploited much faster than they can recuperate.

- Forestlands and grasslands have been used for agricultural purposes. This has led to serious ecological problems.

- Only monoculture single crops are grown. In case, a crop is hit by a pest, whole of the crops can be damaged.

The excessive use of agrochemicals degrades the environmental quality. In case, the traditional varieties are used and a number of different crops are grown, the chance of complete failure is considerably decreased. The use of harmless alternatives to inorganic pesticides and fertilizers is found to be environment-friendly. This is known as integrated crop management.

As far as possible, agriculture should be carried out sustainably. According to the Food and Agricultural Organization (FAO), following sustainable agricultural practices help in conserving land, water, plant, and animal genetic resources. In other words, sustainable agriculture practices are economically viable and do not degrade the environment.

For achieving sustainability in agriculture, biofertilizers are used in place of the usual chemical fertilizers and pesticides. Also, new varieties of seeds are developed through genetic engineering. The use of microbial inoculants—as a source of biofertilizers—is common in most countries.

The atmospheric nitrogen is biologically fixed for plants. A number of free-living and symbiotic bacteria which are known to atmospheric nitrogen are used as biofertilizer in place of nitrogenous fertilizers. Two types of biofertilizers are used in agriculture—bacterial biofertilizer and algal biofertilizer. Japan has developed techniques for the mass cultivation of blue-green algae (BGA), which is used as biofertilizer in paddy fields. In India too, the concept of utilizing BGA as biofertilizer has gained attention. Therefore, efforts are being currently made towards the large-scale production of BGA. In some countries, Azolla water fern cultivation was standardized to be used as biofertilizer in rice fields.

In place of biofertilizers, compost obtained from waste materials can be used as fertilizer. The process is known as vermicomposting and involves the following steps:

(i) A pit of suitable size is dug. The pit's surface is uniformly covered with a polythene sheet and a 3-inch layer, made up of gravel and sand, is spread on the sheet.

(ii) A layer of coconut coir is uniformly spread on the polythene sheet.

(iii) Waste material (from sewage and other sources) mixed with cow dung, slurry, and broth culture of lignocellulolytic microorganisms (300 grams/tonne) is spread on the coconut coir. This makes about 6–8 inches in depth.

(iv) A thin layer of wet rotten cow dung is spread over the waste material.

(v) About 200 earthworms of species *Eisenia foetida* are put on the surface of the cow dung.

(vi) The pit is covered with a gunny bag in order to avoid loss of water due to evaporation from the surface.

(vii) From time to time, water is sprinkled in order to maintain moisture content of about 60% for the survival of microorganisms and earthworms. The earthworms feed on the wastes, consume 2–3 times their body weight, and finally excrete mucus-coated matter as vermicast. The vermicast consists of organic matter which has undergone physical and chemical breakdown by the activity of the muscular gizzard, which grinds waste to a particle size of 1–2 $\mu$m.

(viii) The compost gets matured in about 45–50 days.

(ix) For large-scale preparation, a number of compost pits can be used in sequence. The pits must be covered with sheds to avoid direct sunlight and rainwater.

At the end of the composting process, the pits are flushed with water and washings (known as vermiwash). Finally the compost is collected and used as fertilizer. Vermicast or vermiwash are good sources of macronutrients, micronutrients, vitamins, enzymes, and antibiotics. These nutrients are taken up by the plants. Vermicast is applied in different doses to various types of crops.

## 8.2  MAJOR CROPS IN INDIA

India is home to a variety of climatic conditions. As a result, there is variation in the cropping pattern. We next discuss the different crops and their favourable climatic conditions.

### 8.2.1  Rice

Rice is one of the three most important crops in the world. The other crops are wheat and maize. Rice is the staple diet for about 2.7 billion people worldwide. The leading producers of rice are India, China, Indonesia, Bangladesh, Thailand, Japan, Myanmar, Vietnam, Malaysia, Pakistan, and Sri Lanka. Conditions that are favourable for rice cultivation, include rainfall of 100–150 cm, temperature of

15–27°C, and heavy clayey-to-clayey loamy soil. Thailand is the world's leading exporter of rice.

In India rice is grown in Kuttand valley of Kerala, Kashmir valley, Jharkhand, Odisha, and West Bengal (Purulia and Bankura districts). More than 60% of the total rice is cultivated in West Bengal, Uttar Pradesh, Madhya Pradesh, Chhattisgarh, and Bihar. Most of the rice produced in the country is consumed locally. Basmati—a variety of long, slender-grained aromatic rice—is exported to Gulf countries, Russia, and East European countries.

The Central Rice Research Institute, Cuttack has developed a rice-based integrated farming system. It involves other beneficial components such as fish or prawn, vegetable, and fruit crops. This procedure is found to be three times more productive and four times more economical than the other rice-producing cultures.

## 8.2.2 Wheat

Wheat is the second most important crop in India after rice. India's contribution to the total food grain production of the world is 30%. Worldwide, it ranks third in the production of wheat, the top two being China and the USA. On a global scale, India contributed about 12% (that is, 606 million tonnes) to the total wheat production in 2010–11.

Wheat is grown during winter in the country, hence it is a rabi crop. Wheat cultivation requires temperature of 12–25°C, rainfall of 25–75 cm, and well-drained light to heavy clay. After the USA, India, and China, the world's leading producers of wheat are Russia, Australia, Canada, Pakistan, France, and Turkey. The USA is the world's top exporter of wheat. In India, more than 97% of the total wheat is produced in Punjab, Haryana, and Rajasthan.

## 8.2.3 Barley *(Hordeum vulgare)*

Barley is one of the most important cereal crops in the world, ranking next to rice, maize, and wheat. Each year, the world produces about 136 million tonnes of barley. In India, barley is an important winter crop (rabi) and mainly cultivated in Punjab, Rajasthan, Madhya Pradesh, Uttar Pradesh, and Bihar. Barley is mainly consumed by the poor population of the country. It is also used as cattle feed. In developed countries, it is the chief raw material for manufacturing beer. Barley is also used to make *sattu*. Barley is best cultivated on well-drained fertile loam or light clay soil. It is also grown on the coastal saline soils of the Sundarbans of West Bengal.

## 8.2.4 Maize or Corn *(Zea mays)*

Maize is the fourth most important food crop after rice, wheat, and millets. Also known as corn, the USA accounts for 20% of the total production in the world. For maize cultivation, temperature of 15–27°C and rainfall of 65–125 cm are required. The best soil for maize cultivation is deep heavy clay to light sandy loam. Besides the USA, the major maize-producing countries include India, China, Brazil, Mexico, Russia, Romania, and South Africa.

In India, maize is grown in Uttar Pradesh, Rajasthan, Madhya Pradesh, Bihar, Himachal Pradesh, Jammu and Kashmir, and Punjab. Besides, used as a staple food for humans and quality feed for animals, it is also used as raw material for a large number of industrial products including starch, oil, protein, and alcoholic beverages. Corn has also been used for the production of ethyl alcohol as discussed later in this chapter.

### 8.2.5  Millets *(Sorghum bicolor)*

Millets can be of different varieties and sizes. Millets are important staple food crops of some developing countries. Sorghum (*Sorghum bicolor*), also known as jowar, is an important food and fodder crop in India. However, in the last few decades, areas under sorghum cultivation have considerably decreased. Jowar is considered a drought-hardy crop and is an important component of dry land agriculture. It is cultivated in areas which have 40–100 cm of annual rainfall, 20–55°C of temperature, and sandy loam to clayey loam soil. Besides India, jowar is produced in China, the USA, Nigeria, Ukraine, Thailand, Russia, and Turkey. The USA is the largest exporter of jowar in the world.

### 8.2.6  Bajra *(Pennisetum typhoideum)*

Bajra is an important staple food crop of India. It grows well in regions where temperature ranges between 25°C and 30°C and rainfall is about 30–50 cm per annum. It is grown mainly in Rajasthan, Maharashtra, Gujarat, Uttar Pradesh, Haryana, Karnataka, Tamil Nadu, and Andhra Pradesh. There has been a steady decline in bajra cultivation as it is less popular amongst farmers due to its low-remunerative value.

### 8.2.7  Pulses (Legumes)

Pulses are an important source of dietary protein. Cultivation of pulses makes the soil fertile and sustainable through atmospheric nitrogen fixation. The pulse crops add approximately 35–40 kg nitrogen per hectare. In India, the most commonly grown pulse crops are Bengal gram or chickpea, pigeon pea, green gram, black gram, red lentil, and kidney bean.

(i) Bengal gram or chickpea or gram (*Cicer arietinum*): It is grown in all types of soils and needs temperature of 15–25°C and 25–60 cm annual rainfall. The soil should be ploughed by a soil turning plough, after the harvest of the monsoon (kharif) crops. The Bengal gram is normally rotated with maize, rice, cotton, soya bean, and sunflower.

(ii) Pigeon pea or *arhar/tur* (*Cajanus cajan*): A native crop of India, pigeon pea is cultivated in tropical and subtropical regions. This dal is extensively consumed in some parts of India. The green pods are used as vegetable. The plants of pigeon pea shed large amounts of leaves which add organic matter to the soil. *Tur* dal needs temperature in the range of 20–35°C for cultivation. In India, it is grown in Maharashtra, Karnataka, Andhra Pradesh, Uttar Pradesh, Madhya Pradesh, Gujarat, Odisha, Tamil Nadu, Chhattisgarh, and Bihar. The average yield of pigeon pea is about 1200–1500 kg/ha.

(iii) Green gram (*Vigna radiata*): Green gram or *moong* dal has been cultivated in India since ancient times. It is cultivated at 25–35°C in a wide variety of soils, ranging from sandy to heavy loam. Green gram crop is sensitive to water logging.

(iv) Black gram or *urad* beam (*Vigna mungo*): Like green gram (or *moong*), black gram (or *urad* bean) has also been cultivated in India for thousands of years. It is cultivated as a kharif crop in almost all states. It is used as a dal or made into flour to further produce food items such as papad, dosa, and vada. Black gram is cultivated in a wide variety of soils. Well-drained, moisture-retentive, deep-loam soils, free from excessive soluble salts are ideal for black gram cultivation.

(v) Lentil or *masoor* (*Lens culinaris*): Lentil or *masoor* is an age-old crop which developed near the East and Mediterranean regions and, subsequently, reached India, China, and Europe. In India, lentil is grown in different types of soils, ranging from light loamy, sandy to heavy clay soil in northern parts, and deep, light, black soils in Madhya Pradesh and Maharashtra. The crop is best cultivated in the temperature range of 15–25°C.

(vi) French bean or *rajmah* (*Phaseolus vulgaris*): French bean is native to Mexico and Guatemala. Subsequently, it spread to other parts of the world. In India, it is cultivated in Madhya Pradesh, Maharashtra, Gujarat, Andhra Pradesh, and Jammu and Kashmir. It is best cultivated in the temperature range of 15–27°C. The variety grown in Jammu and Kashmir is a valuable cash crop mainly due to its small size.

## 8.2.8 Oilseeds

India is the fifth largest oilseed-producing country in the world after the USA, China, Brazil, and Argentina. It accounts for about 12%–15% of the world's total oilseed production. The oil obtained from oilseeds is used as edible oil (seven varieties in total) or non-edible oil. An example of non-edible oil is castor which is now being used to manufacture diesel oil by transesterification.

The most important oilseeds include groundnut, rapeseed, mustard, oil-palm, and flax.

(i) Groundnuts or peanuts (*Arachis hypogaea*): Groundnut is believed to be a native of Brazil. The oil content of groundnut varies from 45% to 50%, depending on the variety. Groundnut is cultivated throughout the tropics on different soils. However, the best results are obtained on sandy loam and loamy soils. The rainfall requirement for groundnut cultivation is 50–125 cm. The major groundnut-producing countries are India, China, Nigeria, the USA, Indonesia, Argentina, and Myanmar.

In India, groundnut cultivation is done mainly in Gujarat, Andhra Pradesh, Tamil Nadu, Karnataka, Rajasthan, Maharashtra, Madhya Pradesh, Odisha, and Uttar Pradesh. India produces about 20% of the world's total production. Being a leguminous crop, groundnut cultivation contributes to nitrogen fixation of the soil. It is normally grown in rotation with other crops such as millets, maize, or cotton.

Groundnut is used in the manufacture of *vanaspati ghee* while its oil is extensively used in cooking. It also finds use in the manufacture of soaps, cosmetics, lubricants, and stearin.

(ii) Rapeseed (*Brassica rapa*) and mustard (*Brassica Juncea*): Rapeseed-mustard is the most important oilseed crop. The crop is cultivated in areas having 25–40 cm of rainfall. However, in low-rainfall areas, mustard and paramecia are preferred whereas in medium- and high-rainfall areas, raga and toria are grown. Mustard is normally cultivated as a sole crop in rain-fed areas of kharif fallows.

In India, rapeseed and mustard are mainly cultivated in Rajasthan, Uttar Pradesh, Haryana, Madhya Pradesh, Gujarat, Karnataka, Tamil Nadu, and Andhra Pradesh.

(iii) Oil palm (*Elaeis guineensis*): Oil palm is the highest oil-yielding plant. It is used for meeting the nutritional and energy requirements of people. Oil palm crop is believed to be a crop for the future and a source of import substitution. In India, oil palm plantation is extensively carried out in Andhra Pradesh, Karnataka, Odisha, Tamil Nadu, Tripura, and West Bengal. For its cultivation, temperature of 24–33°C, rainfall of 250–400 cm, and relative humidity of more than 80% are required.

The oil palm plant is propagated through seeds extracted from fruits. The seeds are pre-heated for almost 80 days in 40°C temperature, soaked in running water for 5 days, and then placed in a cool place. It takes about 10–12 days for their germination. The sprouted seeds are kept in polybags.

(iv) Flax (*Linum usitatissimum*): The seeds of linseed are a good source of oil. Fibre is obtained from the stems of flax crops (for more details, refer to Section 8.2.11). Coconut oil is valuable oil and is obtained from coconut trees (discussed in Section 8.2.10).

## 8.2.9   Sugar-producing Crops

Sugar (commonly known as sucrose or cane sugar) is produced mainly for the manufacture of ethyl alcohol which, besides being used as an alcoholic drink, is mixed with gasoline to produce energy. The main sugar-producing crops are sugar cane and sugar beet.

(i) Sugar cane (*Saccharum* spp.): Sugar cane is the main source of sugar, *gur*, and *khandsari*. The molasses left after extraction of sugar is a valuable raw material for ethyl alcohol production. The leftover cane residue is used in paper manufacturing. The upper green part of sugar cane is a nutritious fodder for cattle. Sugar cane is a cash crop of India and the principal source of sugar. For sugar cane cultivation, 20–35°C temperature and 85–165 cm rainfall are necessary.

The soils that support sugar cane cultivation include well-drained alluvium, black, red, and brown regur soils. The chief sugar cane-producing countries are India, Brazil, China, Pakistan, Thailand, Mexico, Cuba, and Colombia. Of these, Brazil is the leading exporter. In India, sugar cane is extensively cultivated in Andhra Pradesh, Assam, Bihar, Gujarat, Haryana, Karnataka, Kerala, Himachal Pradesh, Maharashtra, Odisha, Punjab, Rajasthan, Tamil Nadu, Uttarakhand, Uttar Pradesh, and West Bengal.

(ii) Sugar beet (*Beta vulgaris*): Sugar beet is another sugar-producing crop, accounting for about 22% of the world's total sugar production. It is also a potential source of ethanol and can be blended with gasoline. Sugar beet cultivation requires temperature of 15–25°C and rainfall of 25–50 cm. Well-drained, loamy soil is necessary for cultivation. The main producers of sugar beet are France, the USA, Germany, Russia, China, Ukraine, Poland, and Turkey. The beet pulp—a residue left after extraction of sugar—is a valuable cattle feed.

(iii) Corn (*Zea mays*): Besides sugar cane and sugar beet, sugar is also obtained from corn. For this purpose, corn kernels are ground (using a hammer mill), mixed with water, heated to 104°C (using pressurized steam), and treated with alpha amylase. The formed mesh is kept at 85–90°C for a short period of time, cooled at 32°C, and fermented by glucoamylase and yeast. The formed dextrins (in the mesh) are broken down into monosaccharides or disaccharides which are then converted into ethanol.

## 8.2.10   Nuts

Nuts (dry fruits) are commonly used as a good source of protein. These include cashew nut, walnut, almond, and areca nut.

(i) Cashew nut (*Anacardium occidentale*): Cashew is cultivated throughout the tropics for its kernels. In India, it is cultivated in the west coast, the east coast, and some plains of Karnataka, Tamil Nadu, Kerala, Andhra Pradesh, Maharashtra, and Madhya Pradesh. Cashew can adapt well to dry conditions as the plant is hardy and drought resistant. It grows in almost all kinds of soils such as sandy loams, laterite soils, and coastal sands. Cashew plants start bearing fruits within three years after planting. Generally, the best quality fruits are obtained after 10 years of planting, especially when the nuts fall on their own from cashew trees.

(ii) Walnut (*Juglans* sp.): Walnut is an important nut (fruit) of India. It is grown in Jammu and Kashmir, Himachal Pradesh, and Uttarakhand. The walnut plant grows from seedlings, attain giant sizes, and starts bearing fruits after 10–15 years. Those areas where springtime is free from frost and there is no extreme heat in summer are best suited for walnut plantation. The plant grows in areas with well-spread rains of about 75 cm or more. Temperature within the 25–38°C range near harvesting can yield best results. A well-drained silt loam soil, having abundant organic matter, is best for walnut cultivation. Walnuts are harvested when the nuts' colour change from green to yellowish with the development of cracks.

(iii) Almond (*Amygdalus communis*): Like walnut, almond is also an important nut (fruit) of India. It is mostly grown in Jammu and Kashmir and Kinnaur District (Himachal Pradesh). Most of the orchards in Jammu and Kashmir are of seedling origin. For its cultivation, proper soil and air drainage are necessary. Almonds are harvested when the nuts change colour from green to yellowish and cracks develop.

(iv) Areca nut (*Areca catechu*): Areca nut, also known as betel nut or *supari,* is chewed fresh or after processing. In Assam, Kerala, and northern parts of West Bengal, ripe areca nut is used while in western and northern parts of India, a variety of areca nuts called *chali* is used. The processed green nut, *kalipak,* is favoured in Karnataka and Tamil Nadu. Because of the medicinal properties of areca nut, it is used for treating a number of ailments such as leucoderma, cough, fits, worms, anaemia, and obesity. The tannins in areca nuts are used for dyeing clothes and tanning leather. The husk of areca nuts are used to make plastic, hard boards, and craft paper. The areca nut stem is a useful building material in villages. Areca nut is grown mostly in Kerala, Karnataka, Assam, West Bengal, and Tamil Nadu.

(v) Coconut (*Cocos nucifera*): It is cultivated in India in Kerala, Tamil Nadu, Andhra Pradesh, Karnataka, Goa, Gujarat, and Maharashtra. The dried fruit is used for the extraction of coconut oil which, besides being used as cooking oil, is also used for making sweets. Coconut water is good for health. The cultivation of coconut requires temperature of about 27°C with rainfall of 100–250 cm. The soil used for cultivation is laterite red or sandy alluvial.

Besides the nuts discussed above, groundnut is also a useful source of oil (for more details, refer to Section 8.2.8).

## 8.2.11   Fibre-producing Crops

A number of crops are used for producing various types of fibres which are useful for manufacturing a variety of items. These crops include cotton, jute, mesta, sunn hemp, ramie, sisal, and flax.

(i) Cotton (*Gossypium* spp.): Cotton—also referred to as 'white gold'—is an important commercial crop of the world. The leading producers of cotton are China, the USA, India, Brazil, Pakistan, Uzbekistan, Egypt, and Turkey. The USA is the leading exporter of cotton in the world. India contributes nearly 19% to the total cotton production of the world. Cotton accounts for about 65% fibre used in Indian textiles. Cotton crop cultivation requires temperature within the 18–27°C range and rainfall of 60–110 cm. The soils that suit the cultivation of cotton are the well-drained loam and regur (black earth).

In India, cultivation of Bt cotton hybrid (a genetically modified organism of the cotton variety) was approved by the Government of India in the 2002 crop season. Its large-scale cultivation is carried out in Maharashtra, Gujarat, Andhra Pradesh, Madhya Pradesh, Karnataka, and Tamil Nadu. After partition (1947), India was left with about 60% of its crop production industry. However, it possessed more than 90% of the cotton-based industry. It was mainly due to the introduction of Bt cotton that India not only met its domestic demands but also exported the surplus production.

(ii) Jute (*Corchorus capsularis*): Jute is another cash crop of India and mainly grown in West Bengal, Assam, northern Bihar, south-east Odisha, Tripura, Meghalaya, and eastern Uttar Pradesh. Besides India, jute is also grown in Bangladesh, China, Thailand, Myanmar, Indonesia, Brazil, Nepal, and Africa. Jute requires a warm and humid climate, with temperature range 27–35°C and 150–250 cm rainfall. It is grown in sandy and clay loam soils. Soils with lower pH give low yields. The optimum pH for jute crop is about 6.4.

(iii) Mesta (*Hibiscus sabdariffa*): Mesta fibre is obtained from the stems of kenaf and roselle. The major mesta-growing countries are India, China, Thailand, Malaysia, Indonesia, the Philippines, Egypt, Sudan, Brazil, and Australia. In India, mesta is grown extensively in Andhra Pradesh, Maharashtra, Odisha, Bihar, and West Bengal.

Cultivation of mesta requires a warm and humid climate, with temperature and rainfall of 20–30°C and 50–75 cm, respectively. It can be grown on a variety of soils including new and old alluvium. Higher fibre yields are produced in light textured, well-drained soil, having adequate organic matter.

(iv) Sunn hemp (*Crotalaria juncea*): Sunn hemp belongs to the *Fabaceae* family of legumes and is known for producing quality fibres. The fibre is used for manufacturing tissue paper and paper for currency notes. Besides, it is used for making ropes, twine, nets, canvas, and serums. The sunn hemp crop is best grown in tropical and subtropical climates. The temperature range of 20–30°C and rainfall of 40–50 cm are favourable for the growth of sunn hemp crops. The crop is grown in all parts of India. Well-drained alluvial soils having sandy loam or loamy texture are best suited for sunn hemp cultivation.

(v)  Ramie (*Boehmeria* genus): Ramie is the fibre crop which produces long fibres of plant origin. The crop is indigenous to central and western China. In India, ramie is grown in Assam, Arunachal Pradesh, Himachal Pradesh (Kangra valley), Nilgiri hills, and Tamil Nadu. The fibre of ramie contains about 85% cellulose.

The use of a fibre depends on its gum content. If the gum content is less then 4%, it can be used for manufacturing fibres. The fibres can be blended with cotton, silk, wool to produce yarns.

(vi)  Sisal (*Agave sisalana*): A native of Mexico, sisal provides a creamy-white, hard fibre from its leaves. The major sisal-producing countries are Brazil, Kenya, Tanzania, Madagascar, Angola, Haiti, and China. In India, it is grown in Odisha, Madhya Pradesh, Andhra Pradesh, Maharashtra, Jharkhand, Bihar, and western parts of West Bengal.

Sisal is grown in hot and humid regions. Rainfall of about 100 cm per annum along with plenty of light and sunshine are good for sisal growth. The soil for sisal cultivation should be friable, well-drained, dry, permeable and sandy-loam. The propagation of sisal is done by bulbils. Sisal fibre is used for manufacture of cordage-rope, twine, carpets, and so on.

(vii)  Flax (*Linum usitatissimum*): As already stated, flax is an oil-producing plant (from seeds). Besides oil, flax is used for the production of fibres from its stems. Flax fibres are durable and have good strength and are superior to those of cotton.

## 8.2.12  Spices

Spices, including black pepper, cardamom (small), cinnamon, clove, coriander, cumin, ginger, tamarind, and turmeric, produced in India are valued throughout the world. Most of these spices apart from being used for cooking, are also valued for their various medicinal properties.

(i)  Black pepper (*Piper nigrum*): Black pepper is cultivated on a large scale in India. This puts India among the top black pepper exporters of the world. It is grown in Kerala, Karnataka, Tamil Nadu, Andhra Pradesh, Anadaman and Nicobar Islands, and Puducherry. For its cultivation, black pepper requires temperature of 15–40°C and rainfall of 200–300 cm. Soils rich in humus, red loam, sandy loam, and red laterite sandy loam are ideal for black pepper plantation. In India, different types of black pepper are cultivated, including white pepper, green pepper, and bottled-green pepper.

(ii) Cardamom (small) (*Elettaria cardamomum*): India is the leading producer and exporter of cardamom. It is cultivated in Kerala, Karnataka, and Tamil Nadu. For its cultivation, temperature of 10–35°C and rainfall of 150–400 cm are favourable. It is best grown in soils rich in humus.

(iii) Cinnamon (*Cinnamomum verum*): Cinnamon is an evergreen tree, having a height of 6–15 m. The dried inner barks of cinnamon are used as spice. It is cultivated in the states of Kerala, Karnataka, and Tamil Nadu. Being a hardy plant, cinnamon can tolerate a range of climatic conditions. Normally, cinnamon is grown in laterite soils and sandy patches. It needs a rainfall of 200–300 cm for efficient growth.

(iv) Clove (*Syzygium aromaticum*): Since ancient times, clove is being used in India. Cloves are dried, aromatic, unopened flower buds. Clove oil finds use in dental treatments and has other medicinal properties. Clove grows in the rich, loamy soil of the humid tropics.

(v) Coriander (*Coriandrum sativum*): It is commonly used as a flavouring substance. Stem, leaves, and fruits of a coriander have a pleasant aroma. In medicine, its seeds are used as a carminative refrigerant and diuretic. In India, coriander is cultivated in Andhra Pradesh, Rajasthan, Gujarat, Madhya Pradesh, Karnataka, Tamil Nadu, and Uttar Pradesh. Loamy soil is best suited for coriander cultivation.

(vi) Cumin (*Cuminum cyminum*): Cumin seeds are used extensively in Ayurvedic medicine for treating stomach pains and dyspepsia. In India, it is mainly cultivated in Gujarat and Rajasthan. The cumin grows well in well-drained, loamy soils.

(vii) Ginger (*Zingiber officinale*): Ginger has a distinct flavour and pungency. It is used as a flavourant in soft drinks, alcoholic and non-alcoholic beverages, confectionary, pickles, and pharmaceutical preparations. India is the largest producer of ginger in the world. It is also grown in West Indies, Brazil, China, Japan, Indonesia, and Vietnam. In India, it is grown in Kerala, Meghalaya, Uttar Pradesh, Uttarakhand, and West Bengal.

Ginger grows well in warm and humid climate. Early planting helps in better growth and the development of rhizomes, thus resulting in better yields. For its cultivation, rich soil with good drainage and aeration is preferred. It grows well in sandy and clayey loam, red loam, and lateritic loam soils.

(viii) Tamarind (*Tamarindus indica*): Tamarind is an important tree that grows in semi-arid tropical conditions. Each and every part of this tree can be used for different purposes. Its fruit pulp is sweetish/ acidic in taste and is commonly used in curries, chutneys, and soups. The pulp is carminative and laxative and is given as an infusion in biliousness and febrile conditions. Tamarind kernel powder is used as a sizing material in the textile and leather industry. The seeds yield a fatty oil which is used in paint and varnish production. The wood of the tamarind tree is used for making agricultural implements. In India, it is grown in Bihar, Jharkhand, Chhattisgarh, Odisha, Maharashtra, Karnataka, Andhra Pradesh, Madhya Pradesh, Uttar Pradesh, and Tamil Nadu. For efficient growth, tamarind tree needs rainfall between 75 cm and 100 cm and gravelly to deep alluvial soils.

(ix) Turmeric (*Curuma longa*): Turmeric is used as a spice, a dye, and in the cosmetic industry. It is also valued for its medicinal properties. In India, it is cultivated in Andhra Pradesh, Odisha, West Bengal, Tamil Nadu, Karnataka, and Kerala. Turmeric grows best in well-drained sandy or clayey loam or red loamy soil, having an acidic to a slightly alkaline pH.

## 8.2.13  Beverage Crops

Worldwide, a number of beverage crops are grown to produce a number of potable beverage products including tea, coffee, and cacao.

(i) Tea (*Camellia sinensis*): Globally, tea is the most popular beverage. It is extensively drunk in China, Japan, India, Sri Lanka, Great Britain, and Russia. India is one of the leading tea exporters in the world. The major tea-producing states are Assam, West Bengal, Tamil Nadu, and Kerala. On a small scale, it is also grown in Tripura, Karnataka, Himachal Pradesh, Uttarakhand, Sikkim, Bihar, Manipur, Odisha, Nagaland, and Arunachal Pradesh.

Tea plantation needs a temperature of 15–55°C and rainfall of 100–250 cm. Well-drained alluvial is the best soil for tea plantation. For cultivation of tea, young tea plants are grown in nurseries. The saplings are transplanted in the field when they are about a year old. The process of plucking of leaves is done after 3 years of plantation. Best yields are achieved when tea plants become 6 years old. Constant pruning of tea bushes gives tender new leaves, which is the only part of the plant that is harvested. Tea leaves once plucked are processed which involves withering, fermenting, and firing. This makes black tea. Green tea is obtained when withered leaves undergo steaming to stop fermentation. Nowadays, green tea is becoming extremely popular all over the world because of its health benefits.

(ii) Coffee (*Coffea*): Coffee is a stimulating beverage crop. The stimulating effect is due to the presence of caffeine. Originally, coffee was grown in tropical rainforests of Ethiopia and Central Africa. In India, coffee cultivation started in the 17th century.

Three important variations of coffee are (i) arabica, also known as Mocha Coffee, native to Yemen (Arabian Peninsula), (ii) robusta, a west African variety which can survive arid conditions and is disease resistant, (iii) liberica, indigenous to Liberia.

Coffee plantation requires hot and humid climate, with temperature ranging from 15°C to 27°C. It requires more than 100 cm of rainfall. The best soil for coffee plantation is well-drained alluvial soil. The leading producers of coffee are Brazil, Colombia, Indonesia, Vietnam, Ivory Coast, Mexico, Ghana, Cameroon, and India. Brazil is the leading exporter of coffee in the world. In India, majority of coffee is grown in Karnataka, followed by Tamil Nadu and Kerala. Coffee is propagated from seeds or through cuttings in a nursery. In the latter case, coffee plants are planted 3 m apart in the field.

(iii)  Cocoa or cacao (*Theobroma cocao*): Cocoa is an important beverage crop. It is used for manufacturing soft drinks and chocolates. The raw material for these products is obtained from the seeds of the cocoa tree.

The cocoa is indigenous to tropical America. Spain subsequently developed methods for cocoa cultivation. The leading producers of cocoa are Ivory Coast, Ghana, Indonesia, Brazil, Cameroon, Nigeria, Ecuador, and Costa Rica. Ivory Coast is the leading cocoa exporter in the world.

Cocoa plantation needs temperature between 18°C and 35°C with 100–250 cm of rainfall. The best soil for its cultivation is well-drained alluvial. The cocoa plant is propagated through seeds and the seeds are planted about 3 m apart. Occasional weeding and manuring help improve the quality of the beans.

## 8.3  SOME MISCELLANEOUS CROPS

Besides the crops stated above, rubber and tobacco are also cultivated in India.

(i) Rubber (*Hevea brasiliensis*): Rubber is the latex obtained from the rubber tree. The major rubber-producing countries include Malaysia, India, China, Sri Lanka, Liberia, and Brazil. The leading rubber exporter in the world is Thailand. Rubber plantation needs temperature of about 27°C with 150–250 cm rainfall. Well-drained alluvial soil is suitable for cultivating rubber trees.

In India, rubber plantation districts include Ernakulam, Kollam, Kottayam, Kozhikode (Kerala), Coimbatore, Madurai, and Nilgiri. It is worth mentioning here that natural rubber is being replaced by synthetic rubber, mainly to fulfil the increasing demand for rubber and to overcome the limitations of natural rubber.

(ii) Tobacco (*Nicotiana tabacum*): Originally tobacco was cultivated by the Portuguese in 1508. Subsequently, its cultivation spread to other countries. India is the leading producer of tobacco in the world. Tobacco is used mainly for smoking in the form of cigarette, *bidi*, cigar, cheroot, and *hookah*. It also finds use for the manufacture of insecticides. In India, tobacco is cultivated in Andhra Pradesh, Maharashtra, Gujarat, Uttar Pradesh, Bihar, Tamil Nadu, Karnataka, Kerala, Odisha, Madhya Pradesh, Rajasthan, and West Bengal. The ideal temperature range for tobacco cultivation is 18–25°C. It requires a rainfall of 100–250 cm. Well-drained soil is ideal for tobacco cultivation. The Government of India is trying to curtail the habit of smoking as it is one of the major causes of cancer.

## 8.4  FRUIT CROPS

A variety of fruits are grown in India. These include mango, citrus fruits, banana, guava, apple, papaya, grape, litchi, arid fruits, pineapple, and so on. Being a perishable crop, fruits must be used within a reasonable time after cultivation. Some of the major fruits grown in India are discussed here.

  (i) **Mango:**  Commonly known as the king of fruits, mango is extensively grown in India. The country accounts for 55% production of the total mangoes produced worldwide. It grows well in areas with annual rainfall of 75–150 cm with little irrigation. Major mango-growing states in India are Uttar Pradesh, Andhra Pradesh, Odisha, West Bengal, Maharashtra, Gujarat, and Karnataka. Many varities of mangoes are grown in India including Dasheri, Langra, Chaunsa, Bombay Green, Amrapali, Fazli, Alphonso, Pusa Surya, and Konkan Ruchi.

 (ii) **Citrus:**  Various citrus fruits are grown in India. These include lime, lemon, sweet orange, and so on. The citrus-producing states in India are Maharashtra, Andhra Pradesh, Punjab, Haryana, Karnataka, and North-Eastern states. An important citrus fruit is Kinnow which is widely grown in Punjab, Haryana, Rajasthan, and Himachal Pradesh.

(iii) **Banana:**  In India, banana is produced in Tamil Nadu, Maharashtra, Karnataka, Gujarat, Andhra Pradesh, Assam, Bihar, and Madhya Pradesh. Cultivation of Dwarf Cavendish banana is done in dry climate. Many varieties of banana are grown in India.

 (iv) **Guava:**  Guava is an important fruit of India and grown in almost all states and union territories. Many varieties of guava are grown in India including L-49 Chittidar Allahabadi, Safeda, Red flesh, and Lalit.

  (v) **Papaya:**  The papaya plant requires warm and dry summer and cool winter. Papaya develops better in bright sunshine. In India, it is mainly grown in Andhra Pradesh, Karnataka, Maharashtra, Gujarat, Tamil Nadu, Madhya Pradesh, Punjab, Haryana, and Uttar Pradesh. A number of varieties of papaya are grown in India.

 (vi) **Grape:**  In India, grapes are grown in Maharashtra, Andhra Pradesh, Karnataka, Tamil Nadu, and to a limited extent in northern states. Different varieties of grapes are grown in India. These include Anab-e-shahi, Bangalore blue, Bangalore purple, Thompson seedless, and PUSA seedless.

(vii) **Litchi:**  It is produced mainly in Uttarakhand, Bihar, West Bengal, Assam, Punjab, and Haryana. It is a valuable fruit and used for making drinks. It has a great economic significance due it its high return and export potential.

(viii) **Arid fruits:**  These include aonla, ber, pomegranate, date palm, and fig. Some other fruits include jackfruit, jamun (*Syzgium cumine*), bel (*Aegle* *marmelos)*, star fruit (*Averrhoa carambola*), phalsa (*Grewia asiatica*), wood-apple (*Limonia acidissima*), mulberry (*Morus alba*), and lasoda (*Cordia myxa*). All these fruits have varied uses. Recently, cultivation of olives and kiwi fruit has started in Jammu and Kashmir, Himachal Pradesh, and Uttarakhand.

   (ix) **Pineapple:**  Pineapple plantation needs temperature of 20–30°C and rainfall of about 150 cm. It is grown in Meghalaya, Tripura, Kerala, West Bengal, Bihar, Tamil Nadu, Karnataka, and Andaman and Nicobar Islands.

## 8.5  VEGETABLE CROPS

Vegetables are known to contain a number of nutrients that are essential for human growth. India is the world's second largest producer of vegetables, after China. The following are the major vegetables produced in India:

   (i) **Tomato:**  Tomato is the most important vegetable crop in India. It is grown in Bihar, Karnataka, Odisha, Maharashtra, Madhya Pradesh, Andhra Pradesh, Punjab, Haryana, Uttar Pradesh, and Karnataka. The optimum temperature for its cultivation is 18–27°C.

   (ii) **Brinjal:**  Brinjal is the second most important vegetable crop in India and is grown almost all over the country. The major brinjal-growing states are West Bengal, Odisha, and Bihar. Different varieties of brinjal such as purple, yellow, round, thin, and short are grown in India.

   (iii) **Cabbage:**  India occupies third position in cabbage production in the world. It needs moist climate for cultivation. The major cabbage-growing states in India are West Bengal, Odisha, Bihar, Assam, Karnataka, Uttar Pradesh, Punjab, and Haryana.

   (iv) **Onion:**  India ranks second in onion production in the world. It is the fourth most important commercial crop of India. The major onion-growing states are Gujarat, Maharashtra, Karnataka, and Uttar Pradesh.

   (v) **Cauliflower:**  It is the fifth most important vegetable of India. India holds the top position in the list of major cauliflower producers of the world. It needs a cool and moist climate for cultivation. The optimum monthly temperature for efficient growth of cauliflower crop is 15–20°C. It is grown in almost all states of India.

   (vi) **Potato:**  India ranks fifth in terms of cultivation area and production of potatoes. India annually produces 225 lakh tonnes of potato on an area of 13 lakh hectares. Almost 90% of the total potato production is carried out in northern plains during winter and about 6% share is grown in hilly areas in summer. The major potato-producing states in India are Uttar Pradesh, Bihar, West Bengal, Punjab, Haryana, Karnataka, Assam, and Madhya Pradesh.

**(vii) Carrot:**   Carrot is grown mostly in winter and needs a temperature of 15–20°C. In warm climate, the colour of the carrot changes due to light. Carrots are mostly grown in northern plains of India.

**(viii) Peas:**   Peas are grown in winter. It grows best in regions where there is a low transition from cool to warm weather during spring.

Besides the vegetables mentioned above, certain other vegetables are also grown in India including raddish, turnip, cucumber, lady finger (*okra*), and greens such as spinach and mustard. Most of the crops need good irrigation which is provided by various sources such as canals, tube wells, and tanks. The sprinkler system is an efficient method for irrigation as it uses less water and yields maximum results.

# SUMMARY

- India is an agricultural country. A large number of people depend on products obtained from agriculture.
- In India, agriculture provides livelihood to about 70% of the population.
- Agrochemicals such as fertilizers, insecticides, and herbicides used for increasing yield contribute considerably to environmental degradation.
- Use of better technologies is primarily responsible for the Green Revolution.
- India has a variety of climatic conditions in different parts of the country and so there is great variation in the cropping system.
- The major crops in India are cereals, pulses, oilseeds, sugar-producing crops, nuts (dry fruits), fibre-producing crops, spices, beverage crops, fruit crops, and vegetable crops.
- Almost all crops need good irrigation which is provided by various sources such as canals, tube wells, and tanks.
- The sprinkler system is the best system for irrigation. It uses less water and yields maximum result.

# EXERCISE

## [A] Multiple-choice questions

1. Which of the following statements are correct about agriculture?
    (a) Production of a number of agricultural crops.
    (b) Employment to more than 50% of the population.
    (c) Agriculture is necessary for sustenance of life.
    (d) All are correct

2. For the increasing population of India
   (a) More land is required by deforestation
   (b) Use of agrochemicals for increasing yield causes environment problems
   (c) A large amount of water is necessary for irrigation
   (d) All are correct

3. The most important agricultural crops all over the globe are
   (a) Rice, wheat, pulses
   (b) Oilseeds, nuts
   (c) Sugar cane, spices
   (d) Fibre-producing crops
   (e) Fruit and vegetable crops

4. Pulses are
   (a) Important sources of dietary proteins
   (b) Pulse crops make the soil fertile due to fixation of atmospheric nitrogen
   (c) Both (a) and (b) are incorrect
   (d) Both (a) and (b) are correct

5. The oil obtained from oilseed is used for
   (a) Cooking medium
   (b) Manufacturing diesel oil
   (c) Mostly non-edible oil is used for producing diesel oil
   (d) A number of oils are known for their medicinal properties
   (e) All are correct

6. Flax is
   (a) An oil-producing plant
   (b) A plant with stems that are used for the production of fibres
   (c) Both (a) and (b) are incorrect
   (d) Both (a) and (b) are correct

7. The main sugar-producing crop is
   (a) Sugar cane
   (b) Sugar beet
   (c) Corn
   (d) Depending on the availability of different crops used

8. The importance of areca nut is due to
   (a) Its medicinal properties
   (b) Tannins which are used for dyeing clothes and tanning leather
   (c) The husk of areca nut is used to make plastic and craft paper
   (d) The stem of areca nut is used as building material in villages
   (e) All are correct

9. The most important fibre-producing crops is/are
    (a) Cotton and jute               (b) Mesta
    (c) Sunn hemp                     (d) Ramie
    (e) Sisal

10. Globally, which of the following beverage crops is used maximum?
    (a) Tea                           (b) Coffee
    (c) Cocoa                         (d) All are equally important

11. India holds first position in the world in the production of
    (a) Tomato                        (b) Brinjal
    (c) Cabbage                       (d) Cauliflower
    (e) Potato

12. Least amount of water should be used for irrigating various crops. This can be made possible by using
    (a) Canals                        (b) Tube wells
    (c) Tanks                         (d) Sprinkler system

### Answers

| | | | | |
|---|---|---|---|---|
| 1. (d) | 2. (d) | 3. (a) | 4. (e) | 5. (e) |
| 6. (d) | 7. (d) | 8. (e) | 9. (a) | 10. (a) |
| 11. (d) | 12. (d) | | | |

## [B] Fill in the blanks.

1. In India, agriculture provides employment to about _______ % of the population.

2. In agriculture, considerable environmental problem is caused by _______ and use of______.

3. For sustainable agriculture, ______ and ______ are used.

4. Worldwide, the most important crops are ______, ______ , and ______.

5. Cultivation of pulses makes the soil ______.

6. Diesel oil is obtained mostly from non-edible oils by ______.

7. In India, sugar is produced from ______.

8. Different parts of the ______ plant are used for different purposes.

9. In India, the main fibre-producing crops are ______ and ______.

10. The only plant whose seeds are used for producing oil and stem for producing fibres is the ______.

11. The most popular beverage of the global population is ______.

12. India ranks number one in the production of the vegetable ______.

### ANSWERS

| | |
|---|---|
| 1. 70 | 2. deforestation, agrochemicals |
| 3. biofertilizers, biopesticides | 4. rice, wheat, maize |
| 5. fertile | 6. transesterification |
| 7. sugar cane | 8. areca nut |
| 9. cotton, jute | 10. flax plant |
| 11. tea | 12. cauliflower |

## [C] Short-answer questions

1. India is an agricultural country. Comment.
2. Why is agriculture important in India?
3. What environmental concerns are associated with agriculture?
4. Write a note on the Green Revolution?
5. What is sustainable agriculture? How can it be achieved?
6. What are the major crops of India?
7. What do you understand by 'transesterification'?
8. Which crops are used as sources of protein?
9. What are the uses of spices?
10. Which fruit is the most popular in India?

# Environmental Engineering

## 9.1 INTRODUCTION

Environmental engineering deals with wastewater management, air pollution control, and other environmental problems. Besides it also deals with the supply of water, intake of water, and sewage characterization including treatment of sewage and solid waste.

## 9.2 HYDROLOGY

It deals with the study of water at different levels.

### 9.2.1 Availability of Water

Water is the most important and essential component of life; without it life is not possible. Water is abundant on earth. However, the main concern is the availability of water in the right place, at the right time, and in the right form. Water exists in liquid, solid, or gaseous state in a number of places such as oceans, glaciers, and the atmosphere. Table 9.1 lists the availability of water at different locations on earth.

Water has some properties and characteristics which makes it a special component of the biosphere. Some of these properties are discussed here:

**Table 9.1** Availability of water

| Location | Percentage of water |
|---|---|
| Oceans | 97.2 |
| Atmosphere | 0.001 |
| Rivers and streams | 0.0001 |
| Groundwater | 0.31 |
| Lakes | 0.009 |
| Glaciers | 2.15 |

- Water possesses the highest heat of fusion and evaporation, collectively known as latent heat, of all known liquid substances at ordinary temperature. Latent heat is responsible for moderating the temperature of the biosphere. It also plays a vital role in the evaporation of water and its condensation (precipitation) as rain and dew (for details, refer to the next section).

- The high surface tension of water (75 dyne $cm^{-1}$ at 20°C) is important in many physical and biological processes involving movement of water through and into organisms.

- The high viscosity of water (0.01 poise at 20°C) enables organisms to swim using simple movements.

- Ice, which is the solid form of water, is lighter than its liquid form. This enables ice to float on the surface of water. If waterbodies froze from the bottom up, it would result in the death of all aquatic life.

- Water is transparent and allows sunlight to pass through it; this permits organisms to live below the surface of water.

## 9.2.2　Hydrological Cycle

Also known as water cycle, the hydrological cycle is the most important of the various cycles of the environment. In the hydrological cycle, water circulates between the atmosphere and various waterbodies such as oceans, rivers, lakes, seas. There is movement of water (i) from oceans to the atmosphere (through evaporation), (ii) from the atmosphere to oceans and land (through precipitation), (iii) from land to ocean runoff, and (iv) from streams and rivers to the atmosphere (through evaporation). The sun in the form of solar energy provides the energy required for the hydrological cycle. Figure 9.1 gives the schematic representation of the hydrological cycle.

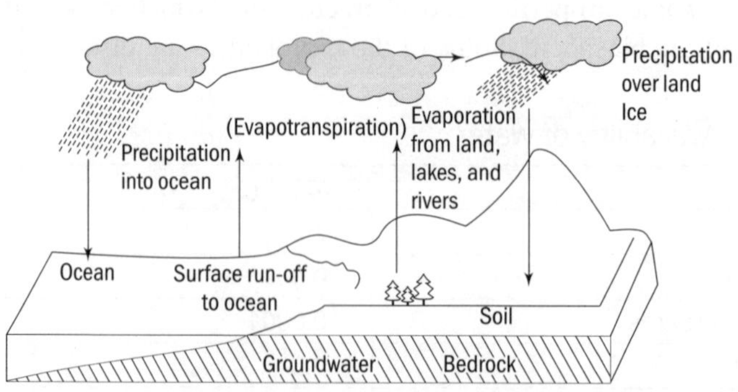


**Fig. 9.1**　Hydrological cycle

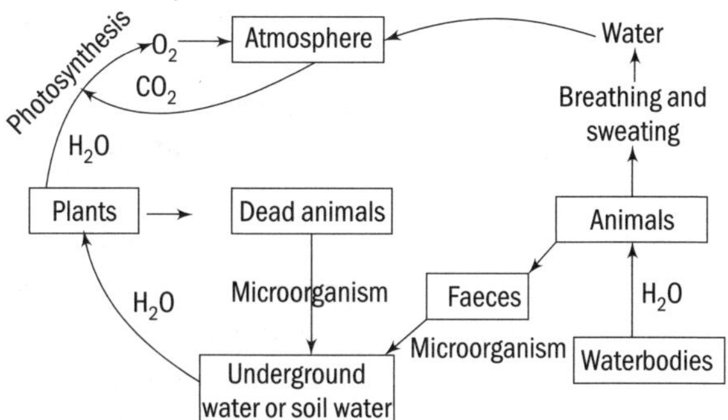


**Fig. 9.2**   Alternative pathway of hydrological cycle

In addition to the water circulations described above, water as groundwater (or soil water) is also circulated by plants, animals, and the atmosphere. Plants absorb soil water through their roots. A part of this water is used by plants for photosynthesis and the excess goes off into the atmosphere during transpiration (the loss of water from the leaves of plants via evaporation).

Transpiration is the main source of water in the atmosphere. Water is released back into the soil when microorganisms cause dead plants to decay. The alternative pathway of the hydrological cycle is shown in Figure 9.2 (for details, refer to Chapter 2, Section 2.3).

## 9.2.3  Groundwater

Groundwater, normally, refers to the water below the water table where saturated conditions exist (up to about 800 m depth). It constitutes about 0.31% of the total global water and is expected to be available for thousands of years. The water table refers to the upper level of an underground surface in which the soil or rocks are permanently saturated with water. It is the boundary that separates the groundwater-saturated zone (below it) from the unsaturated zone (above it). The water table of a region fluctuates on the basis of precipitation, climate variations, irrigational activities, and the kind of vegetation found in the region. Pockets of water existing below the water table are called aquifers. In some advanced countries, such as the USA, about half of the population depend on groundwater for their water requirements. In India and other developing countries, groundwater is the main source of potable water required for human consumption, agriculture, and other needs. It is generally believed that groundwater is pure and safe to drink. This is not, however, true. In fact, groundwater can be easily polluted.

In general, groundwater contamination is irreversible. Groundwater gets polluted due to human activities which include industrial, domestic, and agricultural activities. This is responsible for the degradation of water quality, which results in water with objectionable taste, odour, and excessive hardness. Groundwater can also be polluted by septic tanks and refuse dumps. In view of this, it is necessary to take appropriate steps to prevent groundwater pollution. In case, it does get polluted, it should be suitably treated to remove harmful pollutants. The average composition of groundwater is given in Table 9.2. For comparison, the chemical compositions of surface water (river) and seawater are also given.

Polluted groundwater is a major cause for the outbreak and widespread occurrence of chronic diseases such as typhoid, jaundice, dysentery, diarrhoea, tuberculosis, and hepatitis. The use of polluted groundwater for irrigation damages crops and decreases the agricultural yield. Polluted groundwater affects fertility by killing bacteria and other microorganisms. A severe case of groundwater pollution from Medak District of Andhra Pradesh (India) was reported by *The Hindu* (18 September 1988). According to the report, the groundwater contamination was very high. This was primarily due to the release of poisonous chemicals from chemical industries, set up in the district. Due to pollutants, the groundwater became greenish in colour, emitted a foul smell, and was responsible for causing a number of diseases such as dysentery, jaundice, and diarrhoea. This resulted in a number of deaths.

In view of the incident, it is extremely necessary to protect groundwater from getting polluted. This can be achieved by taking appropriate measures regarding predisposal treatment of toxic industrial effluents and municipal discharges. Also, the location of wells for drinking water supplies should be very carefully decided. Moreover, too much withdrawal of groundwater is unsustainable. It results in a decrease in the earth's water level as replenishing groundwater takes a very long time.

**Table 9.2** Average composition of groundwater, surface water, and seawater

| Parameters (ppm) | Groundwater (well) | Surface water (river) | Seawater |
|---|---|---|---|
| Chloride | 9.6 | 13 | $19 \times 10^3$ |
| Bicarbonate | 330 | 110 | 140 |
| Calcium | 92 | 36 | 400 |
| Magnesium | 34 | 8.0 | $1.35 \times 10^3$ |
| Iron (III) | 0.09 | 0.02 | 0.01 |
| Nitrate | 13 | 0.1 | – |
| Potassium | 1.4 | 1.2 | 380 |
| Silica | 10 | 1.2 | 6.0 |
| Sulphate | 84 | 22 | $2.65 \times 10^3$ |
| Sodium | 8.2 | 6.5 | $10.5 \times 10^3$ |
| TDS | 434 | 1.65 | – |

ppm – parts per million; TDS – total dissolved solids

## 9.3  IRRIGATION ENGINEERING

Besides human consumption, water is an essential requirement for various crop irrigation. Depending on surface and underground water availability, a number of irrigation methods are employed in India. These include irrigation by canals, wells and tube wells, tanks, and other sources.

**(i) Canal irrigation:** In India, canals are an important source of irrigation, especially in plains. In 1950–51, about 44% of all agricultural irrigation was carried out by canals. This, however, decreased to 28.8% by 2010–11. Canal irrigation has been commonly used in Punjab, Haryana, and Uttar Pradesh.

Canals are the main source of irrigation since their sources originate from rivers or the reservoirs of dams. Canals carry considerable amounts of  river sediments. These sediments get deposited in agricultural fields, increasing soil fertility. Canals are a cheap source of irrigation as the farmer has to pay only irrigation charges per annum. However, the initial cost of construction of a canal is very high. Additionally, a considerable amount of water is lost through evaporation and seepage. Canals may also lead to water logging. The waterlogged areas become breeding grounds for parasites like mosquitoes which can transmit diseases such as malaria, yellow fever, dengue, encephalitis, and chikungunya.

**(ii) Well and tube well irrigation:** Well irrigation is usually carried out in areas where sufficient underground water is available. These days, water is drawn from wells by using electricity. Tube wells are the main source of irrigation in Punjab, Haryana, Uttar Pradesh, Rajasthan, Madhya Pradesh, and Bihar. As per Statistical Abstracts of India, only 32% of the total agricultural area utilized wells and tube wells for irrigation. However, this dependency increased to over 62% in 2010–11.

Wells and tube wells are independent sources of irrigation. A tube well's pumping set can be installed in a short time and irrigation can be carried out effectively. Additionally, there is much less wastage of water. However, well and tube well irrigation has some drawbacks: (i) the methods are better suited for the irrigation of small farm areas, (ii) the level of groundwater may fall during droughts, leading to shortage of water, and (iii) the cost of electricity adds to the total expenses.

**(iii) Tank irrigation:** In this type of irrigation, tanks are used for carrying water from ponds and lakes to fields. It is commonly used in Andhra Pradesh, Karnataka, Tamil Nadu, Odisha, West Bengal, Madhya Pradesh, Chhattisgarh, and Maharashtra. The problem arises when the water level of ponds and lakes considerably reduces, particularly in the absence of rain in dry seasons.

### 9.3.1  Economical Use of Water for Irrigation

Agriculture requires large amounts of water. Using improved irrigation systems, such as drip irrigation or sprinkler irrigation, the amount of water required for crops can be substantially reduced.

(i) **Drip irrigation:** The traditional methods for irrigation involve surface irrigation. This method is not suitable for water-scarce areas and involves the use of large amounts of water. A lot of water is lost via evaporation and percolation. In comparison to traditional methods, drip irrigation and sprinkler irrigation techniques are much superior. Drip irrigation involves distribution of water through water pipes running through the land; the pipes contain holes which drip water directly to the soil near the root system. This is a convenient procedure for conservation of water in agriculture.

(ii) **Sprinkler irrigation:** Like drip irrigation, sprinkler irrigation is also an effective method of irrigation that helps in conserving water. In this method, water is sprinkled using jets. These jets, which can move in different directions, spray water on the field and irrigate crops in a rainfall-like pattern. In comparison to the 95% efficiency of drip irrigation, sprinkler irrigation offers an efficiency of 75%.

## 9.4 WATER RESOURCE ENGINEERING

Water is essential for the sustenance of various life forms on earth. Though water is available in considerable amounts, particularly in oceans and seas, there is scarcity of freshwater in the world. The importance of water is evident from the fact that a number of early civilizations have flourished on river banks. Freshwater, one of the most important substances for sustaining life, is among the five vital elements; the others being earth, fire, air, and space.

Potable water is scarce. This is basically due to modern development, overexploitation, and mismanagement of water resources by humans, especially over the last two decades. For a large section of the population, shortage of water means epidemics, hunger, despair, and death.

It is known that less than 3% of the globally available water is freshwater and only a fifth of this is available in liquid form. More than 90% of this scarce commodity exists in the form of groundwater and only 1% is available in the form of lakes and ponds. India is fortunate in terms of its total annual rainfall.

It is essential that the world rethinks its management of water resources. It is known that the world's population has crossed the 6 billion mark. This implies that the demand for freshwater has increased. It is estimated that a person needs a minimum of 20–40 L of water per day for drinking and sanitation purposes. This has placed enormous pressure on the world's limited supply of freshwater. It is believed that more than are 1 billion people worldwide have virtually no access to clean water. The shortage of clean water has led to many conflicts. As an example, in India, Karnataka and Tamil Nadu are fighting over the waters of the Cauvery River while Karnataka and Andhra Pradesh are involved over the Krishna River dispute. Therefore, it is necessary to make people aware about the importance of safe water access. In fact, no drop of water should be wasted in any form.

## 9.4.1  Water Conservation

As already mentioned, almost 75% of the earth's surface is covered with water. However, only 1% of this water is available for use. Of this scarce 1%, about 73% is used in agriculture, 20% is used by various industrial establishments, and the rest is used domestically.

Next to air, water is the most important element for the survival of humankind. However, it is continuously shifting towards becoming a scarce commodity. The scarcity of water threatens us all. The United Nations Population Fund predicted in 2001 that in the next 25 years or so, about one-third of the world's population is likely to experience severe water scarcity. Presently, more than 1 billion people in the world do not have access to safe drinking water. The problem has become more acute because of population growth, industrialization, and urbanization. This is compounded by the fact that about 90% of all sewage produced, particularly in developing countries, is discharged into fresh waterbodies such as rivers, ponds, and lakes. Due to this, the water in these waterbodies becomes unfit for human consumption.

In view of the above discussion and owing to increase in water consumption over the years, water conservation has become a priority at a global level. Water conservation is primarily aimed at the careful use of water resources, in terms of preserving both the quality and the quantity of water. Conservation is an essential component of sustainable water use. We have already discussed how water is used in agriculture, in industries, and for domestic purposes as well as the amount of water availed for each of these. The following procedures discuss how conservation of water can be achieved by reducing the use of water or using water economically and avoiding any waste.

**(i) Agricultural use:** Agriculture is the largest consumer of water. About 80% of all freshwater is utilized in agriculture. Consumption of water can be reduced by 25%–30% when improved methods of irrigation are adopted. The following procedures can be used for the purpose:

- Reduction of seepage and evaporation of water through covered or lined canals.
- Use of computer monitoring and scheduled water release for maximum efficiency. This method is commonly used in some advanced and developed countries.
- Irrigation should be done when evaporation rate is minimum of fields such as night-time or early morning.

- Use of improved irrigation systems such as sprinklers or drip irrigation. This can lead to substantial conservation of water as these procedures apply water more efficiently to crops.
- Development of crops that use less water.

**(ii) Industrial use:** Industries use considerable amounts of water and discharge wastewater that contains hazardous chemicals into waterbodies. This results in severe water pollution. Industries should follow the procedures discussed here so that both water wastage and waste generation can be avoided to the largest extent possible.

- Water removal for electricity generation through steam could be reduced considerably by using cooling towers that use less water.
- Treatment of wastewaters from industries prior to being discharged.

**(iii) Domestic use:** On an average, about 10% of freshwater is used for domestic purposes such as washing clothes, cleaning dishes, and bathing. The amount of water required for domestic use can be reduced considerably by the following procedures:

- Use of efficient bathroom fixtures, such as low-flow toilets that use 1.5 gallons of water per flush rather than the standard 5 gallons.
- Use of low-flow showerheads that reduce flow rate but still provide sufficient water.
- Not keeping the taps running while doing activities such as brushing teeth, shaving, and washing.
- Flushing toilets only when really necessary.
- Fixing or restoring all water leakages in the shortest possible time.
- Use of washing machines or dishwaters to reduce the consumption of water.
- Watering of lawns and plants during low evaporation times, such as late afternoon, night, or early morning.
- Individually changing the "I pay for the use of water, so why bother" is not correct.
- Collection of wastewater from household water purification processes, such as reverse osmosis. This water should be used for watering plants, washing utensils, or cleaning floors.

**(iv) Use of wastewater:** Wastewater from households and industries should be suitably treated before being discharged into waterbodies. This is an important aspect of water conservation. If wastewater is discharged directly into waterbodies, the water gets heavily polluted and can cause a number of health hazards.

The global water shortage can be also met by rainwater harvesting and desalination of seawater.

### 9.4.1.1  Rainwater Harvesting

There is a serious shortage of water all over the globe, and so each and every drop of water must be used carefully. A convenient method is the use of rainwater. This is called rainwater harvesting. It involves collecting the maximum amount of freshwater possible during rains and storing it for future use. This practice has been traditionally followed in many parts of the world. The stored water must be kept clean and pollutant free in such a way that it can be used even for drinking. Otherwise, there are likely chances of the development of microscopic organisms such as algae and zooplankton, which are known to cause infections in unclean stored water. Therefore, uncontaminated storage of rainwater is very important.

Rainwater harvesting requires rainwater to be collected in a covered tank for storage and use after the monsoon. The main concern is the construction of large storage tanks which are expensive. For small domestic use, ferrocement tanks can provide a low cost and easy solution to store rainwater. Alternatively, rainwater can be collected and allowed to percolate into the ground in order to recharge groundwater resources, such as wells, rather than being allowed to flow into rivers. In fact, the recharging of groundwater by harvested water from rooftops increases the water level of the underground water.

In cities such as Delhi where metros have elevated stations, large amounts of rainwater can be harvested. In fact, there should be separate underground pipes which can carry water directly to waterbodies, such as rivers, rather than allowing freshwater to mix with sewage discharges and then reaching the waterbodies. If we can harvest all the rainwater in the world, then we will never run short of clean water.

### 9.4.1.2  Desalination of Seawater

Desalination is the process of removing dissolved salts from seawater or blackish water to yield potable water for human consumption. We know that oceans and seas account for about 97.2% of the global water. However, seawater is saline and contains dissolved salts to the extent of about 3.5%. On an average, 1 m$^3$ of seawater contains about 40 kg of dissolved salts, which makes it unfit for human consumption (or agricultural purposes). Before seawater can be used, it has to be desalinated. A number of processes are used in different parts of the world in order to desalinate seawater and render it fit for human consumption. These processes that are used for the desalination of seawater require large amounts of energy, which makes potable water costly.

A process that is used for the desalination of seawater is reverse osmosis. In this process, seawater is separated from dissolved salts and is made to flow through a semi-permeable membrane under applied pressure in excess of normal osmotic pressure. The dissolved salts are retained in the semi-permeable membrane and clean water passes through. It is difficult to use this process on a large scale due to the high costs involved.

Electrodialysis is another method of seawater desalination. In this method, the low-electrical conductivity of pure water and the migration of ions from dissolved solids in the presence of applied electric current are made use of. Like reverse osmosis, electrodialysis is also a membrane-based filtration technology for removing ions from seawater. In this method, two types of membranes are used— cation permeable and anion permeable. These two membranes are utilized alternatively for carrying out large-scale purification of seawater. The cation-selective membrane is a polystyrene polymer with sulphonic acid group and the amino-selective membrane has quaternary ammonium group. The seawater gets desalinated due to the movement of cations and anions through the membrane selective to them.

The most effective method of desalination involves the use of solar energy. The principle involved is to focus the sun's energy on a relatively small amount of seawater in a suitable container. The sun's energy is focused with the help of mirrors. Water evaporates and gets converted into steam, which is condensed back to water. This procedure is basically distillation. In fact, distilled water is prepared by this process. Desalination is a costly process and is generally utilized only when alternate sources of clean water are not available.

It is appropriate to state that huge quantities of water are lost through floods, one of the most frequently occurring natural disasters. However, this water could be saved for accomplishing various purposes (for details refer to Chapter 6, Section 6.3.1).

## 9.4.2  Potable Water

It is well known that water is an essential component of life and no life is possible without it. Only about 1% of the total water is potable (suitable for drinking and consumption). This is because water contains a large amount of impurities, which render it unsuitable for use. The main problem is the availability of water at the right place and in right form. In fact, water is called blue gold. It is a precious commodity without which life cannot survive.

Water is known to perform a number of vital roles in humans and other living beings. It is present in each and every cell in a human body. The concentration of water in blood is 80%, 75% in the brain, 90% in lungs, 75% in muscles, and 20% in bones. Water helps to absorb nutrients from the intestines and carries them to all parts of the body. It helps to eliminate water-soluble products through the kidneys. It plays an important role in regulating body temperature, serves as a lubricant for joints, forms saliva, keeps the mucosal membrane soft, and alleviates constipation and acidity.

The only natural resource that is used in large quantities is water. Its demand has increased considerably due to rapid increase in population, industrialization, and agriculture. It is, therefore, necessary to look for other sources of water. Two such possibilities are the use of groundwater and desalination of seawater.

Water is regarded as a universal solvent. In fact, there is no other liquid that can be compared to water as a solvent. Natural water is slightly acidic (pH 5.6) due to the presence of dissolved carbon dioxide (forming carbonic acid or $H_2CO_3$). Table 9.3 summarizes the principle physical properties of water. Some of them are elaborated here as follows:

(a) Water density decreases as the temperature falls to 0°C. Density also decreases when the temperature exceeds 3.98°C. It reaches the same density as ice at about 70°C.

(b) Water has the highest specific heat of all substances.

(c) Water has the highest surface tension of all liquids. The surface tension decreases with temperature.

(d) Viscosity of water changes with temperature.

### 9.4.2.1  Water Contaminants

Contaminants in water include pathogens, suspended particles, dissolved salts, organic compounds, radioactive elements, and some gases. Pathogens are disease-causing microorganisms which come mainly from human and animal faecal waste. Deadly water-borne diseases caused by these microbes include typhoid, cholera, and diarrhoea. Cryptosporidium is the cause of a number of gastrointestinal disorders. The microbes in water can be killed by disinfectants.

Particulates are particles such as dust, sand, rust, and other substances which are insoluble in water and must be removed to make it potable. Dissolved salts, such as sodium chloride, are another class of water impurities. Sodium chloride is the dissolved salt most responsible for the salinity of water. The presence of calcium and magnesium salts makes water hard. Iron is another impurity. Sometimes, toxic metals are also present in water and are responsible for causing a number of diseases as discussed here:

- **Aluminium salts:**  These salts can cause Parkinson's and Alzheimer's diseases.

- **Hexavalent chromium:**  It reaches waterbodies from effluents, is rich in chromium, is released from commercial setups, and causes dermatitis, asthma, internal bleeding, and liver and kidney damage.

- **Lead:**  Natural erosion is the primary agent of water-based lead contamination. Its exposure can delay physical and mental growth in children and cause kidney-related problems and high blood pressure in adults.

- **Mercury:**  Mercury reaches water as run-off from landfills and mercury-using industrial units. Certain microbes convert mercury into methyl mercury, which in turn causes neurotoxicity, reproductive toxicity, and kidney damage.

- **Arsenic:**  Arsenic comes in contact with water as a result of erosion of natural deposits, copper smelting, and glass and electronic production

**Table 9.3** Principal physical properties of water

| | |
|---|---|
| Density, g/mL (3.98°C) | 1.0 |
| Melting point, °C (at 760 mm Hg) | 0.0 |
| Boiling point, °C (at 760 mm Hg) | 100 |
| Temperature at maximum density, °C (cal/g°C) | 3.90 |
| Specific heat (cal/ g°C) | 1.00 |
| Surface tension, mN/m (20°C) | 72.75 |
| Dynamic-viscosity, (mNs)/m$^2$ (20°C) | 1.000 |
| Specific electric conductivity, s/m (25°C) | $5.10^{-6}$ |
| Critical temperature, °C | 374 |
| Critical density, g/cm$^2$ | 0.322 |
| Critical specific volume, cm$^2$/g | 3.11 |
| Dielectric constant (20°C) | 80.20 |

waste. Its exposure causes skin problems, affects the circulatory system, and increases the risk of skin, bladder, kidney, and lung cancers.

- **Inorganic anions:** Inorganic anions such as nitrate, nitrite, fluoride, and cyanide also reach waterbodies through different routes (mainly industrial effluents), and are responsible for causing a number of health problems.

Organic compounds are released in massive amounts from industries engaged in the production of polymers, herbicides, insecticides, and pharmaceutical and petroleum products. The contamination of water by radioactive elements is a very serious problem of the modern world. Gases such as $H_2S$, $SO_2$, and $NH_3$ also contaminate water. Table 9.4 lists some contaminants and their permissible limit in drinking water.

**Table 9.4** Drinking water specification (IS 10500,1992)

| S. No. | Parameter | IS: 10500 require-ment (desirable limit) | Undesirable effect beyond the desir-able limit | IS: 10500 permissible limit |
|---|---|---|---|---|
| Essential characteristics | | | | |
| 1. | pH | 6.5–8.5 | Mucus membrane is affected | No relaxation |
| 2. | Colour (Hazen units) | 5 | Consumer accep-tance decreases | 25 |
| 3. | Odour | Unobjectionable | – | – |
| 4. | Taste | Agreeable | – | – |
| 5. | Turbidity NTU | 5 | Consumer accep-tance decreases | 10 |

*Contd...*

**Table 9.4** *Contd...*

| S. No. | Parameter | IS: 10500 requirement (desirable limit) | Undesirable effect beyond the desirable limit | IS: 10500 permissible limit |
|---|---|---|---|---|
| Following results are expressed in mg/L | | | | |
| 6. | Total hardness as $CaCO_3$ | 300 | Adverse effect on domestic use | 600 |
| 7. | Iron as Fe | 0.30 | Adverse effect on domestic use | 1.0 |
| 8. | Chloride as Cl | 250 | Taste and palatability | 1000 |
| 9. | Residual-free chlorine | 0.20 | – | – |
| Desirable characteristics | | | | |
| 10. | Dissolved solids | 500 | Palatability decreases and causes gastrointestinal irritation | 2000 |
| 11. | Calcium as Ca | 75 | Adverse effect on domestic use | 200 |
| 12. | Magnesium as Mg | 30 | Same as Ca | 100 |
| 13. | Sulphate | 200 | Gastrointestinal irritation | 400 |
| 14. | Nitrates | 45 | Methemoglobinemia takes place | 100 |
| 15. | Fluoride | 1.0 | Fluorosis | 1.5 |
| 16. | Mercury as Hg | 0.001 | Toxic | No relaxation |
| 17. | Arsenic as As | 0.05 | Water becomes toxic | No relaxation |
| 18. | Cyanide | 0.05 | Water becomes toxic | No relaxation |
| 19. | Lead as Pb | 0.05 | Water becomes toxic | No relaxation |
| 20. | Chromium as $Cr^{6+}$ | 0.05 | Carcinogenic | No relaxation |
| 21. | Pesticides | Absent | Toxic | 0.0001 |
| 22. | Radioactive materials<br>$\alpha$ emitters (Bq/L)<br>$\beta$ emitters (pCi/L) | – | – | – |
| 23. | Alkalinity | 200 | Water becomes unpleasant | 600 |
| 24. | Aluminium as Al | 0.03 | Cumulative effect | 0.2 |

### 9.4.2.2  *Water Quality Parameters*

Depending on it use, water must possess the right parameters. As an example, if water is to be used for cleaning purposes, no special treatment is required, and it is not necessary to judge water quality on any parameter. On the other hand, if water is to be used for washing purposes (for example, laundry), it should be ascertained that the water used is soft water. Hard water consumes lots of detergents (or soaps) for cleaning. In addition, hard water is not suitable for use in boilers as it leads to the formation of scales. For drinking purposes, water should be pure and free of any pollutant. In the case of pharmaceutical industries, water must be free of any dissolved salts. In view of the use of water for different purposes, it is helpful to know the quality of water. Physical parameters and maximum containment levels have been prescribed by different regulatory bodies. Tables 9.5 and 9.6 give the standards for industrial and drinking water (human consumption) by the Bureau of Indian Standards (BIS).

**Table 9.5**  BIS standards for water for industrial and drinking purposes

| Physical parameters | BIS standard |
| --- | --- |
| Colour | Colourless |
| Odour | Odourless |
| Taste | Light, sour-sweet |
| pH | 6–8.5 |
| Specific conductance | 300 µmho cm$^{-1}$ |
| DO | 4–6 ppm |

DO–Dissolved oxygen; ppm–Parts per million

**Table 9.6**  Maximum contaminant-level permissible for potable water

| Contaminant | Maximum contaminant level (ppm) as per BIS standard |
| --- | --- |
| Chloride | 600 |
| Sulphate | 1000 |
| Cyanide | 0.0001 |
| Fluoride | 3 |
| Nitrate + nitrite | 12 |
| Phosphate | 0.1 |
| Calcium | 100 |
| Magnesium | 30 |
| Barium | 1 |
| Copper | 1 |
| Arsenic | 0.002 |

*Contd...*

**Table 9.6** *Contd...*

| Contaminant | Maximum contaminant level (ppm) as per BIS standard |
|---|---|
| Lead | 0.1 |
| Iron (filterable) | 0.3 |
| Chromium | 0.05 |
| Zinc | 0.05 |
| Pesticides | 0.005 |
| Total bacterial count | $1 \times 10^6$ |

ppm–Parts per million

The quality of water is mainly judged by four parameters: dissolved oxygen (DO), biochemical oxygen demand (BOD) chemical oxygen demand (COD), and total dissolved solids (TDS). These parameters are also used for determining sewage characteristics. The various parameters for determination of sewage characteristics are discussed next.

**(i) Dissolved oxygen:** Oxygen is soluble in water to the extent of 14.6 mg/L at 0°C and about 7 mg/L at 35°C under 1 atm of pressure. DO in water is essential for aquatic life. A minimum of 4 ppm DO is necessary for the survival of aquatic species. In water, atmospheric oxygen is the main source of oxygen. It is also produced by photosynthesis carried out by aquatic plants. Depending on the DO content in water, it is possible to determine the suitability of water for aquatic life, for industrial use, and also for public distribution supply systems. DO contents in water can be determined by Winkler's method, involving treatment of water with a solution of $MnSO_4$, NaOH, KI, and $NaN_3$. The reaction between $MnSO_4$ and NaOH gives $Mn(OH)_2$ which reacts with DO in water to form $Mn(OH)_3$.

$$MnSO_4 + 2\ NaOH \longrightarrow Mn(OH)_2 + Na_2SO_4 \qquad \ldots(i)$$
White precipitate

$$4\ Mn(OH)_2 + O_2 + H_2O \longrightarrow 4\ Mn(OH)_3 \qquad \ldots(ii)$$
Brown precipitate

Addition of $H_2SO_4$ converts $Mn(OH)_3$ into $MnSO_4$, and oxygen is liberated.

$$4\ Mn(OH)_3 + 4\ H_2SO_4 \longrightarrow 4\ MnSO_4 + 10\ H_2O + 2(O) \qquad \ldots(iii)$$

The liberated oxygen is treated with KI solution, liberating equivalent amount of iodine.

$$4\ KI + 2\ H_2SO_4 + 2(O) \longrightarrow 2\ K_2SO_4 + 2\ H_2O + 2\ I_2 \qquad \ldots(iv)$$

The liberated iodine is estimated by titration against a standard sodium thiosulphate solution using starch as an indicator.

$$4\ Na_2S_2O_3 + 2\ I_2 \longrightarrow 2\ Na_2S_4O_6 + 4\ NaI \qquad \ldots(v)$$

From Equations (iii) and (v), one can find

Number of moles of $Na_2S_2O_3$/Number of moles of $O_2 = 11/1$ ...(vi)

$$M_1V_1/M_2V_2 = 4/1 \text{ or } M_2 = M_1V_1/4\,V_2 \qquad \text{...(vii)}$$

where $M_1$ and $V_1$ are the morality and volume of $Na_2S_2O_3$ solution, respectively.

$V_2$ is the volume of water sample and $M_2$ is the morality of DO in the water sample.

Therefore, DO concentration in water sample

$$= M_2 \times \text{molar mass of } O_2 \times 1000$$

$$= 32{,}000\ M_2$$

Substituting the value of $M_2$ from Equation (vii), we get DO concentration in the water sample

$$= (M_1V_1/4\,V_2) \times 32{,}000$$

$$= 800\ [\text{morality of } Na_2S_2O_3 \text{ solution/volume of } Na_2S_2O_3$$

solution/volume of water sample]

**(ii) Biochemical oxygen demand:** BOD is defined as the standardized measurement of the amount of oxygen required by microorganisms for the biological oxidation of organic matter under aerobic conditions to $CO_2$ and $H_2O$ at 20°C over a period of 5 days. The result obtained is called five-day BOD and is expressed in milligram of oxygen per litre of water (mg/L). The oxidation is represented as

$$CH_2O + O_2 \xrightarrow[\text{Anaerobic oxidation}]{\text{Microorganisms}} CO_2 + H_2O$$

Organic matter DO  +  Bacterial cell

The 5-day BOD analysis is a standard test. The BOD values of some water samples collected from different sources are given in Table 9.7.

The method for the determination of BOD involves measurement of the amount of oxygen consumed by a water sample of known volume. The water sample is collected in an airtight bottle and incubated at a specified temperature for 5 days. The DO is measured initially and after incubation, and the BOD is computed from the difference between initial and final DO values.

**(iii) Chemical oxygen demand:** The COD (like BOD) is also a measure of the amount of oxygen required to oxidize organic matter. The oxidation is affected by chemical oxidizing agents such as $K_2Cr_2O_7$. The unused $K_2Cr_2O_7$ is determined by back titration with a suitable reagent such as Mohr's salt. The amount of $K_2Cr_2O_7$ is determined by substration.

Amount of $K_2Cr_2O_7$ consumed = Amount of $K_2Cr_2O_7$ (initially added) – Amount of $K_2Cr_2O_7$ (determined by back titration)

The amount of oxygen used for oxidation can be calculated from the strength of $K_2Cr_2O_7$ consumed as per the following equation:

$$K_2Cr_2O_7 + 4\ H_2SO_4 \longrightarrow K_2SO_4 + Cr_2(SO_4)_3 + 4\ H_2O + 3(O)$$

The results are expressed in terms of amount of oxygen (in parts per million or ppm) required to oxidize the contaminents. On the basis of COD status, the quality of water can be measured (Table 9.8). COD determination suffers from the drawback that aromatic hydrocarbon derivatives are not easily oxidized by the oxidizing agents used. Hence, its presence cannot be ascertained.

**(iv) Total dissolved solids:** TDS are the amount of non-volatile substances present in water and are expressed in milligram per kilogram (mg/kg). To determine TDS in water, calcium and magnesium bicarbonates are converted into carbonates. In addition to TDS, three other types of solids also occur: (i) fixed residue solids, (ii) mineral residue solids, and (iii) sulphate solids.

Fixed residue solids are determined by carrying out calcination of total solids (for about 15 minutes at 800°C). The residue obtained is the fixed residue solid content. Mineral residue contains all anions and cations in water including $CO_3^{2-}$, $Al_2O_3$, $Fe_2O_3$, and $SiO_2$ in water. Treatment of TDS with concentrated $H_2SO_4$ gives corresponding sulphates, the total mass of which is the sulphate solid.

## 9.4.3  Treatment of Sewage

In most places, sewage and domestic wastes combined are responsible for water pollution. Waste must be treated before being discharged into waterbodies. Wastewater, particularly municipal wastes including sewage and domestic waste,

**Table 9.7**  BOD values of some water samples collected from different sources

| BOD (mg/L) | Source |
| --- | --- |
| 1 | Very clean water |
| 2 | Clean water |
| 3 | Fairly clean water |
| 5 | Not used for drinking and pharmaceutical preparations |
| 10 | Contaminated water |
| 15 | Unfit for fish reproduction |
| 150 | Domestic sewage discharge |
| 200 | Wastewater from industries |
| 350 | Wastewater from paper industries |
| 1000 | Wastewater from food processing units |
| 2000 | Discharge from dairies |

**Table 9.8** COD status of some water samples

| COD (mg/L) | Status |
|---|---|
| 0–5 | Very clean water, used for drinking |
| 5–20 | Fairly clear water |
| 20–100 | Unfit for drinking but can be used for washing and agriculture |

is treated in three stages: (i) primary treatment, (ii) secondary treatment, and (iii) tertiary treatment.

In the first stage, known as primary or preliminary treatment, the waste sewage is passed through a series of screens to remove most of the floating material. By this process, all non-biodegradable solids such as rocks, sand, grit, plastic, and metal parts are filtered. The filtered water is then passed through a grit chamber, which is packed with sand and small stones. This procedure removes the suspended dirt particles. Next, the resulting filtered water is passed through a sedimentation tank in which the particulate matter settles down at the bottom in the form of sludge. It may be helpful to add alum, which hastens the settling process. The sludge is then removed and can be used after processing as manure.

The second stage, known as secondary treatment or biological oxidation process, involves aeration of the filtered water (from the first stage). In this treatment, some sludge is added from the final (second) sedimentation tank. The sludge contains aerobic bacteria, which break down organic pollutants in the water. This treatment takes several hours. Subsequently, the water is taken to the sedimentation tank in which most of the sludge settles down. The total sludge is subjected to microbial digestion, and the evolved methane gas is used as fuel. Finally, the water from the sedimentation tank is treated in disinfection tanks, usually by chlorine, to remove disease-causing organisms. In some countries, ozone is used for sterilization.

The combination of the first and second steps (primary and secondary treatment) constitutes the complete treatment. This water can be either discharged in waterbodies (from which municipalities draw water) or subjected to the final treatment, called the tertiary treatment. During tertiary treatment, highly soluble salts are removed as precipitates by adding flocculating agents or alum. Addition of lime makes the water alkaline which precipitates the phosphates. A more advanced tertiary treatment involves reverse osmosis and disinfection through ultraviolet rays. This treated water can be used for drinking purposes. Figure 9.3 diagrammatically shows the working of a sewage treatment plant.

### 9.4.3.1 Harmful Effects of Sewage and Domestic Wastes

Sewage is an ideal medium for the growth of pathogenic bacteria, viruses, and protozoa. *Vibrio cholerae* present in sewage causes cholera, *Salmonella typhosa* causes typhoid, and *Shigella dysenteriae* causes bacillary dysentery. In addition, some of the other water-borne diseases include viral hepatitis, polio, and amoebiasis.

## 9.5  RADIOACTIVE POLLUTION

Till date, radioactive pollution is the worst type of environmental pollution and is responsible for untold misery to humans, leading ultimately to death. It occurs when living organisms are continuously exposed to radiation from various radioactive sources, which include natural sources and man-made sources. During the testing of nuclear devices in the air (above the ground), the radioactive fallouts spread in the atmosphere in the form of clouds. These radioactive fallouts consist mostly of radioisotopes which spread over a large surface and finally fall on the ground. The generated radioactive dust affects humans via the food chain (for more details, refer to Chapter 1, Sections 1.4.1 and 1.4.2.2).

### 9.5.1  Sources of Radioactive Radiation

The most important and harmful sources of radioactive radiations include X-rays, radioisotopes, nuclear tests, radioactive fallouts, nuclear reactors, nuclear power plants, processing of radioactive ores, and nuclear accidents. The most important aspect of nuclear reactors, including nuclear power plants, is the disposal of radioactive waste.

Radioactive waste is dangerously harmful for humans and must be stored safely. The best procedure is to store such waste in geologic formations. For this, identification of the storage site is very important. The storage site must meet the criteria of ground stability and slow movement of groundwater. There should be no variation in climates, groundwater flow, erosion, and earth movement for such sites. Most of the geologic formations must remain undisturbed for millions of

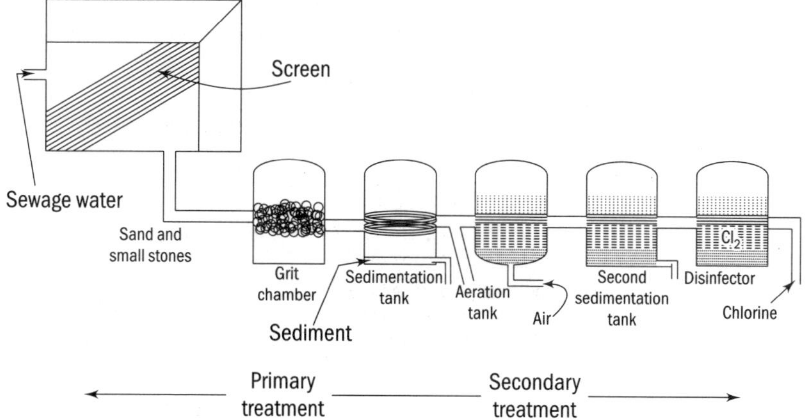


**Fig. 9.3**  A sewage treatment plant

years. The radioactive waste should be buried in repositories (storage facilities) which must be at least 600 m below the earth's surface in a stable geologic formation. The radioactive waste must be packed in containers which should be durable and leak and corrosion resistant. The bottom of such 'secure landfill' is lined with compacted clay using gravel. The clay is flexible and resists cracking in case the ground shifts. A thick polythene sheet is placed over the layer of gravel. A layer of absorbent cushions the inner layers. The radioactive waste is packed in drums and put into a landfill. The landfill is finally covered with clay, plastics, and soil. Vegetation is then placed for stabilizing the surface and improving appearance. A diagrammatic representation of a landfill is shown in Figure 9.4.

## 9.6  SUSTAINABLE DEVELOPMENT

Sustainable development is the basis of our existence. The issue of environment and development has led to the concept of sustainable development. According to the World Commission on Environment and Development (1987), sustainable development refers to development that meets the need of the present without compromising on the ability of future generations to meet their own needs.

Development should not degrade the natural systems that support life on earth. In the industrialized world, many people believe that the world has an unlimited supply of resources for human use. This is far from being correct. In fact, the concept of sustainable development leads us to new resource consumption strategies which are as follows:

- Conservation or reduction of excessive resource use
- Recycling and reuse of materials wherever possible
- Use of renewable resources, such as solar energy and tidal energy, more than non-renewable resources such as oil and coal wherever possible.

Sustainable development must also look after the basic needs of the deprived sections of society (the poor and unprivileged). Poor people also aspire to a

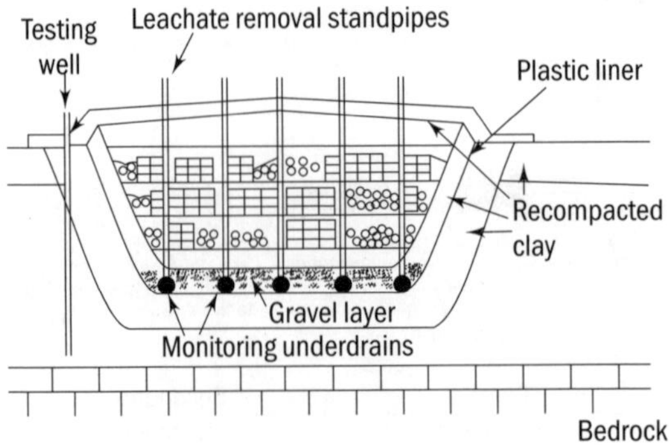


**Fig. 9.4**  A schematic diagram of a secure landfill

better life. There may be ecological and other crises if poverty and inequality are endemic. Mahatama Gandhi's famous quote that "earth provides enough to satisfy every man's needs, but not every man's greed" adeptly clarifies the concept of sustainable development.

The United Nations Conference on Environment and Development was held in Rio de Janeiro in 1992. The outcome of this conference was to take measures to ensure sustainable development. These measures were outlined in Agenda 21 to promote sustainable development at a local level in both developed and underdeveloped countries. Subsequently, the World Summit on Sustainable Development was held in Johannesburg, South Africa in August 2002 (the Earth Summit 2002). An important outcome of this summit was to establish a world solidarity fund to eradicate poverty and to promote social and human development in the developing countries.

Sustainable development can be achieved by some policy changes at the global level and basic changes in the way people deal with environmental issues. Some of these are discussed as follows:

(i) **Technology:** Advanced technology (developed by advanced, rich countries) is responsible for environmental deterioration throughout the world, even though it is a boon to society. In fact, the challenge is to make technology more energy efficient, less risky, cleaner, and more humane. Such technology, referred to as appropriate technology, relies on the use of smaller, repairable machines with production methods that consume optimum energy and materials and cause minimum pollution. Countries such as India, where manpower is abundant, should look for labour-intensive rather than capital-intensive technologies. Although sophisticated technologies increase production, they put people out of work. Ideally, appropriate technology should utilize local and biodegradable resources and consume minimum amounts of energy (preferably renewable energy).

(ii) **Economics:** In most countries (rich or poor), the process of economic growth should be based on the availability of renewable and non-renewable resources. However, in the majority of the cases, it is not so. For example, incomes from mining and forestry operations are generally measured in terms of cost of extraction of products (in the case of mining) and value of timber (in the case of forestry). The cost of reclamation of the land after mining or cost of regeneration of the forest is not taken into account.

(iii) **Population:** Sustainable development can be pursued easily if the growth of population is stabilized at a level consistent with the productive capacity of the ecosystem.

(iv) **Conservation:** For sustainable development, the earth's natural resources must be conserved. This can be particularly achieved by restricting the use of oil and coal (non-renewable sources) for energy generation and opting for technologies that use renewable resources such as solar energy and wind energy. Reuse of waste is helpful for sustainable development; for example, production of biogas from organic wastes is a good procedure. In a similar way, wastewater from industries can be purified appropriately and reused.

(v) **Agriculture:** The principles of sustainable development should be incorporated in agriculture practices so that environmental damage can be avoided to the largest extent possible. This can be achieved through the use of biofertilizers and biopesticides in place of the usual chemical-based fertilizers and pesticides. Also, new and better varieties of seeds should be developed using genetic engineering.

The use of microbial inoculants as a source of biofertilizers has become common in most countries. Atmospheric nitrogen gets biologically fixed for plants with the use of microbial inoculants. A number of free-living and symbolic bacteria are used as biofertilizers in place of nitrogen fertilizers; for example vermicompost obtained from waste materials can be used as a fertilizer. The process is known as vermicomposting.

## 9.7 ENVIRONMENT PROTECTION ACTS

With the progress of civilization, humans began altering the natural environment to meet their own needs. This resulted in slow depletion of natural resources and degradation of the environment. There has been a lot of strain on natural resources and also on the environment because of the increase in human population, industrialization, urbanization, and numerous development projects. The problem is compounded by air, water, and land pollutions. The situation has deteriorated to such an extent that the environmental problems pose a threat not only to the health of humans, but also to their very existence. To protect the environment from further deterioration, a number of legislations have been enacted at national and international levels. The various acts enacted for the protection of the environment at the national level are discussed next.

### 9.7.1 Water (Prevention and Control of Pollution) Act, 1974, Amended in 1988

This act was passed by the Parliament in 1974 under Article 252 of the Constitution of India. The administrative machinery for the act is called the Water Pollution Board and it exists at the central and state levels. Its objective is to control and prevent pollution of water, including streams, river water courses, inland waters, subterranean water, seawater, and tidal water. The water pollution boards are given the power to advice, coordinate, and provide technical assistance for the prevention and control or abatement of water pollution. The Water Act prohibits dumping of poisonous, noxious, or polluting matter into waterbodies. Some problems in the administration of the act led to its amendment in 1988. According to the amendment, water pollution boards are empowered to issue directions and order closures, prohibition, or regulation of any industry or its operation and stop its water, electricity supplies, or any other services. Strict penalties and punishments are imposed for not complying with the procedures of the act.

### 9.7.2   Air (Prevention and Control of Pollution) Act, 1981, Amended in 1987

This act was passed for the prevention and control of air pollution under Article 235 of the Constitution of India. Its objective is to control and abate air pollution from automobiles and industrial plants. The act defines various terms such as air pollution and air pollutants. The Central Board for Prevention and Control of air pollution is authorized to implement and enforce the rules outlined in the act.

### 9.7.3   Biodiversity Act, 2000

The Biodiversity Act, 2000 enables the establishment of state-level biodiversity management committees to deal with matters concerning conservation of biodiversity as well as sustainable use and equitable sharing of biological resources. The National Biodiversity Authority came into being on 10 October 2003 under this act.

## 9.8   ENVIRONMENT IMPACT ASSESSMENT

Before any development project can be initiated, permission from the Ministry of Environment, Forest and Climate Change is necessary. The Ministry of Environment, Forest and Climate Change, in order to consider such requests, needs an environment impact assessment (EIA) report, which should be carried out by a competent organization. The EIA should reflect the likely impact of the proposal on waterbodies, soil, and air, if it is accepted. The EIA must also specify if the project is likely to have an adverse effect on the habitat of any endangered species. The Ministry of Environment, Forest and Climate Change has listed 30 different industries that need clearance before they are set up. The projects are not passed if the anticipated impacts are likely to be severe.

## SUMMARY

- Hydrology deals with the study of water at different levels.
- Water is the most important and essential component of life without which no life is possible.
- The latent heat of water is responsible for moderating the temperature of the biosphere.

- The hydrological cycle involves movement of water from oceans to the atmosphere (evaporation), from the atmosphere to oceans and land (precipitation), and from land to oceans and the environment.
- The energy required for the hydrological cycle is derived from the sun in the form of solar energy.
- In India, irrigation is carried out by canals, wells, tanks, and some other sources including drip irrigation and sprinkler irrigation.
- Water must be conserved, particularly when used for agricultural, industrial, and domestic purposes.
- The shortage of water all over the globe can be met by rainwater harvesting and desalination of seawater.
- The quality of water is judged by parameters such as DO, BOD, COD, and TDS.
- Sewage and domestic wastes together account for water pollution. These are treated (before being discharged into waterbodies) in three stages: primary, secondary, and tertiary treatment.
- Sewage and domestic wastes are harmful for human health.
- Radioactive pollution is the worst type of environmental pollution and is responsible for untold misery to humans, leading ultimately to death.
- The most important sources of radioactive radiations include nuclear tests, radioactive fallouts, nuclear power plants, and nuclear accidents.
- The most important aspect of nuclear reactors, including nuclear power plant, is the disposal of radioactive wastes, which is dangerously harmful for humans and must be stored safely in secure landfills.
- Sustainable development is the basis of our existence. It refers to the development that meets the need of the present without compromising on the ability of future generations to meet their own needs.
- Sustainable development involves conservation or reduction of excessive resource use, recycling, reuse of materials (whenever possible), and use of renewable resources.
- Various acts have been enacted for the protection of the environment at the national level.

# EXERCISE

## [A] Multiple-choice questions

1. The maximum amount of water is present in
   (a) Rivers and streams      (b) Groundwater
   (c) Oceans      (d) Lakes

2. Which of the following statements is correct?

   (a) Natural water is slightly acidic due to dissolved $CO_2$.

   (b) Water is regarded as a universal solvent.

   (c) Ice is lighter than water.

   (d) Water has the highest specific heat of all substances.

   (e) All of the above

3. The most harmful water contaminants are

   (a) Pathogens              (b) Suspended particles

   (c) Domestic wastes        (d) Radioactive wastes

4. Conservation of water is best achieved by

   (a) Treatment of sewage and domestic waste

   (b) Treatment of wastewater from industries

   (c) Rainwater harvesting

   (d) Desalination of seawater

5. Economical use of water involves

   (a) Using sprinklers for irrigating crops

   (b) Using drip irrigation for irrigating crops

   (c) Irrigating crops when evaporation loss is minimum

   (d) All of the above

6. Desalination of seawater can be achieved by

   (a) Reverse osmosis

   (b) Using solar energy to get distilled water

   (c) Rainwater harvesting

   (d) Flood water

   (e) All of the above

7. The quality of water is judged by

   (a) Dissolved oxygen       (b) Biochemical oxygen demand

   (c) Chemical oxygen demand  (d) All of the above

8. Maximum penetrating power is exhibited by

   (a) $\alpha$ particles     (b) $\beta$ particles

   (c) $\gamma$ rays          (d) All are equally penetrating

9. Radioactive isotopes enter the environment through

   (a) Fallouts from nuclear tests   (b) Radioactive wastes

   (c) Nuclear installations         (d) Nuclear accidents

   (e) All of the above

10. Treatment of sewage and domestic waste involves
    (a) Filtration
    (b) Aeration
    (c) Treatment with ozone or UV rays
    (d) A combination of all the above procedures
11. Sustainable development involves
    (a) Conservation or reduction of excessive resource use
    (b) Recycling and reuse of materials wherever possible
    (c) Using renewable resources
    (d) All of the above
12. Sustainable agriculture involves use of
    (a) biofertilizers
    (b) biopesticides
    (c) developing new and better varieties of seeds
    (d) All of the above

### ANSWERS

| | | | | |
|---|---|---|---|---|
| 1. (c) | 2. (e) | 3. (d) | 4. (c) | 5. (d) |
| 6. (e) | 7. (d) | 8. (c) | 9. (e) | 10. (d) |
| 11. (d) | 12. (d) | | | |

## [B] Fill in the blanks.

1. The maximum amount of water is available in ________.
2. The property of water which is responsible for the moderation of temperature of biosphere is ________.
3. The best procedures for irrigation are ________ and ________.
4. The disease-causing microorganisms in water are known as ________.
5. For the survival of aquatic life, the DO should be in the range of ________ ppm.
6. The worst type of environmental pollution is ________.
7. For sustainable agriculture, it is necessary to use ________ and ________.
8. For any new project, it is helpful to get the ________ done.

### ANSWERS

| | |
|---|---|
| 1. Oceans | 2. Latent heat |
| 3. Drip irrigation, sprinkler irrigation | 4. Pathogens |
| 5. 4–6 | 6. Radioactive pollution |
| 7. Bio-fertilizers, bio-pesticides | 8. EIA |

## [C] Short-answer questions

1. What do you understand by the term 'environmental engineering'?
2. Give the salient features of the hydrological cycle.
3. How are high latent heat, high surface tension, and high viscosity of water helpful?
4. How do organisms survive below the surface of water?
5. Write a note on irrigation engineering and water resource engineering.
6. How can conservation of water be achieved?
7. Write notes on:
   (a) Rainwater harvesting
   (b) Desalination of seawater
   (c) Potable water
8. What parameters are generally used for finding the quality of water?
9. Give the various steps involved in the treatment of sewage.
10. What are the important sources of radioactive pollution?
11. Write a note on 'sustainable development'.

# Multiple-choice Questions

1. Biodiversity includes the following forms of life:
   1. Plants
   2. Animals
   3. Microorganisms
   4. Biological wealth of earth

   Select the correct answer using the codes given below
   (a) 1, 2, and 3
   (b) 2, 3, and 4
   (c) 1 and 4
   (d) 1, 2, and 4

2. Biodiversity can be
   1. Genetic diversity
   2. Species diversity
   3. Economic diversity
   4. None of the above

   Select the correct answer using the codes given below.
   (a) 1
   (b) 1 and 2
   (c) 1, 2, and 3
   (d) 4

3. Consider the following:
   1. Oxides of nitrogen
   2. Oxides of sulphur
   3. Carbon dioxide

   Select the correct answer using the codes given below
   (a) 1
   (b) 2 and 3
   (c) 1 and 3
   (d) 1, 2, and 3

4. The formation of ozone hole in the Antarctic region is due to
   1. Chlorofluorocarbons
   2. Methane and chlorofluorocarbons
   3. Global warming
   4. Acid rain

   Which of the above is/are correct?
   (a) 1
   (b) 2 and 3
   (c) 4
   (d) 1, 2, 3, and 4

5. Consider the following kinds of organisms:
    1. Fungi
    2. Bacteria
    3. Flowering plants

    Which of the above kinds of organisms are employed as biopesticides?

    (a) 1                        (b) 2 and 3

    (c) 1 and 3           (d) 1, 2, and 3

6. Consider the following kinds of organisms:
    1. Bees
    2. Bird
    3. Bat

    Which of the above is/are pollinating agent(s)?

    (a) 1 and 2           (b) 2

    (c) 1 and 3           (d) 1, 2, and 3

7. Which of the following groups of animals belong to the category of endangered species?

    (a) Asiatic wild ass, cheetah, Blue Bull, and great Indian bustard

    (b) Kashmir stag, great Indian bustard, and musk deer

    (c) Snow leopard, saras crane, and swamp deer

    (d) Blue bull, grey langur, and cheetah

8. What would happen if phytoplankton of an ocean is completely destroyed?
    1. The ocean as a carbon sink would be adversely affected
    2. The food chain in the ocean would be adversely affected

    Select the correct answer using the codes given below.

    (a) 1                        (b) 2

    (c) 1 and 2           (d) Neither 1 nor 2

9. What is the role of ultraviolet radiation in the water purification systems?
    1. It kills harmful organisms in water
    2. It removes undesirable odour
    3. It removes turbidity

    Which of the statements given above is/are correct?

    (a) 1                        (b) 2 and 3

    (c) 1 and 3           (d) 1, 2, and 3

10. Chlorofluorocarbon, the ozone depleting agent, is used
    1. for production of plastic foams
    2. for production of tubeless tyres

3. for cleaning certain electronic equipment

4. as pressurizing agents in aerosol cans

Which of the statements given above is/are correct?

(a) 1, 2, and 3                 (b) 4

(c) 1, 3, and 4                 (d) 1, 2, 3, and 4

11. Acid rain is caused by the presence of

(a) $CO$ and $N_2$             (b) $CO_2$ and $N_2$

(c) $O_3$ and $CO_2$           (d) $N_2O$ and $SO_2$

12. Photochemical smog is due to the reaction of

(a) $CO$, $O_2$, and peroxyacetyl nitrate in the presence of sunlight

(b) $NO_2$, $O_2$, and peroxyacetyl nitrate in the presence of sunlight

(c) $CO$, $CO_2$, and $NO_2$ at low temperature

(d) High concentration of $NO_2$, $O_3$, and $CO$

13. Which of the following organisms is/are known as decomposer organism(s)

    1. Fungi

    2. Virus

    3. Bacteria

Select the correct answer using the codes given below:

(a) 1                          (b) 1 and 3

(c) 1 and 2                  (d) 1, 2, and 3

14. Which of the following is responsible for releasing $CO_2$?

    1. Volcanoes                  2. Respiration

    3. Photosynthesis            4. Decay of organic matter

Select the correct answer using the codes given below:

(a) 1 and 3                  (b) 2

(c) 1, 2, and 4               (d) 1, 2, 3, and 4

15. Soil erosion is associated with

    1. Deforestation

    2. Tropical climate

    3. Terrace cultivation

Select the correct answer using the codes given below:

(a) 1 and 2                  (b) 1

(c) 1 and 3                  (d) 1, 2, and 3

16. Which of the following have coral reefs?

    1. Andaman and Nicrobar Islands    2. Gulf of Kutch

    3. Gulf of Mannar                 4. Sunderbans

Select the correct answer using the codes given below:

(a) 1, 2, and 3

(b) 2 and 4

(c) 1 and 3

(d) 1, 2, 3, and 4

17. Which of the following are some important pollutants released by steel industry in India?

1. Carbon dioxide

2. Carbon monoxide

3. Oxides of sulphur

4. Oxides of nitrogen

Select the correct answer using the codes given below:

(a) 1, 3, and 4

(b) 2 and 3

(c) 1 and 4

(d) 1, 2, 3, and 4

18. Use of excess nitrogenous fertilizer in agriculture leads to

1. Proliferation of nitrogen-fixing microorganisms in soil

2. Increase in acidity in soil

3. Leaching of nitrate in groundwater

Select the correct answer using the codes given below:

(a) 1 and 3

(b) 2

(c) 2 and 3

(d) 1, 2, and 3

19. Fly ash from coal-fired power plants is used for

(a) production of building components such as bricks

(b) partial replacement of Portland cement in concrete

(c) Fly ash made up of $SiO_2$ and $CaO$ only and does not contain toxic element

## ANSWERS

| | | | | |
|---|---|---|---|---|
| 1. (d) | 2. (c) | 3. (d) | 4. (a) | 5. (d) |
| 6. (d) | 7. (b) | 8. (c) | 9. (a) | 10. (c) |
| 11. (d) | 12. (b) | 13. (b) | 14. (c) | 15. (b) |
| 16. (a) | 17. (d) | 18. (c) | 19. (a) and (d) | |

# Index

# About the Author

Professor V K Ahluwalia is Professor (Retd) of Chemistry, University of Delhi. His tenure in this university spanned for more than 30 years. For these three decades, he taught numerous graduate, postgraduate, and MPhil students and provided guidance to about 70 students for their MPhil and Doctoral degrees. He was also Visiting Professor at Dr B R Ambedkar Centre for Biomedical Research, University of Delhi.

Professor Ahluwalia worked as a Post-doctoral Fellow for two years (1960–62), and had the opportunity to work with Professor Harold Shechter at the Department of Chemistry, Ohio State University. He also worked with Professor Herbert C Brown (Nobel Laureate) at the Department of Chemistry, Purdue University.

Professor Ahluwalia has published more than 250 research papers in national and international journals. He is the distinguished author of a number of books on reaction mechanism, green chemistry, environmental chemistry, and organic synthesis. Some of these include *Green Chemistry: environmentally benign reactions*, *College Practical Chemistry*, and *Comprehensive Practical Organic Chemistry Qualitative Analysis*. His co-authored books include *New Trends in Green Chemistry; Green Chemistry in 21st Century and Beyond; Organic Reaction Mechanisms*; *Chemistry of Natural Products: amino acids, peptides, and enzymes*; *Comprehensive Practical Organic Chemistry: preparation and quantitative analysis*; *Comprehensive Practical Organic Chemistry: quantitative analysis*; *Environmental Science*; *A Textbook of Organic Chemistry*; *Organic Synthesis: special techniques*, and *Advanced Environmental Chemistry*. His book *Green Chemistry: environmentally benign reactions* is winner of 2009 Choice Award of Outstanding Title.